Artificial Intelligence
and
The Environment

Artificial Intelligence
and
The Environment

AI Blueprints for 16 Environmental Projects

Pioneering Sustainability

EDITED BY DR. C. L. MASON

Artificial Intelligence and The Environment
ISBN 978-1-7335248-0-3

Ebook ISBN 978-1-7335248-1-0

Library of Congress Control Number: 2019909945
First printing 2019 at Harvard Book Store
First Amazon printing 2020.
First e-book printing 2020.

Front Cover design by Studio Schaad Design,
Victoria Evans and Cindy Mason.

Book design and titles by Studio Schaad Design.
Cover photo by Ondrej Prosicky in Svalbard, Norway.

Chapter illustrations digitally recreated by Cindy Mason,
Cathleen Schaad, Mehede, Andew, Dawood, and Bill Daul.

Content with permissions by individual authors.

www.aiandenvironment.org

@ai_environment

Ordering information: for a copy of the book made
by book-making robot order from Harvard Book Store,
see www.harvard.com

weborders@harvard.com

1.800.542.READ

Carl Linnaeus, famous for naming all things in nature, shines a light on goddess Mother Earth removing the shroud of darkness (ignorance). Both AI and the human mind rely heavily on names of things. Image adapted from Fragment of Frontispiece by Jan Wandelaar (1690–1759) of Linnaeus, C. (1738), Hortus Cliffortianus.

About This Book

"This is not your usual collection of science papers, and these are not usual times."
– Tim Foresman, former chief environmental scientist for the United Nations

WE NEED TO BUILD a more sustainable human experience on our planet and AI can help. The book contains AI blue prints for 16 different important environmental projects. Created by more than 50 scientists, engineers and AI researchers around the globe, the chapters include AI systems for firefighting resource planning, toxic algae bloom prediction, waste water treatment, sustainable forestry, weather prediction, flood prediction, and systems for cooperation and sharing.

If you chose this book because you are hoping to use AI technology to help with the environment crisis, you have come to the right place. Scientists, educators and administrators from all different disciplines and all areas of the world are learning how to use AI technologies for the public good. Each chapter comes from a collection of papers from the first international AI and Environment workshop where pioneers used every AI trick in the book to produce blueprints to problems that plague us now. The AI methods used here are the brick and mortar of today's AI and includes software agents, neural nets, learning, search, genetic algorithms, integrated and hybrid AI and so on. The AI architectures in these chapters depict compositions of computing components that are as interconnected and interdependent as GAIA herself.

If you chose this book because you are an educator, or a student, I hope you will find the section "Classroom Connections" and the sets of questions at the end of each chapter useful and inspiring. Composed by world class AI and environmental scientists, each chapter has been reviewed and screened through a peer review process at IJCAI, the world's foremost international AI conference. All the chapters are from projects conducted at institutions with a long history of important contributions. Historically, the projects in these chapters were the first AI systems in the world to work on environmental problems. And as Tierney Thys, the National Geographic Explorer said, we have a lot of *caring* technologists.

During the book-making process The Extinction Rebellion began – students in more than 270 cities across the world went on strike to demand action on environmental issues. On 21 February 2019, the President of the European Commission, Jean-Claude Juncker, stated his intent to spend hundreds of billions of euros on climate-change mitigation, a fourth of the EU budget. Weather maps now have 2 additional colors for heat and new records for heat set with each passing day. The Intergovernmental Panel on Climate Change (IPCC) made an announcement that the early figures were wrong, and things are worse than we thought. Also during this time, the U.S. pulled out of the Paris Accord. News programs now have regular segments on pollution.

The good news is that we have a lot of technology and it can help deal with what is happening in the world. But we also need cooperation. In the US, beliefs about environmental problems are often highly political. Each of us has overcome obstacles to create these chapters. Despite the obstacles each scientist faced at the time, cooperation, friendship and love enabled us to overcome these obstacles. With the publication of this volume we share pioneering AI blueprints (software agents, system structures, and algorithms) for 16 environmental problems. As you skim, read, or study the Environmental AI systems described here, it is my hope that you have a spark or connect the dots to something or someone you already know, and this can give rise to something that helps us now – in our cities, in our classrooms, in our world.

Foreword

BY TIERNY THYS

*National Geographic Explorer, marine biologist,
educator, and founder of oceansunfish.org*

DECADES AGO, the researchers whose work appears in this volume saw into the future and knew how crucial it would be for humanity to create extensive and innovative tools for long-term monitoring of our fast-changing environment. Nowhere is this more evident than in studies of our dynamic world ocean – that vast realm which hosts a mere 99% of Earth's habitable space. Our consumption and combustion of fossil fuels, as you know, is not only warming the ocean but shifting its pH to be more acidic, from 8.2 to 8.1 While this change may seem small, past natural shifts have taken between 5,000 and 10,000 years. We have made this shift happen at relatively lightning speed – 50-80 years.

The ocean is our bright blue planet's dominant feature – and to this day – remains our biggest unknown. If we are to make any meaningful progress in understanding our home and preparing for our future, we really need to dive inside the ocean and maintain a 24/7 presence. Alas, being air breathing, land-lubbing hominids, our undersea residency options are somewhat limited. That's where the combination of AI, underwater robotics and remote sensing from satellites come in as our most economical and time-efficient tools for exploring and documenting large expanses of the ocean. The workshop Cindy Mason organized, where the work in this volume of papers was first presented, helped catalyze interest, action and progress in this realm as well as many others.

The workshop was truly an important gathering, both nationally and internationally, and expansive in its coverage of the planet and its range of topics.

It included the first underwater robot in Antarctica, a software agent that monitored for nuclear testing, software agents for storm warnings, water level monitoring, pollution monitoring, and so many things we now find essential to our future. From this workshop, it appears more scientists took up the mantle in Europe and continued the work, although it's odd in the U.S. there was a large time span with no further research in this area. It's helpful these papers are now to be finally published.

Today with such tools at the Oculus Rift virtual reality headset, Google Ocean and Caitlin Seaview's Underwater Streetview, Synthetic Aperture Radar and Sonar (SAR and SAS) imagery as well as Planetlabs, Skybox and our growing ability to image the ocean – coupled with aerial drones – wave gliders, Argo floats, slocum gliders, DIY ROVs and more – we are sailing ahead at full tilt, assisted by smart machines at our sides.

As Cindy has pointed out in some of her other papers, the machine/man partnership is absolutely crucial to increase our mechanistic understanding of ocean dynamics and, perhaps even more importantly, to reinvigorate our increasingly urbanized indoor masses to care deeply about the wonders and workings of the wild.

This volume of papers represents a group of people who are definitely forward-thinking and caring technologists and scientists. We need more people like this if we are to sustain ourselves into the bright future.

With gratitude, Tierney

Introduction

BY DR. C. L. MASON

*AI researcher, computer scientist, educator, and
founder of 21stcenturymed.org*

PIONEERING A SUSTAINABLE FUTURE means engineering environmental systems as dynamic and complex as nature itself. The data for an environmental problem is not just big, its big and hairy and lumpy. Environmental problems are often ill defined with incomplete, uncertain and sometimes totally absent information. There is not just an enormous amount of data, but complex combinations of time-series, satellite, weather station, flood and water instrumentation, human logs, etc. that can also vary in time and scale from a small collection of regions to the entire planet. There is also a need to integrate information and *the meaning of that information* across different kinds of media from hydro, spatial, topo and Landsat maps to images of species and handwritten notes. These varied kinds of data, formats and their meanings are also integrated across differing governments and organizations, each with their own rules and policies for use. AI technology is particularly well suited to help with big hairy data and complexity – they are AI's *raison d'être*. Each chapter in the book presents a pioneering AI system that takes on the challenges of an environmental problem. In Part I, 'Boots on the Ground', AI takes on projects like sewage treatment, water supply control, algae bloom prediction and fire fighting. In Part II, 'Data, Data Everywhere', the chapters lay out AI blueprints for biodiversity cataloging, product life cycle design and cross governmental, cross agency digital resource sharing. The authors pioneered AI systems using every trick in the AI hand book and then some – from fuzzy sets to automated planning to machine learning.

To address these complex scenarios of environmental projects, many of the pioneers here used what is called *hybrid AI*. Hybrid AI means using more than just one kind of AI, or using AI in combination with other kinds of computing like databases or high performance digital signal processing. Hybrid AI is used to solve a problem when just one AI method is not enough. So just machine learning, just fuzzy inferencing or language understanding or qualitative modeling... alone, these are not enough to work on most environmental problems. It is only through combining AI methods in novel ways that hairy environmental problems get solved. Environmental AI researchers knew this a long time ago, before AI was popular, and before the Paris accord existed and certainly before there was an inter governmental panel on climate change (IPCC). Perhaps it is because GAIA's ecosystems are so interconnected and interdependent that these hybrid AI solutions seem naturally suited for these problems.

The chapters are authored by individuals belonging to an international community of AI researchers known as IJCAI. So the chapters originate from New Zealand, Italy, Germany, Canada, the US and many other countries. Newcomers to AI will benefit by knowing that AI methods vary according to which part of the world you're in. For a long time Japan, China and Russia embraced fuzzy methods for all areas of AI, while in the US, fuzzy methods were very slow to be adapted, and scientists in the US were skeptical. So you will find many more fuzzy AI techniques used outside the US. Also there are periods of time when symbolic approaches to knowledge have been important and other times when mathematically centered representation of knowledge was king. Regardless of what is popular in your country or organization at the moment, it's about finding what works for the problem you have.

To find and use AI technology today you no longer need to be part of an elite AI club like IJCAI or AAAI. You'll find much of today's AI know-how, software and data is publicly shared through online courses, videos and websites. For instance, take a look at the website for project "Argo Float." With over 3800 ocean-going robots sampling our seas, the project has posted a data collection on the net that anyone can access, including an active map of the locations of each robot that has transmitted in the past 30 days. Another inspiring project, although not specific to AI, is the Rasperry Pi project. As I write this introduction, Carnegie Melon University has made all their AI software available free online, and the Pi community just announced a toolkit to build AI software agents. The new Pi 4 is out – its a quad processor and costs about 55 dollars, including power supply. The Raspberry Pi is a small unix based computer that fits in the palm of your hand, yet it has USB slots, two display ports and Bluetooth/Wi-Fi. They can be stacked, mounted on a wall, or fit in a pocket. They can also be used to build hybrid AI systems where conventional and AI systems work together.

Machine learning and neural nets help us recognize patterns from our sensor data and networks. Common sense AI methods help explain and share the meaning of data and decisions in a way that is accessible to people. Many AI technologies also help people to consider decisions in the face of uncertainty and incomplete information. AI automation, unlike us humans, can run 24/7 and robots can take us where we cannot go. Finding patterns in data, making tough decisions when dealing with imperfect and missing information, explaining and sharing the meaning of what we see… and doing this day after day, week after week, year after years.. These are all key features of most environmental problems. When the Fukushima nuclear disaster happened, robots went where we could not go and showed us what happened. AI is already part of pioneering sustainability.

Each group or individual whose project was represented at the first IJCAI AI and Environment workshop in Montreal has a chapter here.[1] Many of the projects included here have grown, expanded or inspired global environmental systems we use today. We can also learn that if a hybrid AI architecture can't help us, what should we do different. Students and innovative entrepreneurs may look at these systems as case examples of hybrid-AI architectures – adapting and innovating from the designs and architectures… reimagining some of these blueprints with drones, IOT and Raspberry PI's running software agents. These chapters show that AI has already been creatively applied across a number of environmental problems.

At the end of each chapter is the Classroom Connections. If you are a teacher or wish to use this book to instruct or build discussion in a classroom, the questions help stir thinking, deepen understanding and create new ideas. It's also where you can test your understanding. Answers are at the back of the book. There's also a Nutshell, if you're in a rush and just need to get the gist of what's in the book. There are a few entries with just one or a few pages. To me these are equally important to include, *e.g.* the entry on using AI to detect environmental crime. For readers with backgrounds outside of AI, it is helpful to explain how the word "domain" is used throughout the book. Because AI is generally about creating computationally intelligent behaviors, e.g. planning and scheduling, image analysis, learning, natural language understanding, etc., the word domain refers to the application of an AI method to a particular problem or domain. So for instance, firefighting and flood prediction would be considered a domain for applying AI. In attempting to solve a problem, new AI methods are often created. The AI method can then be used on other problems or domains. This is why we can look at the chapters as containing blueprints. I hope they inspire your own ideas for sustainability.

Good luck to us all,
C. L. Mason

1 The meeting was sponsored by NASA Ames, The U.S. National Research Council, the Canadian Meteorological Organization, the Canadian Society for Computational Studies of Intelligence, the International AI establishment called IJCAI and C.L. Mason.

The Pioneers

BECAUSE OF THE EVENTS of the world today, every person who participated in the first International AI and Environment symposium listed below deserves a medal and recognition. If we left you out, please get in touch and we can add you in, no problem. We thank all of you for your sweat and devotion to being caring technologists. I hope that life has been good to you in all ways. *Best wishes, Cindy.*

Paolo Avesani, Italy
Yasunori Baba, Japan
G. Babin, Canada
Bruce Barkstrom, USA
Palma Blonda, Italy
J. Boulais, Canada
Georgio Brajnik, Italy
Daniel Charlebois, Canada
Ulises Cortés, Spain
Robert Cromp, USA
Leland Ellis, USA
Mark Friedman, USA
Lise Getoor, USA
David G. Goodenough, Canada
Francois Guerrin, France
Mandy Haggith, Scotland
Ulrich Heller, Germany
Michael Huhns, USA
Andrew Jackson, USA

Eric K. Jones, New Zealand
Roger King, USA
Takashi Kiriyama, Japan
Amy Lansky, USA
D. Scott Mackay, Canada
J. Marcoux, Canada
Cindy Mason, USA
Stan Matwin, Canada
Heinz Mühlenbein, Germany
Peter Ohm, Germany
R. Parent, Canada
S. Payer, Canada
Jim Peak, USA
Anna Perini, Italy
F. Petrucci, Canada
Gregory E. Pitts, USA
Manel Poch, Spain
Bruce Porter, USA
Francesco Ricci, Italy

Jeff Rickel, USA
Jon W. Robinson, USA
Vincent B. Robinson, Canada
Ignasi R. Roda, Spain
Waldir Roque, Brazil
Aaron Roydhouse, New Zealand
Miquel Sanchez, Spain
Scott Schmidler, USA
Nick Short, USA
Munindar P. Singh, USA
Peter Struss, Germany
Tetsuo Tomiyama, Japan
Yasushi Umeda, Japan
R. Verret, Canada
D. Vigneux, Canada
Keith Wichman, USA
Brian Williams, USA
Steve Young, USA
Byoung-Tak Zhang, Germany

Table of Contents

SHORTS

In a Nutshell...

If You Don't Have Time to Read The Whole Book
READ THIS

Chapter 1 — Fire Fighting

Combining Human Assessment and
Reasoning Aids for Decision-making in
Planning Forest Fire Fighting

This chapter addresses fire fighting. Specifically it addresses the problem of quickly planning how to best use resources during fire fighting. The approach in this chapter is to use a hybrid AI system for automatically planning first attacks to a forest fire. It is based on work organization of fire fighting in an Italian Provincial center. The problem of fire fighting, like many environmental problems, is almost as complex as GAIA herself. Fire is a dynamic phenomenon that changes and whose evolution is determined by weather conditions like wind direction and intensity, by humidity, and by fuel type, which changes rapidly in sometimes unpredictable ways, requiring fast decisions. Data about these operating conditions are often uncertain, incomplete, and in some cases totally absent. The decision making automation is complicated with relevant fire events evolving with different time and spatial scales. The planning problem of a fire emergency, like many environmental emergencies, is complicated because multiple organizations are involved with decision making over the fire territory and cooperation is needed for good decision making on the strategies to fight the fire: which fire front, where to locate resources, what needs most attention (*e.g.* railway, houses, etc.). There are also decisions about which order to do things. In this way past knowledge is very important. Their approach uses multiple AI techniques: lazy learning, case-based reasoning and constraint reasoning. The system is aimed at supporting the user in the whole process of forest

fires management and the user always remains active in the ultimate decisions.

Chapter 2 — Flood Prediction

Introducing Boundary Conditions in
Semi-Quantitative Simulation

The chapter addresses flood prediction and water supply control and describes a hybrid AI method that addresses the problem of incomplete and imprecise information that generally plagues many environmental simulation systems. Predictions with standard numerical simulations for boundary value problems* can be error prone because they require precision but in reality the information is imprecise and incomplete. For example, when flood conditions approach, empirical data on the level/flow-rate curve for rivers becomes less and less accurate. In general, the precise shape and size of a body of water is rarely known. The task of flood control and water supply prediction is both difficult and vitally important. For example, a lake has a dam with floodgates that can be opened or closed to regulate the water flow through power generating turbines, the water level (stage) of the lake, and the downstream flow. The goal of a controller is to provide adequate reservoir capacity for power generation, consumption, industrial use, and recreation, as well as downstream flow. In exceptional circumstances, the controller must also work to minimize or avoid flooding both above and below the dam. The conceptual and practical aspects addressed by the AI system include the ontology (actions vs. measurements), the temporal scale (instantaneous vs. extended changes), the impact of discontinuity on model structure and the consequences of incompleteness in predictions. Environmental simulation tools are useful to careful evaluate the effect of actions in critical and dynamically changing situations. They evaluate empirically derived models and parameters, and help to forewarn of undesired possible future situations. The hybrid AI simulation method extends the application of qualitative AI modelling methods to include simulating dynamic systems and problem of handling boundary conditions*.

*in a simulation system, boundary value problems specifying how external influences on dynamic systems vary over time

| Chapter 3 | *Sewage and Pollution* |

Integrating General Expert Knowledge and Specific Experimental Knowledge in Waste Water Treatment Plant

The chapter addresses pollution level control for waste water treatment plants using a hybrid AI system that combines both learning from past experience and from domain knowledge for real-time control of a wastewater treatment plant (WWTP).The main goal of a wastewater treatment plant is to reduce the pollution level of the wastewater at the lowest cost, that is, to remove, within die possible measure, strange compounds (pollutants) of the inflow water to the plant prior to discharge to the environment. So, the effluent water has the lower levels of pollutants as possible (in any case, lower than the maximum ones allowed by the law).The plants taken as models – in this study – are based on the main biological technology usually applied: the activated sludge process. The target wastewater plant studied is located in Manresa, near Barcelona (Catalonia). This plant receives about 30000 m^3/day inflow from 75000 inhabitants. The automated solution to this real-time control problem is a multi-paradigm reasoning architecture able to input and process the different elements of the knowledge learning process, to learn from past experience (*specific experimental knowledge*)

.

and to acquire the domain knowledge (*general expert knowledge*). These are the key problems in real-time control AI systems design. These problems increase when the process belongs to an *ill structured domain* and it is composed by several complex operational units. Therefore, an integrated AI methodology which combines both learning from past experience and from domain knowledge is proposed. This multi paradigm reasoning provides the target system, a wastewater treatment plant (WWTP), with some advantages over other approaches applied to real world systems. Due to the dynamic learning environment, the system is able to adapt itself to different waste water treatment plants, *making the system to be exportable* to any plant with some minor changes. It is only needed to fill the Case library with an initial set of specific cases (operating situations of the concrete WWTP), which can be obtained semi-automatically from real operational data. All these facts make it more powerful than other single technologies applied to wastewater treatment plants as knowledge-based approaches [Lapointe et al., 1989; Maeda, 1989], statistical process control techniques [Novotny *et al.*, 1990], fuzzy controller methods, etc., as well as to other complex ill-structured domains. With this approach, the plant can be controlled in *normal* situations (mathematical control), in abnormal usual situations (expert control) and in *abnormal unusual* situations (experimental control).

| Chapter 4 | *Sustainable Forests/ Timber Harvesting* |

Planning with Agents in Intelligent Data Management for Forestry

The chapter concerns the sustainability of our forests. The largest vegetation on earth are the forests and we place a great demand on them to provide us with wood products – industrially and as consumers. To make sustainable timber harvesting decisions we need to know the state of growth and health of forests over large areas of the earth is essential. The data comes in at about

1Tb/day, is format and media diverse, exists on multiple computing platforms with different access and use policies and includes topographic, soils, hydrology, geology, remote sensing and forest cover descriptions over large areas of the earth. The AI system helps manage this hairy data problem. It is used in support of human decision making process by automatically monitoring data and detecting changes and trends on the state of the biosphere and vegetation. The hybrid-AI system uses software agents that combine both learning from past experience and from knowledge. One of the main problems that the AI system must tackle is the update of forest cover maps stored in digital form in geographical information systems (GIS) by processing remotely sensed imagery in order to detect changes in the state of the forest. The agents learn to do this automatically through the use of a training interface that allows human experts to describe how each task is performed. It is therefore not required to hand code the agents since they are automatically generated by the training interface. These agents can each give a description of the task they perform. These descriptions are then used by a problem solving system that integrates the use of search based planning, case-based reasoning, derivational analogy and machine learning. The software agent systems learn by unobtrusively observing the manner in which they are used, adapt to the tasks for which they are used, and learn from the circumstances of their use.

Chapter 5	*Water Pollution Prediction*

Water Pollution Prediction with Evolutionary Neural Trees

This chapter addresses water pollution prediction using an evolutionary neural learning method for time series data. The task studied here is to predict nitrate levels a week ahead in the watersheds of the Sangamon River in Illinois, USA, from the previous values. The AI method of evolutionary learning networks is generally used for the modeling and prediction of complex systems. In contrast to conventional neural learning methods, genetic learning makes relatively few assumptions about the models of data. The method is effective in identifying important structures and variables in systems whose functional structures are unknown or ill-defined. It uses tree-structured neural networks whose node type, weight, size and topology are dynamically adapted by genetic algorithms. Since the genetic algorithm used for training does not require error derivatives, a wide range of neural models can be identified. The performance results compare favorable to those achieved by well-engineered, conventional system-identification methods. The original study here also aims at giving some indication of the biochemical and physical relationships among the variables and of the controllability of the system. Application areas for this approach include but are not limited to prediction, monitoring, and diagnosis of complex systems, such as environmental processes.

Chapter 6	*Toxic Algae Blooms*

A Qualitative Modeling Approach to Algal Bloom Prediction

This AI project concerns the problem of toxic algae blooms and is a collaboration between researchers from Brazil, Germany and France. The approach to AI system development is an intelligent model-based systems to support decision making concerning many environmental factors of algae bloom. It is discussed in the context of an algae bloom in the Rio Guaíba in Southern Brazil. Knowledge-based systems support analysis and decision making using a representation of our human knowledge about the involved algae bloom processes. Because of the very nature of these algae and bloom processes, our knowledge about them, and the information available, this is a great challenge for standard qualitative modeling. This chapter presents preliminary results of our work including: using AI-modeling for the phenomena of the algal bloom and an intelligent process-oriented description of some of the essential mechanisms contributing to algal bloom. In particular, two problems have to be addressed that are typical for modeling ecological systems. First, the spatial distribution of parameters and processes relevant to algae blooms has to be taken into account which leads us to locate processes in or between water body compartments, the elements of a topological partitioning of the area. Second, the various processes involved in an algae bloom development act with speeds of different orders of magnitude (*e.g.* chemical reactions vs. changes in fish population), which requires AI techniques of time-scale abstraction. Our approach to modeling the interactions involved in this bloom phenomenon use a language called QPC. QPC allows the automatic direct expression and representation of physical models of compartments and their interaction, and the application of time-scale abstraction in the composition of a scenario model.

| Chapter 7 | *Recycling and Resources* |

The Green Browser: A Proposal of Green Information Sharing and Life Cycle Design

The chapter is about revealing product life cycle information from the raw material stage through use and eventual disposal or recycling. Unlike a general purpose browser, *the Green Browser* uses AI methods to focus selectively on environmental (green) product information extracted from the net. Applying AI methods to general browser technology allows us to quickly reveal products bearing positively on green production and environmental protection. This creates greater public literacy and market selection through a product's potential impacts: from resource usage and extraction to disposal and dispersal. A focused browser finds green product information faster than a normal browser. Faster, easier access to such information supports informed corporate and public decisions and enables stakeholders (*e.g.*, employees, shareholders, consumers, regulators, NGO. etc.) to have automated focused access to all available environmental information. The AI information representation and design schemes proposed for this purpose are called *green life cycle model* and *green life cycle design*. The chapter proposes a representational scheme called *green life cycle model* withhich organizes corporate information for the Green Browser. For the purpose of supporting design for life cycle of green products *(green life cycle design)*, the scheme is built to illustrate a product's potential impacts from the raw material stage through use and eventual disposal or recycling. Firms are encouraged to process their firm-specific information based on the scheme. Second, the chapter discusses how the Green Browser can support information sharing to enable stakeholders to obtain the detailed picture of products.

| Chapter 8 | *Arguments and Decision Making* |

Support for Argumentation in Natural Resource Management

In this chapter AI helps resolve arguments about natural resources among differently interested parties. When decisions to be made involve changes to natural resources such as oceans, forests or the atmosphere, the interests of various stakeholders need to be taken into account, including scientists from different disciplines and local stakeholders with different goals and priorities. Software methods to support participants in these discussions are now widely believed to help make wiser and more sustainable management decisions by more easily weighing up the views of all relevant parties. These parties include land-owners, residents, environmental pressure groups, wildlife biologists and other scientists, governmental bodies and industries. When there is disagreement, people require ways to explore the reasons for the different viewpoints and to seek out areas of consensus which can be built upon. This work uses an AI method based on meta-level representation of argumentation frameworks to explore multiple knowledge bases in which conflicting opinions about environmental change are expressed. A formal meta-language is defined for articulating the relationships between, and arguments for, propositions in knowledge bases independently of their particular object-level representation. A prototype system has been implemented to evaluate the usefulness of this framework and to assess its computational feasibility. The results so far are promising.

Chapter 9	*Underground Nuclear Testing*

An Intelligent Assistant for Nuclear Test Ban Treaty Verification

This chapter addresses treaty verification for underground nuclear testbed agreements using a hybrid-AI software agent assistant that classifies and filters seismic data from Norway's regional seismic array, NORESS. Verification of a Comprehensive Test Ban Tan (zero testing) has driven the development of enhanced seismic verification technology with lower detection levels and better noise reduction signal extraction algorithms. However each detected event must be analyzed to determine if it contains a clandestine nuclear test. Lowering the detection threshold causes an exponential increase in the number of events detected. The volume of events to be analyzed and classified overwhelms human analysts. SEA was developed in the Treaty Verification Research Group at Lawrence Livermore National Laboratory. The overall system is hybrid – it contains hardware and many kinds of software, such as advanced signal processing algorithms that work with SEA. The agent architecture supports a pattern driven application of computationally expensive numerical analysis. Three important aspects of the intelligent software assistant SEA are (1) the user interface permits interactive or human-agent analysis (2) it reduces the workload of the human analyst by filtering and classifying the large volume of continuously arriving data, presenting "interesting" events for human review and explanation of its analysis (3) it emulates the common sense problem solving behavior and explanation capability of the human seismic analyst by using a multi-context Assumption Based Truth Maintenance System.

Chapter 10	*Assembling Satellite Data*

The COLLAGE/KHOROS Link: Planning for Image Processing Tasks

This chapter looks at the assembly of satellite data. It is an overarching and pervasive issue in environmental computer systems. Challenges include how to represent and partition information in a way that fosters extensibility and flexibility and how to do this across many kinds of satellite data and analysis products that are often changing and growing. To solve this problem we use a branch of AI known as *planning*. AI Planning allows us to automatically generate the necessary sequence of image processing steps for examining satellite remote sensing data. Several obvious issues arise when integrating a variety of data and products for viewing/analysis: low-level connection tasks; representation translation tasks; the need to present different kinds of users with a suitably coherent combined architecture. To make the system open to future media and data products we are interested in how to represent and partition information in a way that fosters extensibility and flexibility. We describe our work to do this with two existing systems at NASA called – COLLAGE/KHOROS, which accesses a suite of image processing algorithms that are constantly changing and updating. Our challenge for the planning system is to provide the assembly and viewing of these data and data products to be useable by a variety of users with different skill levels. These kinds of issues, of course, are common among many software engineering enterprises.

Chapter 11	*Forest Ecosystems*

KBLIMS For Forested Ecosystem Simulation Management

This chapter addresses forested ecosystem management with hybrid-AI question answering simulation systems. Answering questions like "what is the effect of clearcutting on watersheds in the Turkey Lakes region of Ontario Canada?" involve complex interactions between simulations and specialized tools about climatic, topographic, hydrologic, pedological and ecological processes. The manual process of answering a question is a laborious task where simulations, tools and modeling systems from multiple disciplines are run like batch processing, generating many cumbersome files. The questions also involve the complex interactions between fundamentally different kinds of data from geographic information system(GIS) and ecosystem simulation modeling. For example, geographic information systems typically represent information as points, polygons, lines and layers, whereas simulation systems use system state, mass and energy flux, and the interaction and dynamics of species or individuals. Automating this process relieves the tedium and speeds the process involved in each q/a so that many more queries can be completed. To manage aggregation and integration across these fundamentally different disciplines, data types and systems, the AI systems use a multi-layered ontology across conceptually different systems with an architecture based on the notion of a query model that executes a set of user-defined queries. The system allows many kinds of queries over many combination and levels of aggregation and scales and includes simulation queries, spatial data queries, deduction queries and an aggregation of these processes. The system can run on either user-defined or system-defined queries. Typical use of the system is done automatically so the user, *e.g.* an ecologist, need not explicitly parameterize and run simulation models. System use of the simulation systems are managed by the knowledge base using its meta knowledge about the tools, modelers, etc. which allows for the integration of either tightly-coupled or loosely-coupled systems. Users interface to the system expressing a simulation experiment by first identifying a set of high level concepts/objects as a spatial query, then specifying some action to be performed on these concepts/objects, such as a combined simulation query and aggregation query. The AI explanation system is based on the same ontological/concepts.

Chapter 12 *Weather Bulletins*

SCRIBE: An Interactive System for Composition of Meteorological Forecasts

This chapter describes work by the Canadian Meterological Center to automatically generate public weather forecasting bulletins from weather matrices and sensors across Canada. The system, SCRIBE, uses hybrid-AI methods to generate plain language public forecast bulletins in French or English from a set of stations or sample points prepared at a three-hour time resolution over a range of Canada. Although the system is created for the purpose of automation it is also run in manual mode and all processing can be monitored and modified by human users. A semantic numerical analysis processes the weather element matrices according to standards of codification. The resulting content is described with more than 40 precipitation concepts (rain, rain heavy at times...), including three types of concepts applicable to thunderstorms (risk, possibility, a few) at up to three levels at the same time (ex.: rain and snow possibly mixed with ice pellets) it can also produce two types of concepts applicable to precipitation accumulation (liquid and frozen), six classes of probability of precipitation concepts, 13 sky cover concepts (11 stationary states and two evolving states), 14 classes of wind speed with eight directions, two types of visibility concepts (blowing snow and fog) and ten types of maximum/minimum temperature concepts. By using the standards of codification the AI system provides a simple way to display the content of the weather element matrices for human editing rather than displaying the raw numbers. Once the editing task is complete at the interface level, the modified concept file is quality controlled before being fed to the knowledge base system again to generate the plain language bulletin. The knowledge base system creates a basic sentence structure that can be matched into different structures representing different semantics expressing the same content, following a case base reasoning approach. The knowledge base system uses approximately 600 rules to generate the standardized ontological weather concepts. It uses approximately 1000 rules to generate the plain language bulletins. The use of rules supports the ability to explain the steps of the automation process.

Chapter 13	*Weather Forecasting*

Retrieving Structured Spatial Information from Large Databases

This chapter addresses weather forecasting with an intelligent software agent assistant. The agent acts as a "memory amplifier" for meteorologists to assist in weather forecasting by rapidly locate and analyze similar kinds of past weather. Much of environmental data, including meteorological, covers a large region of the earth so it is organized as spatially. A challenge is that historical multi media meteorological data includes audio, text, satellite images, laser disks, etc.. The chapter presents the first AI method to intelligently retrieve spatially organized data with a technique known as a case-based reasoning system for the rapid display of historical meteorological data. Case based analysis allows the comparison of similar instances or 'cases' of an example. This work is distinguished by the large size of its case base, by its need to represent structured spatial information, and by its use of a relational database to store spatial data cases. This briefly describes some of the technical issues that follow from these design considerations, focusing on the role of the relational database. The system is called MetVUW Workbench.

Chapter 14	*Sharing Digital Environmental Resouces*

The Environmental Information Mall

The chapter addresses sharing environmental tools and data products across government agencies, institutions and other large organizations. The key to the *Environmental Information Mall project* is an environmental concepts ontology. It supports the interoperation of data and analytical tools from a variety of independent sources. The chapter describes AI tools for the creation and maintenance

of the ontology, and then shows how it can be used including but not limited to: information sources advertise their capabilities; mediators combine analytical tools with the data on which they operate to share data products; end users locate relevant information; and intelligent agents or intelligent user interfaces that fuse information from several sources.

Chapter 15	*Biodiversity and Ecosystem Catalogues*

Biodiversity and Ecosystems Network (BENE)— The Challenge of Building a Distributed Informatics Network for Biodiversity

The chapter addresses biodiversity and ecosystem cataloging in global collaboratives for biodiversity conservation and ecosystem protection, restoration, and management communities. BENE (Biodiversity and Ecosystems Network Environment) fosters enhanced communications and collaborations through the intelligent sharing of networks of biodiversity and ecosystem data and collections. Current estimates of the diversity of life (plant, animal, microorganisms) on Earth (biodiversity) range beyond the ~1.5 million species described to date up to perhaps as high as -130 million species. The number of entries in such a collective are vast and are created by wide ranging diverse social, political and economic members from governments, corporations, academia, private foundations, individual citizens and so on. The data types are also diverse and include samples or specimens themselves, field notes of scientists and taxonomists, museum repositories, geographic information systems and spatial data, genome data, education and television data, etc. BENE project a) points users to new networks of biodiversity data collections using intelligent search b) provides web based user access to an integrated network of collectives using search agents that rely on ontological and meta-data. At present, there are nodes in Australia (4), Brazil (the BIN21 Secretariat resides at the Base de Dados Tropical), Costa Rica, Ecuador, Finland (2), Italy, Japan, United Kingdom and the United States (BENE is the only BIN21 node in the U.S.A.).

| Chapter 16 | *Plant Physiology and Climate Change Modeling* |

Automated Modeling of Complex Biological and Ecological Systems

This chapter concerns plant physiology and climate change modeling, specifically the automatic generation of simulation models that answer prediction questions and explain how climate change may affect plant physiology. It is particularly useful to predict the effects of global climate changes on plants and animals in specific regions. In general, predicting answers to climate change questions takes vast amounts of knowledge, time, people with special knowledge and is error prone. Automating this prediction process speeds it up allowing consideration of many different scenarios and assumption conditions. Equally important to the answer for a prediction question is the reason for that answer. Any system like this must also cough up an explanation. But the automation tools themselves choke on the vast knowledge during computation. To answering climate prediction questions we not only need general principles of plant and animal physiology but species interactions and specific data on individual species, climatic events, and geologic formations. The central issue in automatically answering prediction questions is constructing a model from this wealth of information that captures the important aspects of the scenario and their relationships to the variables of interest. This avoids the problem of working with a sea of knowledge, much of which is irrelevant to a particular question. The novel approach taken to solving this problem makes Siri and Watson look like kindergarten tools. Spoiler – the AI system automatically generates code on the fly for each prediction question. The key to this approach lies in building a meta model of the knowledge, causal-relations and tools. Using the meta knowledge, a predictive question/answering system is coded on the fly based on causal relationship elements needed for each question using only computing simulations and knowledge elements relevant to the question. The causal information is also the basis for the explanation facility. Consider the general form of a prediction question in plant physiology: "How would decreasing soil moisture affect a plant's transpiration rate?" A prediction question poses a hypothetical *scenario* (*e.g.*, a plant whose soil moisture is decreasing) and asks for the resulting behavior of specified *variables of interest,* (*e.g.*, the plant's transpiration rate). Using detailed knowledge of plant physiology and other physical systems, the q/a system is generated by parsing the prediction question and determining the relevant elements and factors needed to answer the question. The authors introduce a modeling program called TRIPEL for answering prediction questions based on causal influences. It defines the modeling task, criteria for distinguishing relevant aspects of the scenario from irrelevant aspects and the algorithm that uses these criteria to automatically construct the simplest adequate model for answering a question. The chain of causal influences provides the basis for an explanation facility. Representing the information in multiple levels of abstraction support explanation styles matched to the kind of user (scientist, decision maker, etc.) This system can be generally used on any body of knowledge to automatically generate predictive q/a systems. In biology and ecology, such questions are important for predicting the consequences of natural conditions and management policies as well as for teaching biological and ecological principles.

Classroom Connections

AT THE END of each chapter you'll find a short section titled 'Classroom Connections'. This section includes a page or two with a unique set of questions that serve as a summary of the main issues surrounding our growing environmental project as well as the AI solution features presented. The questions can be used in several ways. As a general reader, they amplify your memory of what you read before, and they can deepen the connections that you'll make to what you already know. As a student, they help you absorb this subject easier, so that you can truly connect with the key points the author is making. If you plan to use the book to speed up the design of tech solutions by re-using, recycling, or adapting the ideas you see here, the questions can also create some talking points to pitch an AI solution for your own architectural approach.

Some of the questions come straight out of the chapters, while others are really designed to explain the most important parts the chapters. They point out some of the best features of the AI system while also pointing out some of the challenges that help distinguish this particular environmental problem. For example, not everyone realizes just how incomplete and uncertain the information about the perimeter of a lake is, or how algae bloom can form, or that an AI system can automatically extract weather concepts from 10 years of historical weather data.

The answers to Classroom Connection questions can be found at the back of the book. These answers will be in a section titled, "Answers to Classroom Connections."

Some instructors may find that questions of a general nature can stir curiosity and discussion. For example, in each chapter, you might ask:

1. What environmental problem(s) are the authors trying to solve? Why is this important?

2. What AI technologies are they using?

3. Can you think of any problems with this approach?

4. What programming tools would you use to build this system and why?

5. Where is this project now? (feel free to use Google or any other resources)

6. How would you build a solution to this problem?

Here are some questions of a general nature that can stir discussion within our own communities.

1. Has an environmental problem ever affected you or your family?

2. Why is this problem so important now?

3. What technologies are used to address this problem? Are they using AI, machine learning or robotics? How are people working with the system? What about non-AI technologies like databases, networks, crowd source apps, etc.?

In creating community centered discussions and solutions, we need to remember it takes more than technology. We need cooperation and a shared vision of the future to bring together governments, everyday people, and technology, to positively work together. For example, distributed crowd-sourced weather data collection in Canada is helping create new ways of predicting storms and modeling climate. And there is an app called 'litterati' that lets everyday users upload a snapshot of litter and catalogue it to track how much trash, what kind, and where it came from so that cities, shippers, and governments can have real data for budgets and decision making.

The last two general questions help to raise awareness for the widening range of environmental sustainability issues that we continue to face today and well into the future:

1. How can AI/machine learning be used to provide solutions to our increasing list of environmental problems? Here are just a few answers:
   - Extreme environments
   - Extreme data collection
   - Continuous monitoring of environments, lakes, atmosphere, etc.
   - Environmental cleanup – automation & robotics
   - Monitor pollution levels, existence of species, etc.
   - Prevention of spills, fires or other environmental disasters
   - Collecting and testing sea floor samples for pollutants
   - Mapping and monitoring atmosphere and ocean for changes
   - Modeling products, their resources & their life cycles
   - Integrating global maps over time and space
   - Query answering systems
   - Using automation to rebuild or repair reef systems
   - Using robots to re-pollinate or monitor agriculture

- Classifying images
- Predicting bacteria or algae blooms

2. What are some environmental issues that are currently affecting our global environment?
   - Pollution
   - Sewers & wastewater treatment
   - Environmental disasters
   - Forest sustainability
   - Water sustainability
   - Waste and recycling
   - Rising sea levels
   - Encroachment of non-native species
   - Floods and pollution
   - Overpopulation
   - Oil spills

We wish you all some good luck and a lot of common sense.

Happy reading.
Cindy Mason

Part I
Boots on the Ground

Chapter 1

Fire Fighting

Combining Human Assessment and Reasoning Aids for Decision-making in Planning Forest Fire Fighting

Paolo Avesani
I.R.S.T., Italy

Francesco Ricci
I.R.S.T., Italy

Anna Perini
I.R.S.T., Italy

ABSTRACT

In this extended abstract we shall illustrate a work in progress aimed at developing an AI system for planning first attacks to a forest fire. It is based on two major techniques: case-based reasoning and constraint reasoning. This planning component is embedded in an Intelligent Decision Support System aimed at supporting the user in the whole process of forest fires management. The novelty of the proposed approach is mainly due to the use of advanced techniques for lazy learning, the application of the case-based paradigm to the planning of the first fire attack and the integration of the case-based reasoner with a constraint solver, mainly in charge of temporal reasoning.

1 INTRODUCTION

In this extended abstract we shall illustrate a work in progress aimed at developing an AI system for planning first attacks to a forest fire. It is based on two major techniques: case-based reasoning and constraint reasoning. This planning component is embedded in an Intelligent Decision Support System [Ricci *et al.*, 1994] aimed at supporting the user in the whole process of forest fires management. The novelty of the proposed approach is mainly due to the use of advanced techniques for lazy learning, the application of the case-based paradigm to the planning of the first fire attack and the integration of the case-based reasoner with a constraint solver, mainly in charge of temporal reasoning.

2 THE FIRE DOMAIN

The complexity of the forest fire domain comes from features which are typical of environmental problems. Fire is a dynamic phenomenon whose

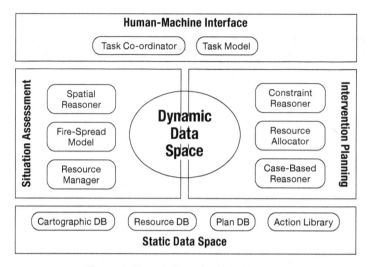

Figure 1. Charade Functional Architecure.

evolution is determined by weather conditions – in particular wind intensity and direction – by humidity, and by fuel type, parameters which usually change rapidly and sometimes in an unpredictable way. Operational constraints impose often quick decisions that drastically limit the possibility to build a plan [Ricci *et al.*, 1993]. Moreover relevant fire events can happen on very different time and spatial scales, from seconds to days, from meters to kilometers, determining a large variety of world states. Data are always incomplete and uncertain, unless, in some cases, totally absent.

In this framework the role of past knowledge is extremely important, sub-optimal solutions are often adopted because of the bias in the decision process. The management of forest fire, as in general environmental emergency, involves organisations which have decisional and operative centers distributed on the territory. So managing a forest fire can require several centers to cooperate. Moreover, complex coordination problems can arise when resources from different organisations, like forestry people, police, ambulances are employed.

These are all general features of the fire domain. To be more specific, the management of forest fires follows a precise operational workflow that is typical of each fire-fighting organisation. We shall concentrate on the work organisation in an Italian Provincial center.

3 THE OPERATIONAL CONTEXT

In order to better understand how the user can be supported in planning an intervention plan

we illustrate the operational context in which the system is to be deployed.

The user of the system is the controller based in a provincial centre. His tools are: a workstation, a dedicated line to acquire data from infrared sensors and meteo sensors, a radio, a fax, a telephone and a printer. The system running on the workstation comprises a Geographic Information System, a graphical simulator of the fire evolution, tools for territorial, meteo and resource assessment and a module for supporting the intervention planning and control.

When a new fire is reported, the alarm is promptly validated and the situation assessed by the user, possibly running the fire spreading model. On the screen the operator can look at the output of the fire spreading model and access, through a graphical interaction, information on the graphical symbols showed by the map. At the end of this phase the operator has acquired enough information for drawing on the map a number of line sectors that subdivide the original fire front.

This operation, called sectorisation, is one of the more crucial decisions because it involves the strategical choices of the fight to the fire: which fire front to take into account in detailing a tactic definition, how far from the fire epicentre to locate the resources, what kind of supply needs a particular attention (for example inhabited houses, railway paths, etc.).

Once the sectors have been identified on the map the operator is now looking for a plan to fight the fire in each sector. The plan may use air forces and/or ground means, and they have to adopt a specific scheme of work. Searching in a database of past sector plans, the system retrieves a set of plans that in a similar context worked succesfully. Follows a modification phase to fit these plans to the current situation. The plans are showed to the operator by means of a predefined form. After this phase of sector plan evaluation the operator may choose to repair a plan editing some subpart. Otherwise he may propose a new one, that seems applicable, based on his experience. The system will check the numeric consistency of the repaired plan: that is verify the temporal constraints, water quantity and resources availability.

At this point the operator has to assign means to actions. He can normally schedule actions or take advantage of an automatic resource allocator. The resource allocator starting from the resource information provided by the assessment looks for a suitable solution that respects the constraints formulated by the intervention plan. If the resource allocator can not find a feasible schedule, the operator can manually perform a partial resource allocation.

The operator finally takes a decision: selects a plan and his related schedule and sends the appropriate orders to the bases all around.

4 THE GENERAL ARCHITECTURE

The general architecture of the Charade decision support system is mainly divided in three subsystems. In Figure 1 both functional modules and data types are shown.

An architecture for a decision support system must enable the co-operation of man and machine capabilities. In Charade the focus of this co-operation between man and computer leads to a task-oriented approach to system design, where analyses of the operator tasks are conducted, and task models are built and exploited in the design process. The architecture of the Man- subsystem uses this model of the operator-system activity (notion of task-model) to drive and control the overall dialogue; in particular the activation of planning and situation assessment computer functions is realized from the task co-ordinator contained in the MMI subsystem.

The situation assessment subsystem roughly implements a blackboard architecture. Different knowledge sources (fire spreading model, spatial reasoner, etc.) collaborate to obtain a global description of the problem domain that is contained in the Dynamic Data Space. The system activity task model included in the MMI can be seen as the main control that activates the different knowledge sources.

Regarding the Intervention Planning subsystem an architecture which integrates constraint reasoning and case-based reasoning is proposed [Avesani *et al.*, 1993]. The case-based reasoner plays the role of assumption maker, suggesting old solution to similar situations, and constraint reasoning filters those assumptions in a feasible solution. The user is always called to an active role, for example refining a hypothesis proposed by the case-based reasoner or browsing the constraint network. The following section gives a more detailed view of the Intervention Planning subsystem components.

5 INTERVENTION PLANNING

The intervention planning subsystem develops a hybrid architecture for planning that integrates a Case-Based Planner and a Constraint Reasoner.

5.1 THE PLAN REASONER

The Plan Reasoner is based on the idea of reusing the previous expert experience in planning initial attacks in order to build a plan for the new situation. This idea yields that we don't need to know the principle of fire fighting planning, but we have to focus on recall of past intervention plans and on their adaptation.

Usually a case-based system starts from an initial assumption on the similarity metric, and its accuracy is related to the number of instances stored in the case memory. But increasing the collection of cases doesn't affect the definition of a similarity metric. In this perspective developing a similarity metric is an empirical task strongly related to the domain knowledge [Kolodner, 1993].

Standards approaches to case-based reasoning adopt a generalization of the Euclidean metric, where the squared differences of two points components is multiplied by a real positive factors called weights, *i.e.*,

$$(d(x,y) = (\sum_{i=1}^{N} w_i |x_i - y_i|^2)^{1/2})$$

These metrics are also called global metrics as they are defined uniformly on the whole input space.

The set of these weights in a case-based reasoning are normally derived from domain knowledge. Such kind of metrics have many limitations, for example, it is not possible to assert that the relevance of a feature f_i depends on the values taken by another feature f_j.

We have introduced a special kind of metric that we called AASM (Asymmetric Anisotropic Similarity Metric), that can lead to a well fitted similarity definition. It is based on two basic assumptions. The first one (anisotropic) states that the metric is defined locally: the space around a trial case is measured using the metric attached to that case. The second one (asymmetric) states that the distance between two points in a continuous feature space F_i is not symmetric, *i.e.*, $d_i(x_i, y_i) \neq d_i(y_i, x_i)$. In fact we use two different weights for the "left" and the "right" directions.

We can define an anisotropic and asymmetric metric on $\bar{C} \times C$ (where C is the case space and $\bar{C} = \{x_1, ..., x_M\}$), which we call δ, such that:

$$\delta : \bar{C} \times C \longrightarrow R_{\geq 0}$$

$$\delta(x_i, y) = (\sum_{j=1}^{N} w_{ij} d_j(x_{ij}, y_j)^p)^{1/p}.$$

for all $i = 1, \ldots, M$, and $y \in C$, where

$$w_{ij} = \begin{cases} p_{ij} & \text{if } x_{ij} \geq y_j \text{ and } F_j = [0,1] \\ q_{ij} & \text{if } x_{ij} < y_j \text{ and } F_j = [0,1] \\ p_{ij} = q_{ij} & \text{if } F_j \text{ is finite} \end{cases}$$

In [Ricci and Avesani, 1995] we proved that AASM can lead to a significant reduction of the number of stored cases while still maintaining good accuracy and therefore to a sensible speed-up in run-time performances.

Moreover our approach in the similarity metric design would take advantage of the interactive nature of the CBR system. After each retrieval step the user can be more or less satisfied with the case proposed by the system. The user evaluation could be a useful feedback to the system in order to modify his behaviour, that is his similarity metric. In this context to update the similarity metric means to modify the feature weights. A good CBR system should evolve towards a similarity metric that meets the user expectation.

In CHARADE we are going to merge a machine learning technique suitable to develop an adaptive retrieval method. The basic idea is to build a learning automata model [Narendra and Thathachar, 1989; Kokar and Reveliotis, 1993] that modifies itself starting from the feedback received by the user interaction. It decreases (reinforcement) the distance between an input case c and the nearest neighbour nn if the user fruitfully can use the past plan; whereas the distance between c and nn is increased (punishment) if the user substantially revises the past plan. This kind of general scheme is called reinforcement learning.

5.2 THE CONSTRAINT REASONER

The Constraint Reasoner manages the constraints defined on a plan, *i.e.* the temporal and domain constraints on actions and respectively on the associated resources [Perini *et al.*, 1994; Perini and Ricci, 1994].

Actions and plans are characterized by a start time and an end time that define the time interval during which the action (plan) is performed.

From a user point of view, the temporal structure of a plan is represented with the temporal relations that can be defined between these time intervals in the form of a set of Allen's interval relations [Allen, 1983]. That is, given two plan components, a conjunction of a set of the thirteen Allen's temporal relations can be stated for them. From the constraint reasoner point of view an Allen's relation between intervals is translated into bounded difference constraints between time points.

A bounded difference constraint between two time points x and y is an inequality like $y - x \leq a$. Qualitative relationships can be represented using infinity values as distance bounds. For example "x less than or equal to y" is expressed constraining the distance between x and y to be between zero and infinity ($0 \leq y - x \leq \infty$).

Action's durations are also represented with bounded difference constraints. These bounds come from evaluation of the resources' capacity and data on fire evaluation. So estimates on minimum and maximum action duration bound the distance between the start and end times of the action, while a sector deadline gives an upper bound to the distance between the start and end times of the sector plan. Note that all this information can be represented with bounded difference constraints.

A set of bounded difference constraints on a set of time points defines a CSP problem on continuous domains [Dechter *et al.*, 1991]. Different computations can be performed on a constraint network, for instance finding the minimal network (computing the Floyd-Warshall all-pair shortest path algorithm), or checking the consistency of a constraint network (computing the Bellman-Ford's single-source shortest path).

For example each time a user adds a new constraint or attempts to modify the definition of a previously installed constraint, the constraint network is checked against possible inconsistencies, and the new domain extensions for the temporal variables are computed using shortest path algorithms. In such a way the user is enabled to incrementally define a plan, by adding or removing actions and constraints, while the system checks the correctness of these operations with respect to the temporal dimension.

ACKNOWLEDGMENTS

Charade Project has been managed by Alenia. The other partners are Alcatel (Software Platform), Thomson CSF/SDC (Man-Machine Interface), Inisel (Situation Assessment), Italsoft (Resource Manager and Resource Allocator), Thomson CSF/LER (cartographic module).

REFERENCES

[Allen, 1983] James F. Allen. Mantaining knowledge about temporal intervals. *Communication of ACM,* 26(11):832-843, 1983.

[Avesani *et al.*, 1993] Paolo Avesani, Anna Perini, and Francesco Ricci. Combining CBR and constraint reasoning in planning forest fire fighting. In *Proceedings of the First European Workshop on Case-Based Reasoning,* pages 235-239, Kaiserslautern, 1993.

[Dechter *et al.*, 1991] R. Dechter, I. Meiri, and J. Pearl. Temporal constraint networks. *Artificial Intelligence,* 49, 1991.

[Kokar and Reveliotis, 1993] Mieczyslaw M. Kokar and Spiridon A. Reveliotis. Reinforcement learning: Architectures and algorithms. *International Journal of Intelligent System*, 8:857-894, 1993.

[Kolodner, 1993] Janet Kolodner. *Case-Based Reasoning.* Morgan Kaufmann Publishers, San Mateo, CA, 1993.

[Narendra and Thathachar, 1989] Kumpati S. Narendra and Mandayam A.L. Thathachar. *Learning Automata.* Prentice-Hall, 1989.

[Perini and Ricci, 1994] Anna Perini and Francesco Ricci. Constraint reasoning and interactive planning. Ithaca, New York, November 18-19, 1994.

[Perini *et al.*, 1994] Anna Perini, Francesco Ricci, and Paolo Avesani. Temporal reasoning and interactive planning. In *Proceedings of the Workshop on Temporal Reasoning, AI*IA*, Parma, 28 September, 1994.

[Ricci and Avesani, 1995] Francesco Ricci and Paolo Avesani. Learning an asymmetric and anisotropic similarity metric for case-based reasoning, technical report 9503-13, IRST, 1995.

[Ricci *et al.*, 1993] Francesco Ricci, Anna Perini, and Paolo Avesani. Planning in a complex real domain. In *proceedings of the Italian planninq workshop*, pages 55-60, Rome, 1993.

[Ricci *et al.*, 1994] F. Ricci, S. Mam, P. Marti, V. Normand, and P. Olmo. CHARADE: a platform for emergencies management systems. Technical Report TR9404-07, IRST, 1994.

CLASSROOM CONNECTIONS

Combining Human Assessment and Reasoning Aids for Decision-making in Planning Forest-Fire Fighting

Multiple Choice

Pick the best answer.

1. What environmental problem is addressed in this chapter?
   A. Putting out forest fires.
   B. Communicating to the public about fire prevention.
   C. Planning the initial attack on a forest fire and predicting spread.
   D. Reducing litter in national parks.
   E. A – C.

2. What kinds of AI technology is used?
   A. Constraint based reasoning.
   B. Temporal reasoning.
   C. Reinforcement learning.
   D. Drones.
   E. Hybrid AI – graphical simulation of fire evolution, resource management tools and sensor data processing together with AI.
   F. A, B, C and E.

3. What kinds of data does the fire fighting planner use?
   A. Infrared and meteo sensed data.
   B. Previous plans.
   C. Geographical information and simulation data.
   D. Input from other locations and organizations.
   E. Incomplete and uncertain.
   F. All of the above.

True or False

Please decide if each of the statements below are True or False.

4. When a new fire is reported, the alarm is promptly validated and the situation assessed by the user possibly running the fire spreading model.

5. The strategical choices to fight a fire include: which fire front to take into account in detailing a tactic definition, how far from the fire epicenter to locate the resources, and what kind of supply needs a particular attention (for example inhabited houses, railway paths, etc).

6. Managing a forest fire can require several centers to cooperate. Moreover complex coordination problems can arise when resources from different organizations, like forestry people, police, ambulances are employed.

7. The role of past knowledge is extremely important, without it suboptimal solutions are often adopted because of the bias in the decision process.

8. Fire is a dynamic phenomenon whose evolution is determined by parameters which usually change rapidly and sometimes in an unpredictable way such as weather conditions, in particular wind intensity and direction, but also by humidity and by fuel type.

Answers can be found at the end of the book.

Chapter 2

Flood Prediction

Introducing Boundary Conditions in Semi-quantitative Simulation

Giorgio Brajnik
Università di Udin, Italy

ABSTRACT

Boundary value problems specifying how external influences on dynamic systems vary over time greatly extend the scope of qualitative reasoning techniques, enabling them to achieve a much wider applicability. This paper discusses conceptual and practical aspects that underlie the problem of handling boundary conditions in SQPC, a sound program for modeling and simulating dynamic systems in the presence of incomplete knowledge. Issues concerning the ontology (actions vs. measurements), the temporal scale (instantaneous vs. extended changes), the impact of discontinuity on model structure and the consequences of incompleteness in predictions are discussed. On the basis of the experimentation done so far it is claimed that given the generality of the assumptions underlying the techniques presented in the paper, and given the relatively low computational cost that is often required to solve a boundary value problem, this approach is viable and can be utilized to widen the applicability spectrum of Qualitative Reasoning.

1 INTRODUCTION

Though qualitative simulation [Kuipers, 1994; Bobrow, 1993] plays a crucial role in many Qualitative Reasoning (QR) tasks (such as control, diagnosis or design), few QR tools are able to deal with boundary conditions that specify how external influences on systems vary over time. In fact, except for a few cases (like [Forbus, 1989]), no qualitative simulator takes as input a description of how certain variables evolve over time, and lets them affect the simulation. These tools solve more or less sophisticated initial value problems where initial conditions of autonomous systems are given. Dealing with non-autonomous systems greatly extends the scope of QR techniques, enabling them to achieve a much wider applicability. In fact, they could encompass capabilities such as:

- simulating, monitoring and diagnosing systems in realistic situations, where they are affected by time-varying controls and environmental parameters;

- evaluating the effects of control laws (*i.e.* sequences of actions) applied to specific systems in dynamically changing situations;

- evaluating consistency of models of dynamic systems with respect to sequences of measurements of observable variables (for data interpretation or theory validation).

Consider for example the problem of water supply control. A lake has a dam with floodgates that can be opened or closed to regulate the water flow through power generating turbines, the water level (stage) of the lake, and the downstream flow. The goal of a controller is to provide adequate reservoir capacity for power generation, consumption, industrial use, and recreation, as well as downstream flow. In exceptional circumstances, the controller must also work to minimize or avoid flooding both above and below the dam. This task is both difficult and vitally important to the residents of surrounding areas. Careful evaluation of the effect of actions in critical and dynamically changing situations is crucial for decision making, and sound modeling and simulation tools could be extremely useful to support this activity. They could also be used to evaluate empirically derived models and parameters, or to forewarn of undesired possible future situations.

This domain is challenging for existing approaches to modeling and simulation, for it poses many requirements. Several forms of incomplete information appear in this domain: for example, the precise shape and capacity of lakes or reservoirs is rarely known; the outflow from opening a dam's floodgates is only crudely measured; empirical data on the level/flow-rate curve for rivers becomes less and less accurate when flood conditions approach. Nonetheless, rough bounds on quantities are usually accurate enough to support decision. Pure qualitative reasoning techniques do not exploit the partial information available and consequently provide too weak predictions. Traditional numeric methods require much more precise information than is available, forcing modelers to make assumptions which may invalidate results and which may be difficult to evaluate. New models need to be constructed to cope with changes in relevant entities, operating modes, and modeling assumptions. Accurate results (instead of approximate ones) are needed to perform an adequate risk evaluation and forewarning.

Considering boundary conditions in qualitative simulation poses a number of basic questions that are independent from the specific framework adopted:

- *Ontology:* which ontology better suits the aim? Some approaches already known in literature exploit the concept of action, while others don't represent actions at all but focus on measurements. What is the relationship between the two concepts?

- *Temporal scale:* shall instantaneous or extended actions be allowed? The former may be adequate in certain situations but they introduce discontinuities difficult to handle, while the latter may impose a too detailed analysis.

- *Model structure:* how do boundary conditions affect the model? Changes in boundary conditions may call for changes in the model to cope with varying modeling assumptions. Do these changes require the same mechanism for revising the model as the ones required when operating regions are crossed? How do these changes interact with the chosen temporal scale?

- *Incomplete knowledge and data:* how will incompleteness in models and incompleteness in boundary conditions affect predictions? What is the sensitivity of predictions with respect to such kinds of incompleteness? What is needed to control the additional ambiguity of predictions caused by considering boundary conditions? How does qualitative time used in simulation correspond to "real" time used in observing and acting upon the system?

This paper discusses the main conceptual and practical aspects that underlie the problem of handling boundary conditions in SQPC (Semi-Quantitative Physics Compiler), an implemented program fulfilling the above mentioned requirements for modeling and simulating dynamic systems.

2   SEMI-QUANTITATIVE PHYSICS COMPILER

SQPC [Farquhar and Brajnik, 1995] performs *self-monitoring simulations* of incompletely known, dynamic, piecewise-continuous systems. It monitors the simulation in order to detect violations of model assumptions. When this happens, it modifies the model and resumes the simulation.

SQPC is built on top of the QSIM qualitative simulator [Kuipers, 1986; 1994] and extends QPC [Farquhar, 1994]. The input to SQPC is a *domain theory* and *scenario* specified in the SQPC modeling language. A domain theory consists of a set of quantified definitions, called *model fragments*, each of which describes some aspect of the domain, such as physical laws (*e.g.* mass conservation), processes (*e.g.* liquid flows), devices (*e.g.* pumps), and objects (*e.g.* containers). Each definition applies whenever there exists a set of participants for whom the stated conditions are satisfied. SQPC smoothly integrates symbolic with numeric information, and is able to provide useful results even when only part of the knowledge is numerically bounded. The domain theory includes *symbolic* or *numeric magnitudes* which represent specific real numbers known with uncertainty (numeric magnitudes constrain such numbers to lie within given ranges); *dimensional information*; *envelope schemas* (they state the conditions under which a specific monotonic function over a tuple of variables is bounded by a pair of numeric functions) and *tabular functions* (numeric functions defined automatically by interpolating multi-dimensional data tables). The specific system or situation being modeled is described by the scenario \definition, which lists objects that are of interest, some of the initial conditions and relations that hold throughout the scenario.

SQPC employs (inheriting it from QPC) a hybrid architecture in which the model-building portion is separated from the simulator. The domain theory and scenario induce a set of logical axioms. SQPC uses this database of logical axioms to infer the set of model fragment instances that apply during the time covered by the database (called the *active* model fragments). Inferences performed by SQPC concern structural relationships between objects declared in the scenario, and the computation of the transitive closure of order relationships between quantities. A database with a complete set of model fragment instances defines an initial value problem which is given to QSIM in terms of equations and initial conditions. If any of the predicted behaviors crosses the operating region conditions, the process is repeated. A new database is constructed to describe the system as it crosses the boundaries of the current model, then another complete set of active model fragments is determined and another simulation takes place.

The output of SQPC is a directed rooted graph, whose nodes are either databases or qualitative states. The root of the graph is the initial database, and a possible edge in the graph may: (i) link a database to a refined database (obtained by adding more facts, either derived through inference rules or assumed by SQPC when ambiguous situations are to be solved); (ii) link a complete database to a state (which is one of the possible initial states for the only model derivable from the database); (iii) link a state to a successor state (this link is computed by QSIM); and (iv) link a state to a database (the last state of a behavior that has crossed the operating region to the database that describes the situation just after the transition occurred). Each path from the root to a leaf describes one possible temporal evolution of the system being modeled, and each model in such paths identifies a distinct operating region of the system. SQPC is proven to construct all possible sequences of initial value problems that are entailed by the domain theory and scenario. Thanks to QSIM correctness, it produces also all possible trajectories.

3 BOUNDARY CONDITIONS AND AUTOMATED MODELING

The problem of performing a self-monitored simulation is extended by providing as input also a *stream of measurements* and by requiring that the output consists of *all possible* trajectories that are *compatible* with measurements.

A *measurement* is a time-tagged mapping of values to a set of variables, which can be either *exogenous*, (*i.e.* representing quantities that can be affected by external influences), or *non-exogenous*. The stream of measurements considered in a simulation must satisfy the following two assumptions: all critical points of all exogenous variables should be measured (*sampling assumption*); and measurements should be chronologically ordered.

For generality, we don't require other properties on measurements. In particular, they need not include *all* variables of the system; they need not concern each time the *same* set of variables; they need not be the result of a *periodic* sampling process, and their time tags and measured values may be expressed as intervals over the real numbers to cope with imprecise data and noise processing.

The following interdependent standpoints provide a rationale for these assumptions and are tentative answers to some of the questions raised in the introduction.

Ontology

An *action* is an activity done by some agent affecting some exogenous variable, while a *change* in such variables is the effect of an action. We prefer to explicitly represent changes and introduce only implicitly actions because appropriate treatment of changes is needed even in case actions are explicitly represented. Explicit representation of actions (like the one adopted in [Forbus, 1989]) could be useful in applications requiring the *generation* of control laws (*i.e.* deciding when to apply a certain action), an issue not tackled in this paper.

Measurements may or may not yield evidence of some action: they do it if they concern exogenous variables (the measured value may reveal that a change occurred or is occurring); they don't if they concern only non-exogenous ones.

Temporal Scales

We envision two kinds of actions (hence of changes): those with a finite duration (*extended changes*) and those occurring instantaneously (*instantaneous changes*). Both are worth considering: instantaneous changes may be used when the time-scale of the action is much smaller than the system's one and limited knowledge is available for modeling the transient during which the action takes place, or the transient is not interesting enough.

For example, given a medium-term analysis (days or weeks), an in-depth investigation of the transient occurring on a dam-lake system *during* a control action of opening a gate is uninteresting. Such a change can therefore be conceptualized as instantaneous. Similarly if no knowledge is at hand for modeling the dynamics during the transient, the effects of operating an electrical switch can be conceptualized again as instantaneous. On the other hand, extended changes could be profitably used when the actual duration is known and predictions of events occurring during the action are wanted; for example, to predict what actually happens inside a servo-controlled turbine when an operator changes the power level requested to the turbine.

While actions (and changes) may be instantaneous or not, measurements are assumed to be instantaneous events. The *sampling assumption* implies that the beginning and end of an extended change are marked by measurements, whereas the occurrence of an instantaneous change is marked by a single measurement. Therefore, during a *segment* (the time interval between two consecutive measurements of the same variable) an exogenous variable may be either constant or strictly monotonic. Of course, some knowledge is required to correctly interpret a measurement (whether it marks an instantaneous change or not) since by itself a measurement does not provide this information. This knowledge derives (in the proposed framework) from properties of measured exogenous variables declared in the scenario description. Such variables may be subject either to extended changes or to instantaneous ones, but not both.

Continuity

Continuity is a fundamental assumption for qualitative reasoning techniques used to constrain the possible intra/inter-model changes that can occur in a system. In order to manage instantaneous changes, we assume that:

1. *state* variables (variables whose time derivative is included in the model) are *piecewise-C^1* (*i.e.* continuous anywhere, and differentiable everywhere but in a set of isolated points);

2. *non-state* variables are at least *piecewise-C^0* (*i.e.* continuous anywhere but in a set of isolated points);

If an instantaneous change occurs on exogenous variables $\Delta = \{V_1 \ldots V_n\}$, in order to correctly deal with the transient, one needs to determine how the discontinuity propagates from Δ onto other variables of the model. Fortunately, the above mentioned continuity assumptions suffice to support a sound and effective criterion (termed *continuity suspension*) for identifying all the variables that are potentially affected by the discontinuity of variables in Δ.

Given a model M, let us say that a variable Z is *totally dependent* on a set of variables A iff the model includes a non-dynamic, continuous functional relation $R(X_1, \ldots X_i, Z, X_{i+1}, \ldots X_n)$ with $n \geq 1$ such that $\forall i : (X_i \in A$ or X_i is totally dependent on A). For example, if the model includes the constraint $((M (+ +)) X Y Z)$ then X is totally dependent on $\{Y, Z\}$. Furthermore, let $TD(A) = \{X \mid X$ is totally dependent on $A\}$.

Let $\mathcal{E}$ be the set of exogenous variables and S the set of state variables of M. Then define PD_Δ (the set of variables that are potentially affected by the discontinuity of variables in Δ) as the maximum set of variables of M that satisfies:

1. $\Delta \subseteq PD_\Delta$ (since variables in Δ are affected by the discontinuity);

2. $S \cap PD_\Delta = \emptyset$ (by continuity assumption, PD_Δ cannot contain any state variable);

3. $\mathcal{E} \cap PD_\Delta = \Delta$ (by the sampling and continuity assumptions, unmeasured exogenous variables must be continuous);

4. $TD(S \cup \mathcal{E} - \Delta) \cap PD_\Delta = \emptyset$ (by definition of total dependency, if Z totally depends on a set of necessarily continuous variables, then Z must be continuous too and cannot belong to PD_Δ).

Continuity suspension handles discontinuous changes of variables in Δ by computing the set PD_Δ so that, during a transient, variables in PD_Δ are unconstrained and can therefore get any new value, whereas those not in PD_Δ will keep their previous value.

Correctness of continuity suspension is easy to prove: if PD_Δ were equal to the set of all the variables in the model, then no restriction would be in effect during the transient, yielding all possible value changes, including the "true" ones. Since conditions 2, 3 and 4 would remove from PD_Δ only necessarily continuous variables, no variable affected by Δ will be ever removed from PD_Δ.

Unfortunately, continuity suspension is not complete, for the set PD_Δ may include also variables that are not affected by Δ (for example, if $y = \frac{dx}{dt}$ belongs to the model and $y \notin TD(S \cup \mathcal{E})$, then $y \in PD_\Delta$). Rules 1-4 are not sufficiently strong to exclude certain variables from PD_Δ. They exclude only variables that are *necessarily continuous*, leaving in PD_Δ those that are *necessarily discontinuous* (like those in Δ) plus those that are *possibly discontinuous* (like y). On the other hand, since PD_Δ is determined on the basis of the model holding before the transient takes place, and nothing is known about what happens during the transient, soundness demands that only necessarily continuous variables are removed from PD_Δ.

Non-exogenous variables can be measured too, but unlike exogenous ones their behavior during a segment is not known in advance, and they do not introduce discontinuities. Such measurements greatly refine predictions (by restricting predicted ranges or by rejecting predictions that are inconsistent with measured values), if they simultaneously involve several variables.

Model structure

Actions may affect the model structure in two ways.

First, they may affect the set of modeling assumptions, calling for a revision of model structure. Model revision may occur either during an extended change (*e.g.* when a valve is being opened the flow regime of the fluid may change from laminar to turbulent), or during the transient of a discontinuous change (*e.g.* if opening a valve is an instantaneous action, then a discontinuous change propagates onto other variables, and new models need to be defined to accurately cover the possible consequences of such a quick action). In the former case no discontinuity is introduced,

reducing model revision to the "normal" revision triggered by the crossing of an operating region (in the previously mentioned example, the region being crossed refers to the variable *Reynolds-number* becoming greater than a certain threshold). In the latter case (model revision occurring during an instantaneous change) the discontinuity in PD_Δ weakens the process of determining the next model(s): referring to the previous example, the discontinuous change in valve section affects other variables (like fluid flow, speed, etc.) whose "next" value will not be constrained by continuity, making it difficult to ascertain whether the flow, after the change, will still be laminar or will became turbulent. In fact, though conceptually being determined by state variables, variables in PD_Δ - Δ usually cannot be given a unique new value if continuity is relaxed because of the inherent ambiguity of the qualitative algebra of signs.

Second, two modeling decisions may be inconsistent. The decision of determining the set of exogenous variables and the decision of determining the set of state variables may lead to two kinds of conflicts: (i) if some state variables are treated as exogenous the resulting model may be overconstrained. Analytically this would lead, in general, to a badly defined model whereas qualitatively this is not necessarily true, since the incomplete knowledge used in the model and state may supply additional degrees of freedom; (ii) state variables may get values which are incompatible with those measured for exogenous variables. Such discrepancies are an indication that the model is clearly a wrong description of the system under study. Both kinds of conflicts are easily identified, though their automatic resolution is far from being trivial since it requires a modeling choice.

4 SEMI-QUANTITATIVE BOUNDARY PROBLEMS

In order to perform a simulation guided by measurements the user has to declare which are the exogenous variables, which are their properties and how to acquire their measurements. This is done in the scenario declaration form (see Figure 1). The property of being piecewise-constant or piecewise-monotonic is invariant in a scenario.

Including a new measurement in a simulation may lead to a model revision and/or a state change. SQPC handles each measurement as a transition (called measurement-transition, or

```
(DefScenario Lake Travis
  :entities ((travis        :type lakes)
             (colorado-dn   :type rivers)
             (colorado-up   :type rivers)
             (mansfield     :type dams)
             (turbine-1     :type mansfield-turbines))
  :structural-relations((flows-into colorado-up travis)
                        (connects mansfield travis colorado-dn)
                        (has-valve mansfield turbine-1))
  :landmarks ((top-of-dam :variables ((stage travis)) : value 714))    ; ft
  :initial-conditions  ((=  (power turbine-1) 20)                      ; Mw
                        (=  (stage travis) (690.25 690.3))             ; ft
                        (=  (flow-rate colorado-up) (900 950))         ; cfs
                        (=  (base turbine-1) 564))                     ; ft
  :exogenous-variables
      (((power turbine-1)         :type  :pw-constant)
       ((flow-rate colorado-up)   :type  :pw-monotonic))
  :measurements (((7.0e5 7.01e5)                ; sec
                  ((power turbine-1) 10))       ; Mw
                 ((4.32e6 4.33e6)               ; sec
                  ((flow-rate colorado-up)   (400 420))))
  ... )
```

Figure 1. Declaration of exogenous variables in scenario definition (clause **:exogenous-variables**): (**power turbine-1**) is declared *piecewise-constant* while (**flow-rate colorado-up**) is *piecewise-monotonic*. Two measurements are given (clause **:measurements**): one after approx. 8 days (between 7.0e5 and 7.01e5 sec.) regarding an instantaneous action which brings (**power turbine-1**) to the value of 10 Mw, the other regarding an action lasting approx. 50 days (4.32e6 and 4.33e6 sec.) specifying a decrease of (**flow-rate colorado-up**) from its initial value to a value comprised between 400 and 420 cfs.

M-transition) between two models. When building a new database SQPC adds measured values in the database and recognizes ongoing actions by looking ahead in the measurement stream for each piecewise-monotonic variable[1]. The new model will include appropriate constraints: **constant** for piecewise-constant variables; **constant, increasing** or **decreasing** for piecewise-monotonic ones, according to the difference of measured values at the ends of the segment.

Two decisions are critical when performing a measurement-guided simulation: realizing when an M-transition occurs and deciding how to revise the model and its initial state.

Recognizing M-transitions

An M-transition occurs when simulation time T_s (the time of the last state being simulated, S) and the time T_m of the next measurement are the same. Unfortunately, unless predictions are very precise, this comparison is usually ambiguous, for time ranges might be overlapping. Even if measured values were extremely precise (*i.e.* singleton ranges), as long as predicted ranges for time have positive length, they would be a source

of ambiguity. In the worst case the three possible orderings between T_s and T_m need to be generated.

Two situations may occur when deciding whether to fire an M-transition: the measurement is taken while some action is ongoing (*i.e.* some exogenous variable is moving towards its final — with respect to the ongoing action — value) or not. In the former case, information of the value of such variables in state S can be used to reduce the ambiguity in T_s and T_m: for example, if such variables reach their values in S and their values are measured at time T_m, then it follows that $T_s = T_m$. In the latter case (only piecewise-constant or non-exogenous variables are involved in the measurement), or when ambiguity is not completely resolved, all three possibilities are explicitly represented (the non-overlap situation is straightforward, and subsumed by the overlap one):

- $T_m = T_s$, and S is indeed the state involved with the measurement; if T_m and T_s overlap, $T_m = T_s$ is asserted in S (usually restricting T_s).

- $T_m < T_s$, which means that the simulation advanced too much. Since the M-transition check is performed at each point state, S must be the first point state whose T_s is greater than T_m. A new state S´ is generated by copying it from the predecessor of S (an interval state), and $T_s = T_m$ is asserted on S´. S is discarded.

---

[1] The depth of such a lookahead is user-defined, and may range from the next absolute measurement to the measurement ending the next segment of each piecewise-monotonic variable.

- $T_m > T_s$, meaning that we should keep on simulating. No M-transition occurs from S, and $T_m > T_s$ is asserted on S.

Revising the model and generating an initial state

When a model has to be revised on the basis of a measurement, the specific details on how it does change depend on which variables are measured and if there are ongoing actions. There are four cases:

1. the next measurement includes only *non exogenous variables*. In this case the model does not change, qualitative values inherited by variables across the M-transition do not change either, and the only thing that changes is their new ranges (*i.e.* measured and predicted ranges are intersected in the initial state);

2. the next measurement includes only *piecewise-constant exogenous variables* **Δ**. Continuity suspension is applied across the M-transition by (i) assigning measured values to variables in **Δ**, (ii) inheriting previous values for variables not in **PD$_Δ$**, and (iii) leaving variables in **PD$_Δ$ — Δ** unspecified. When SQPC constructs a database from the model and the state originating the M-transition, the usual SQPC refinement mechanisms (including QSIM's state completion) will be used to deduce appropriate initial values for variables in **PD$_Δ$ — Δ**.

3. a set of *piecewise-monotonic exogenous variables M* are affected by some ongoing actions. In order to revise the model, SQPC does a lookahead searching for the next measured value for each variable in **M**. By comparing their current values with measured ones, appropriate time-dependent constraints (saying that a variable is either *increasing, decreasing or constant* on its next segment) are added to the model (if no next measurement is available the variable is assumed **constant**). The new model is then initialized with values inherited from the transition state, since all variables are continuous across the M-transition.

4. *any combination of previous cases (1, 2 and 3)*. This is dealt with by a straightforward combination of respective operations, since there is no complex interaction between the effects of simultaneous measurements of variables having different properties.

4.1 IMPLEMENTATION ISSUES

The solution outlined above leads to two pragmatic issues. First, SQPC performs a model revision step for each considered measurement. Since model revision steps are expensive in terms of computing resources (empirically, they consume up to 75% of the time required by a simulation), it is worth investigating whether this activity can be made more efficient. Fortunately, it turns out that model revision triggered by M-transition is limited and well defined. On one hand, if no piecewise-constant variables are involved in the measurement, the only part of the model that is subject to change are the constraints on exogenous variables and their quantity spaces. No complex reasoning is needed to generate the new model nor its initial state: both can be directly derived from previous ones. On the other hand, if the measurement involves some piecewise-constant variables, propagating their discontinuities onto other variables may cause ambiguous evaluation of operating conditions of model fragments, leading to expensive branching in simulation. Even in this case, however, there is a simple syntactic criterion that can be used to detect whether the discontinuity affects the set of active model fragments. In fact, if variables in PD$_Δ$ are not used in conditions of any model fragment, then no model fragment depends on them, the model structure does not change and continuity suspension suffices to compute the next state. This criterion has a dramatic effect on run-times: an activity which requires a few minutes is performed in just a few seconds. Second, measurements introduce a number of distinctions that would go unnoticed in a non-guided simulation.

First, each measured value is normally associated to a landmark, which needs to be totally ordered in respective quantity space. In general, increasing the cardinality of quantity spaces increases the number of distinctions that the qualitative simulator does. In SQPC, landmark creation can be disabled across M-transitions, reducing the resolution of the output (since variables' values across M-transitions are not represented as landmarks labeled with numeric ranges), but reducing also the ambiguity that can occur when suspending continuity.

Second, a three-way branch occurs if simulation time overlaps with measurement time. One branch is marked with the assumption $T_m = T_s$, where T_s is the time of a qualitative event (*e.g.* some variable reaching a landmark). Though theoretically sound, the probability that a measurement — an instantaneous event — is taken at the same time of an independent, instantaneous qualitative event (*e.g.* measuring a gate opening exactly when the lake stage reaches a threshold) is infinitesimal. This is another sort of distinction that can be neglected without much loss of information.

Third, another sort of ambiguity is caused by distinctions made on order relationships between overlapping ranges of consecutive measurements of an exogenous variable. Special purpose user-defined predicates can be used by SQPC for comparing two overlapping ranges in order to reduce ambiguity.

5 AN EXAMPLE

We will demonstrate SQPC on a problem regarding the domain of water supply control. Consider a portion of the system of lakes and rivers to be found in the scenic hill country surrounding Austin, Texas. The Colorado river flows into Lake Travis; the Mansfield Dam on Lake Travis produces hydroelectric power and controls the level of the lake and the flow into the downstream leg of the Colorado.

The problem is to evaluate the effects of some actions in a "what-if" scenario (Figure 1). We are given an initial level for Lake Travis (a value between 690.2 and 690.3 ft), a rough initial inflow from the Colorado river (between 900 and 950 cfs) and an initial requested rate of 20 Mw for the power delivered by the hydroelectric plant. In addition it is known that the input flow is decreasing — its minimum rate has been estimated between 400 and 420 cfs after 50 days. The task is to determine what happens to the lake level and evaluate the effect of reducing the requested power from 20 to 10 Mw after 8 days.

Several model fragments describe the behavior of lakes, rivers, dams, turbine, etc., and envelope schemas provide numeric bounds on relations between quantities. Most envelopes are derived from tabular data resulting from engineering estimates. Table 1 partially describes

Head (ft)	Power (Mw)	Discharge-rate (cfs)
120	8	1,054
120	9	1,150
...	...	...
125	8	1,026
...	...	...
150	30	2,936

Table 1. A portion of the table describing turbine behavior. *e.g.*, given a head of 120 ft and a power setting of 8 Mw, the discharge rate is expected to be 1054 cfs.

the behavior of turbines in Mansfield Dam.[2] In this example, tables are interpolated stepwise by SQPC to provide piecewise-constant (rather imprecise, but accurate) upper and lower bounds. Turbines are controlled by servo-mechanisms designed to generate the desired amount of power regardless of the hydraulic pressure, which is determined by the head at the turbine. This is possible as long as there is sufficient head: when it drops below the minimum threshold for a given power output then less power is released. Different sets of model fragments capture these operating modes accurately.

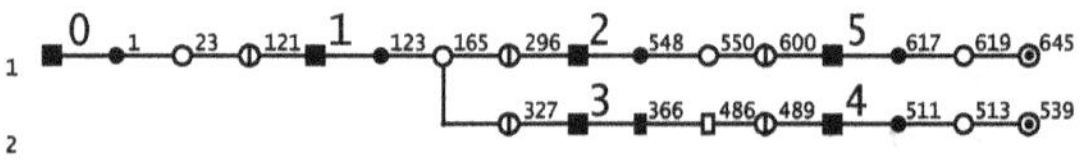

Figure 2: Two behaviors are predicted for the scenario, ending both in quiescent states. Each involves four models (black squares), two M-transitions and one transition (from model 2 to 5 for the first behavior, from 1 to 3 for the second one) from a servo-controlled to a non controlled operating regime of the turbine.

Figure 2 shows the two predicted behaviors. They are generated because of the time-ambiguity between the second measurement and the transition of the turbine to a new operating region (the latter event occurring between 9 and 87 days). Figure 3 shows the time plot of some of the variables in the first behavior. Under the specified boundary conditions the power level of 20 Mw will surely be maintained until time T1, the time of the first measurement (8 days); then, though reducing the requested power, eventually there will be insufficient hydraulic pressure to supply

[2] The Lower Colorado River Authority has contributed actual tables of empirical data to the Qualitative Reasoning Group of the University of Texas for evaluation.

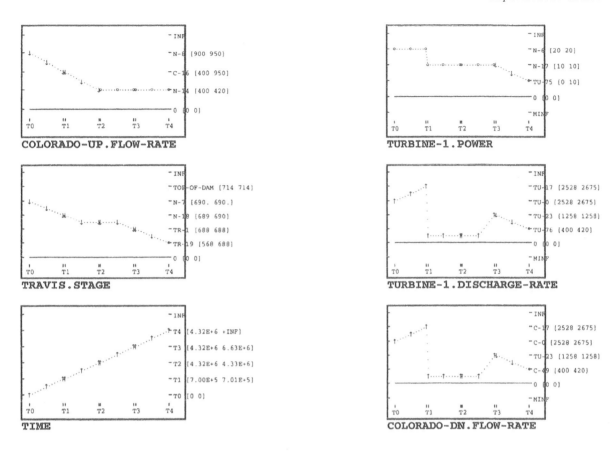

Figure 3. Plot of some of the variables for the first of two behaviors predicted for the scenario. The first M-transition occurs at time **T1** (notice the sudden drop of **TURBINE-1.POWER** and affected variables **TURBINE-1.DISCHARGE-RATE** and **COLORADO-DN.FLOW-RATE**). The second one at **T2**, where **COLORADO-UP.FLOW-RATE** becomes constant. Finally, at **T3** a transition occurs to a region where the turbine is no longer servo-controlled (TRAVIS. STAGE reaches the threshold 688 ft). **TURBINE-1.POWER** is no longer treated as an exogenous variable (since the servo-mechanism does not operate any more) and it becomes a dependent variable.

the requested power. This will happen for the first behavior (Figure 3) at time T3, between 50 and 76 days (*i.e.* after the measurement of the input flow rate is taken). For the second behavior, not shown, after at least 8 days and not beyond 50 days (*i.e.* before the measurement). Finally, the lake system reaches equilibrium with the lake level stabilized between 568 and 588 ft.

Notice the instantaneous change occurring on variable **TURBINE-1.POWER** at time **T1** which affects other variables like **TURBINE-1. DISCHARGE-RATE**. Continuity suspension is applied to these variables and their behavior across the M-transition occurring at **T1** is not constrained. On the other hand, the second M-transition occurs when the input flow rate reaches its lowest value and since it involves a piecewise-monotonic variable, all variables are continuous across the transition.

If measurements included observations for other (non-exogenous) variables, then the ambiguity in times could disappear and certain ranges shrink. For example, if the second measurement were

```
((4.32e6  4.33e6)
 ((flow-rate colorado-up) (400 420))
 ((stage travis) (688.5 688.7)))
```

(*i.e.* of the same input flow-rate, taken at the same time [4.32e6 4.33e6] but involving in addition the non-exogenous variable **stage travis**), then only the first behavior would be consistent with the observed value of the lake stage. In fact, only in the first behavior, the ordering of the events "head reaching the minimum threshold (when stage= 688 ft)" and "measurement at time [4.32e6 4.33e6]" is compatible.

5.1 IMPLEMENTATION STATUS

SQPC is fully implemented in Lucid Common Lisp as an extension to QPC, which in turn uses QSIM. We are currently experimenting with SQPC in the water supply control domain and in economics. It has been run on several examples comparable to the one shown in this paper. The runtime for this example is around 8 minutes on a Sun 20. The bulk of this time is spent computing order relations with interpreted rules during the three full-fledged modeling steps. Using a special purpose inequality reasoner, whose implementation is underway, will result in a substantial (orders of magnitude) speedup.

6 RELATED WORK

Several efforts facing the issues discussed in this paper have been reported in literature, but none of them covers the whole problem or provides viable and sound solutions.

[Kuipers and Shults, 1994] and [Forbus, 1989] provide some means to represent external influences on a system and to implement a guided simulation. *Expressive Behavior Tree Logic* [Kuipers and Shults, 1994] is a temporal logic (integrated in QSIM) that can be used to specify, in logical statements, the qualitative behavior of variables and have QSIM generate a simulation compatible with them. This method, still under development, is complementary with respect to the one presented in this paper, since it does not handle model revisions caused by external influences nor quantitative information.

Forbus [Forbus, 1989] explicitly introduces the concept of action, with pre and post-conditions. The purely qualitative total envisionment that is generated includes all possible instantiation of known actions. Forbus allows only instantaneous actions and adopts heuristic criteria to handle discontinuities. No provision is made to handle quantitative information, nor to focus the envisionment process.

One work that centers on discontinuities either caused by external influences or autonomous, is that of [Nishida and Doshita, 1987]. Nishida and Doshita describe two methods for handling discontinuities: (i) approximating a discontinuous change by a quick continuous change and (ii) introducing mythical states to describe how a system is supposed to go through during a discontinuous change. The former requires a complex machinery to compute the limit of the quick change, whereas the second is based on heuristic criteria for selecting appropriate states.

Many other approaches have been described which aim to interpret measurements of dynamic systems. Some of them do not perform a simulation, like DATMI [DeCoste, 1991] which interprets measurements with respect to a total envisionment. Others, like MIMIC [Dvorak, 1992], though performing a semi-quantitative simulation and refining predictions with measured data, do not cope with model revisions nor with guided simulations. (Indeed, some of the ideas presented in SQPC descend from techniques first applied in MIMIC, *e.g.* for integrating measurements into simulations.)

7 CONCLUSION

The main issues arising from considering measurements in a self-monitoring simulation have been discussed. Boundary conditions expressed in terms of instantaneous or extended changes of exogenous variables are used to guide and refine an online or offline (depending on the depth of the lookahead) incremental simulation of incompletely known lumped-parameters systems.

From the conceptual analysis and from the experimental activity done so far, it appears that considering boundary conditions by itself does not aggravate the uncertainty of predictions. If measurements are added to a scenario of an incompletely known situation, the precision of the output does not change significantly. Nor does it change if measured values become less precise. It does worsen considerably though if uncertainly affects the time of events, because of range overlap, which is dealt with by representing the different orderings of events. If inter-dependent variables are simultaneously measured, however, the output precision increases since ranges can be restricted and inconsistent behaviors refuted. Furthermore, it would be straightforward to extend SQPC in such a way to suggest to the user when some additional measurement would be needed to reduce the ambiguity.

Discontinuous changes are comparatively more difficult to handle. The adopted criterion to handle the transient, continuity suspension, limits the combinatorial growth of possible trajectories taking place during the transient by restricting the number of variables that could be affected by discontinuities. The method is correct and, though incomplete, it has not proven yet to be a bottleneck. Furthermore, though used only on M-transitions, continuity suspension is a general criterion that could be used also to handle other kinds of transitions imposing discontinuous changes on variables (for example to model abrupt faults).

Computationally, the cost of handling non-autonomous systems is often relatively low (even in cases where a limited model revision is needed). It may well happen, however, that dealing with instantaneous changes requires a complex modeling activity. Even though appropriate precautions are taken to limit the number of such activities, a substantial number of measurements with ambiguous events quickly leads to intractable problems.

In conclusion, we believe that given the generality of the assumptions underlying the techniques presented in the paper, and given the relatively low computational cost that is often required to solve a boundary value problem, it seems worthwhile employing them to widen the applicability spectrum of Qualitative Reasoning.

ACKNOWLEDGMENTS

Part of the research reported in this paper took place while I was visiting the UT Qualitative Reasoning Group, at Austin, TX during 1992. I'm indebted to Ben Kuipers for many illuminating discussions, and to Adam Farquhar for letting me use his QPC program. Many thanks to Dan Clancy and Bert Kay for making me understand several parts of QSIM and to Franco Ceotto for his help in implementing SQPC.

REFERENCES

[Bobrow, 1993] D. Bobrow. Special volume: AI in perspective. *Artificial Intelligence*, 59(1-2):103-146, 1993.

[DeCoste, 1991] D. DeCoste. Dynamic across-time measurement interpretation. *Artificial Intelligence,* 51, 1991.

[Dvorak, 1992] Daniel L. Dvorak. Monitoring and diagnosis of continuous dynamic systems using semiquantitative simulation. Technical Report AI 92-170, Artificial Intelligence Laboratory, The University of Texas at Austin, 1992.

[Farquhar and Brajnik, 1995] Adam Farquhar and Giorgio Brajnik. A semi-quantitative physics compiler. In *Tenth International Conference on Applications of Artificial Intelligence in Engineering*, Udine, Italy, July 1995. Presented also at the Eighth International Workshop on Qualitative Reasoning on Physical Systems, 1994, Nara, Japan.

[Farquhar, 1994] A. Farquhar. A qualitative physics compiler. In *Proc. of the 12th National Conference on Artificial Intelligence*, pages 1168-1174. AAAI Press / The MIT Press, 1994.

[Forbus, 1989] K. Forbus. Introducing actions into qualitative simulation. In *IJCAI-89*, pages 1273-1278, 1989.

[Kuipers and Shults, 1994] B. Kuipers and B. Shults. Reasoning in logic about continuous systems. In *8th International Workshop on Qualitative Reasoning about physical systems*, pages 164-175, Nara, Japan, 1994.

[Kuipers, 1986] Benjamin Kuipers. Qualitative simulation. *Artificial Intelligence*, 29:289-338, 1986.

[Kuipers, 1994] B. Kuipers. *Qualitative Reasoning: modeling and simulation with incomplete knowledge*. MIT Press, Cambridge, Massachusetts, 1994.

[Nishida and Doshita, 1987] T. Nishida and S. Doshita. Reasoning about discontinuous change, In *AAAI87*, pages 643-648, 1987.

CLASSROOM CONNECTIONS

Introducing Boundary Conditions in Semi-Quantitative Simulation

Multiple Choice

Pick the best answer.

1. **What are the main problems of monitoring and controlling water supply?**
   A. The systems change over time and environmental conditions.
   B. Evaluating effects of laws and how they apply in various situations.
   C. To provide adequate reservoir capacity for power generation, consumption, industrial use, recreation, down-stream flow and minimize or avoid flooding both above and below the dam.
   D. Evaluating the effects of actions such as opening or closing gates to turbines and flood gates in dynamical and critical situations.

2. **What kinds of imprecise or incomplete information can be found in environmental systems such as flood prediction or water supply control?**
   A. Precise shape and size of lake or reservoir is rarely known.
   B. Empirical data on the level/flow-rate curve for rivers becomes less and less accurate when flood conditions approach.
   C. The outflow from opening a dam's floodgates is only roughly measured.
   D. All of the above.

3. **What kinds of AI tools can be helpful in solving this problem?**
   A. Qualitative representation of imprecise and incomplete information.
   B. Ontologies – knowledge representation of concepts like boundary conditions and their relationships to time and action.
   C. Qualitative models.
   D. All of the above.

True or False

Please decide if each of the statements below are True or False.

4. Knowledge is required to interpret a measurement.

5. Purely qualitative models (as opposed to AI based qualitative models) make weaker predictions because they cannot exploit the available partial information.

6. Simulations based on qualitative concepts and ontologies allow for more continuous and changing situations to be evaluated under imprecise information.

7. Numerical models can help predict problems, but they require precision and force modelers to make assumptions that can invalidate results.

8. Precise shape and size of water systems are rarely known.

Answers can be found at the end of the book.

Chapter 3

Integrating General Expert Knowledge and Specific Experimental Knowledge in Waste Water Treatment Plants

Miquel Sànchez,
Universitat Politècnica de Catalunya, Spain

Ulises Cortés,
Universitat Politècnica de Catalunya, Spain

Ignasi R. Roda,
Universitat de Girona, Spain

Manel Poch,
Universitat de Girona, Spain

ABSTRACT

The development of an architecture able to manage efficiently the different elements of the process (*integrated architecture*), to learn from past experience (*specific experimental knowledge*) and to acquire the domain knowledge (*general expert knowledge*) are the key problems in real-time control AI systems design. These problems increase when the process belongs to an *ill-structured domain* and it is composed by several complex operational units. Therefore, an integrated AI methodology which combines both kinds of knowledge is proposed. This multi-paradigm reasoning provides the target system – a wastewater treatment plant (WWTP) – with some advantages over other approaches applied to real world systems.

1 INTRODUCTION

1.1 WASTEWATER TREATMENT PLANTS AND AI

The main goal of a wastewater treatment plant is to reduce the pollution level of the wastewater at the lowest cost, that is, to remove within the possible measure strange compounds (pollutants) of the inflow water to the plant prior to discharge to the environment. So, the effluent water has the lowest levels of pollutants possible (in any case, lower than the maximum ones allowed by the law).

The plants taken as models in this study are based on the main biological technology usually applied: the *activated sludge* process [Robusté, 1990]. The target wastewater plant studied is located in Manresa, near Barcelona (Catalonia).

This plant receives about 30000 m^3/day inflow from 75000 inhabitants. The activated sludge process directly depends on live beings (microorganisms), and therefore, on changes experienced by them. It could be possible to get a good plant operation if the supervisory control system is able to react to the changes and deviations of the system and can take the necessary actions to restore the system's performance.

These features reveal that supervision and control of activated sludge processes could only be treated in a multi-disciplinary integrated way [Venkatasubramanian, 1994] that includes: *monitoring* (sensor developing, continuous analysis equipment), *modelling* (equations that model the bioreactors' behaviour), *control* (maintaining good effluent water quality and reducing operation costs), *qualitative information* (microbiological information, water's colour and odour, water's appearance, etc.), *expert knowledge* (supplied by the large experience from plants' managers, biologists and operators) and *experimental knowledge* (specific knowledge supplied by the previous solved problems in the system). Last features, commonly provide the systems with incomplete, uncertain or approximate information. Therefore, AI can play a good role in WWTP supervision [Stephanopoulos, 1990; Patry and Chapman, 1989; Stephanopoulos and Stephanopoulos, 1986].

1.2 GOALS

This paper presents an approach to integration of general knowledge (coming from experts' domain knowledge or expert knowledge) with specific knowledge supplied from previous solved problems in the system (experimental or practical knowledge). The expert knowledge will be modelled through explicit inference rules, while the experimental knowledge will be modelled by means of cases or experiences. This cooperation tries to get benefit from the advantages of both kinds of knowledge, and to cope with typical shortcomings either from knowledge-based systems: do not learn from experience, the knowledge acquisition problem, the brittleness; or from automatic control systems: complexity of the processes, ill-structured domains, non-numerical or qualitative information, uncertainty or approximate knowledge. This paradigm combination integrates in a single architecture some cognitive processes as knowledge-based reasoning, case-based reasoning, learning, knowledge acquisition, problem solving [Plaza *et al.* 1993].

2 GENERAL EXPERT KNOWLEDGE

In this paradigm, the knowledge about the domain is modelled with inference rules. The process of extracting these rules (knowledge acquisition) from experts – with interactive sessions where the experts try to make explicit their knowledge and reasoning processes – is quite often described as a bottleneck. Therefore, much effort in AI has been addressed to overcome it. In this case, the knowledge acquisition process have been done with Linneo+ [Béjar, 1995] (a semiautomatic classification tool). The main objective of Linneo+ is to build classifications for ill-structured domains; where much imprecise information exists, it is assumed that observations vary in their degree of membership with regard to each class. Bearing all this in mind, the use of the conventional concept of distance as a fuzzy similarity value is used.

A crucial point for the WWTP supervision is the concept of working situations. *A situation is an operational working state of the plant, described by measures of the relevant attributes of the process.* The experts characterized 20 *working situations* of a plant using 23 attributes [Serra *et al.*, 1994]:

bulking-non-filamentous	normal
bulking-sulphures	rising
bulking-not-enough-oxygen	foaming
bulking-too-much-oxygen	underaeration
bulking-F/M	overareation
bulking-toxic-substances	surging
high-plant-inflow	storm
bad-clarifiers-operation	overloading
bad-primary-settlers-operation	bad-wasting
in-plant-overloading	
toxic-substances-loading	

Each situation could be defined in terms of raw descriptions and relationships. For example, the *bulking-non-filamentous* situation was defined as follows:

Outflow-COD	–> High
Sludge age	–> Old
Filamentous	–> Normal
SVI	–> High
Volatile SS-recircul.	–> Low
All-other-attr.	–> Nought-value (don't care)

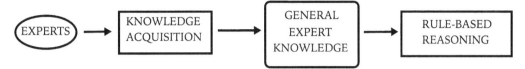

Figure 1. General expert knowledge.

The results of the classification process with Linneo+ provide intensive and extensive description of the generated classes (*situations*) and a *fuzzy membership matrix* that relates observations (data) to generated classes. At this point, inference rules can be generated. This process is depicted in Figure 1. Bearing in mind the *prototype* of a class and the superclassification structure, inference rules that lead the *diagnosis* process in the target system, can be derived. These rules *identify* to which class (set of situations) belongs a given observation (data). *Identifying rules* characterize the values that descriptors of new data must show for being member of a class. For instance a rule as the following could be generated:

```
(if      (COD-EXIT HIGH
         SVI HIGH
         SS-RECIRCULATION LOW
         SSV-RECIRCULATION LOW)
    VERY-POSSIBLE
         (INFER CLASS-3A))
```

Other *discriminating rules* must be provided to discriminate to which situation -within a class- belongs a given observation. For this task is taken into account the *fuzzy membership matrix*. For example:

```
(if      (CLASS-3 A
         SLUDGE OLD
         FILAMENTOUS NORMAL)
    ALMOST-SURE
    (INFER BULKING-NON-FILAMENTOUS))
```

This process is semi-automatic, so that requires the experts' final validation. All these rules are analyzed (subsumption detection, synonymy analysis, etc.) and, afterwards, they are organized in a hierarchical way to guide the diagnosis process. The results are made known to the experts who can accept and confirm them, or have the chance to go back to the classification process.

When all these actions are over, rules can be validated using new observations not previously included in the classification sample. As soon as rules are accepted by experts, they can be incorporated into the KB's of the distributed architecture. These rules capture the subjective domain knowledge of the experts in their daily work at the WWTP. From the several KB's can be done the diagnosis process that leads to identify the *generic working situation(s)* of the plant.

3 SPECIFIC EXPERIMENTAL KNOWLEDGE

In this approach, the knowledge about the practical problem solving in the domain is represented by means of cases or experiences (in this case *situations*), which are organized in the Case library. This Case library contains information about previously detected situations and solutions given to them, as well as their efficiency (specific experimental knowledge). A Case-based reasoning can be performed in order to get benefit from these past experiences and cases. The Case library will be modified accordingly with the new information [Kolodner, 1993; Schank and Slade, 1991; Riesbeck and Schank, 1989].

Cases denote a *working situation* of the plant. These cases are previously experienced situations, which have been captured and learned – in such a way – that they can be reused in the solving of future situations. The reasoning process in the Case-Based Reasoning and Learning agent is performed by a general cycle described by the following steps:

- *Retrieving* the most similar case(s) (previous working situations) by means of some heuristic functions or distances, possibly domain dependent.

- *Adapting* or reusing the information and knowledge in that case to solve the new problem (the current working situation of the plant).

- *Evaluation* of the proposed solution. Usually, it is performed by simulation, by questioning the human oracle or by future checking of effectiveness.

- *Learning* the parts of this experience likely to be useful for future problem solving. The agent can learn both from successful solutions and from failed ones. This retaining is made by updating the Case library accordingly.

The initial Case library is fitted with some situations obtained by Linneo+ classification, from a real data stream of 521 data (days) corresponding to the period 1990–1991. Each datum is described by means of the daily mean of 39 variables. That study [Sànchez *et al.*, 1994a] provided a classification of the real *specific working situations* of the concrete plant. It is interesting to notice that with these data Linneo+ discovered that there are four subtypes of *normal situations* (usually not considered by the experts) and revealed that about 20% of the variables provided by the plant's operators were not relevant for the characterization of *situations*. The resulting situations were:

Toxic substances loading	Normal (4)
Primary-treatment problems	Solid's shock
Plant problems	Storm
Secondary-treatment problems	

So, the Case library contains a set of experienced situations of the plant (specific situations). It evolves from initial contents and captures the experimental knowledge of the concrete plant under control, learning either from its successfully solved situations (plans) or from its failed ones (objective knowledge). All this process is shown in Figure 2.

4 THE INTEGRATED AND DISTRIBUTED SUPERVISORY MULTI-LEVEL ARCHITECTURE

The proposed architecture (called DAI-DEPUR [Sànchez *et al.*, 1994b]) is a distributed and integrated supervisory multi-level system (see Figure 3). It is a *distributed* architecture so that is formed of several interacting subsystems (agents) that can be executed in parallel. For instance, the supervisory agent, the case-based reasoning

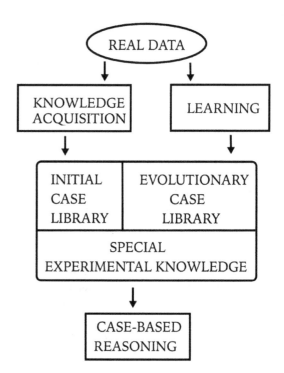

Figure 2. Specific experimental knowledge.

agent, primary settler-KBS agent, biological reactor-KBS agent, etc. Distribution criteria are based on spatial and semantic distance [Bond and Gasser, 1988]. The main reason to choose a Supervisory Distributed AI System is because for WWTP there is a set of fixed *abnormal* situations as *Storm, Bulking, Toxic load,* etc., that may be treated with a predetermined plan or strategy, in a more efficient way than other types of DAI architectures as Blackboard Systems or Contract Nets (see [Sànchez *et al.*, 1994b] for a more detailed description).

DAI-DEPUR is an *integrated* architecture because of joining in a single system several cognitive tasks as learning, reasoning, knowledge acquisition, problem solving, etc. Moreover, focusing on the *expertise level* [Steels, 1990] – that is the aim of this paper, – there is the integration of the two paradigms of knowledge modelling.

Also, the architecture is *multi-level*, and provides independence to all the levels. Taking into account the domain theory (models), it can be structured as a four-level architecture: 1) data level, 2) expertise level, 3) situations level and 4) plans level.

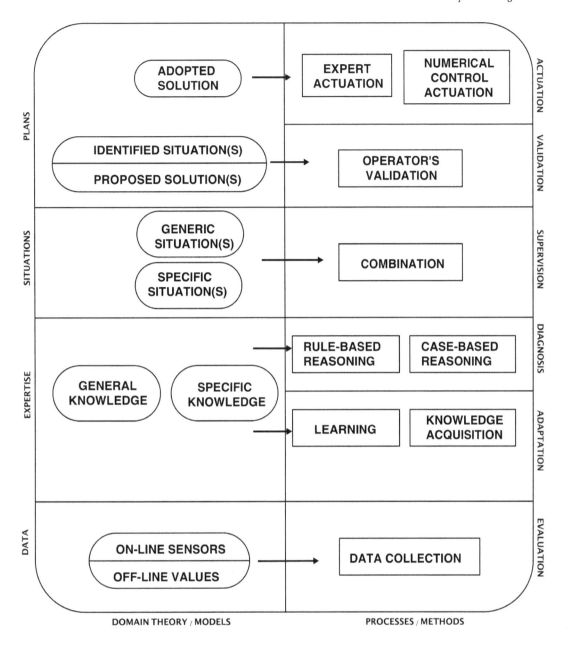

Figure 3. Integrated supervisory multi-level architecture.

Data level

It is formed of on-line data gathered from sensors and off-line values provided by the operator as laboratory analysis, subjective information, etc.

Expertise level

Modelled by the two paradigms or approaches explained in this paper: general expert knowledge and specific experimental knowledge.

Situations level

The *global operating situation* of a plant is obtained by combination of its several subsystems' *local situations*.

Plans level

At this level, the identified *whole situation*, some previous solved similar situations as well as predefined (canned) plans are taken into account to propose a first solution, that has to be validated against the operator, who can modify the proposed plan. Then, an arranged plan can be executed to cope with the actual operating situation of the plant. *Plans* are a sequence of actions to be taken in order to restore the plant performance.

On the other hand, considering the processes acting over the models (methods), the architecture can be decomposed into a six-level process or 6 phases: 1) evaluation level, 2) adaptation level, 3) diagnosis level, 4) supervision level, 5) validation level and 6) actuation level. The system activates a new supervisory cycle at fixed intervals of time.

Evaluation process

For this purpose it is necessary to know some values for certain variables of the process. All this data can be extracted from the evolutionary Data Base, fitted either with the on-line sensors values coming from the data collecting systems or with some other features provided by the operator (like a laboratory analysis, qualitative observation, etc.).

Adaptation process

This is a process that is sometimes performed either by dynamic learning from past proposed solutions and its efficiency -that can update the Case library- or by acquiring some new knowledge from (new) experts or (new) sources through classification techniques

Diagnosis process

In a new cycle the Supervisory agent activates the Knowledge-based agents to diagnose the state of the different subsystems of the plant by means of rule-based reasoning. At the same time in the diagnosis phase the Case-Based Reasoning and Learning agent (CBRL) is activated to retrieve similar cases recorded in the Case library (this means concurrent execution of all agents involved). And is updated to the most similar one in order to adapt it to actual situation of the plant. Because this task needs access to the Data Base, results are communicated to the Supervisory agent.

Supervision process

The Supervisory agent combines all information coming from the several KBS agents (*general knowledge*) and from the CBRL agent (*specific knowledge*) to infer the current global situation of the plant and the suggested actions to be taken. It sends this information to the operator through the User Interface Module.

Validation process

The system can be inquired by the operator in various ways, such as, asking for explanations, retrieving certain values, etc. The Supervisory agent waits for the operator's validation of actions to be taken in order to update the current working state of the plant.

Actuation process

The Supervisory agent recognizes *situations* and uses the right strategy or plan in order to keep the process controlled, or if *normal situation* has been detected, then, the automatic numerical control is maintained or activated. If there are on-line actuators, the plant can be automatically updated through the Actuator system. If not, manual operation is required.

5 PRELIMINARY RESULTS AND EVALUATION

The knowledge-based paradigm (expert knowledge) is already built-up. Knowledge-based agents are implemented using the G2 shell (in prototype status). They are incrementally validated with some real data stream taken from the plant, against the experts' opinion and some simulation studies, yielding good results [Serra *et al.*, 1993]. Also, Linneo+ -the knowledge acquisition module- is already implemented.

The case-based reasoning approach (experimental knowledge) is under development. The Case library is being implemented as a prioritized discrimination network, where the priority of node-attributes is obtained from experts' opinion and from an inductive learning method (such as ID3, etc.). Cases, retrieving, and adding tasks are designed and now we are working on adaptation and evaluation steps. This agent, and other agents (supervisory, etc.) are implemented in Lisp.

Data collection module is also developed. It gathers the values from status of turbines, pumps, automatic grids, etc., from the control panel of the plant under supervision, with 6 PLC's (SISTEL 8512). These 96 digital signals are transmitted through RS-422 to the monitoring computer (PC) for evaluation process. It also receives 9 analogical signals (inflow, wasting flow, recirculation flow, biogas produced, DO- line-1, pH, temperature-digester-1 and temperature-digester-2) converted by an AD/DA card. It will be connected to the main computer (SUN Sparc station) where are running all the other agents and processes.

After the validation on the simulation of the plant, the prototype system is currently being validated -in an incremental way- in a real plant under contract between our universities and "Junta de Sanejament de la Generalitat de Catalunya" as the responsible organization of wastewater treatment plants management in Catalonia. Until now, the results obtained with the system are promising.

6 SUMMARY

From what has been previously described, one can state that the combination of both paradigms at the *expertise level* let the system model the subjective knowledge (supplied by the experts) as well as the objective knowledge (supplied by the real operation of the concrete plant under control)[1]. This integration presents some advantages over knowledge-based reasoning, from case-based reasoning, from dynamic learning and from semiautomatic knowledge acquisition, that are the methods acting at the expertise level:

- It makes it possible to *reason in a poorly understood and ill-structured domain*, where in other kinds of reasoning systems such as model-based reasoning or algorithmic reasoning it would not be possible.

- The system learns from previously solved problems and adapts to the available experimental knowledge from the domain (*dynamic learning environment*).

- Overcoming the *brittleness* of KBS' in coping with unforeseen situations (not previously considered by the general expert knowledge), by trying to solve them by means of the most closely situation in the Case library.

- Capturing the knowledge provided by the experts (*knowledge acquisition*) which is very important – although subjective – to get a central corpus of knowledge about the domain.

- Dealing either with prototypical situations (*general knowledge*) or with idiosyncratic or exceptional ones (*specific knowledge*).

- Due to the dynamic learning environment, the system is able to adapt itself to different wastewater treatment plants, *making the system portable* to any other plant with some minor changes. It is only needed to fill the Case library with an initial set of specific cases (operating situations of the concrete WWTP), which can be obtained semi-automatically from real operational data.

All these facts make it more powerful than other single technologies applied to wastewater treatment plants as knowledge-based approaches [Lapointe *et al.*, 1989; Maeda, 1989], statistical process control techniques [Novotny *et al.*, 1990], fuzzy controller methods [Czoagala and Rawlik, 1989; Alex *et al.*, 1994], etc., as well as to other complex ill-structured domains. With this approach, the plant can be controlled in *normal* situations (mathematical control), in *abnormal usual* situations (expert control) and in *abnormal unusual* situations (experimental control).

ACKNOWLEDGEMENTS

Currently, this approach is been partially supported by the "Junta de Sanejament de la Generalitat de Catalunya" and the Spanish CICyT project ROB94-679 and EEC project VIM ERBCHRXCT 930401. Also the authors wish to acknowledge the cooperation of Ricard Tomàs, manager of the Manresa wastewater treatment plant.

REFERENCES

[Alex *et al.*, 1994] J. Alex, U. Jumar and R. Tschepetzki. A Fuzzy Controller for Activated Sludge Wastewater Plants. In *Procc. of the 2nd IFAC/IFIP/IMACS Int. Symp. on Artificial Intelligence in Real Time Control (AIRTC'94)*, pages 75-80, València, October, 1994.

[Bond and Gasser, 1988] Alan H. Bond and Les Gasser (editors). *Readings in Distributed Artificial Intelligence*. Morgan Kaufmann Publishers, San Mateo, CA, 1988.

---

[1] So that it is commonly known – and has been shown out in the performed study [Sànchez et al, 1994a] – that not all the considered situations by the experts occur in the practice, and vice versa, certain situations not taken into account by the experts can occur in the WWTP.

[Béjar, 1995] Javier Béjar. Knowledge acquisition in ill-structured domains. Ph. D. Thesis. Dept. de Llenguatges i Sistemes Informàtics. Universitat Politècnica de Catalunya, 1995. (In Spanish).

[Czoagala and Rawlik, 1989] E. Czoagala and T. Rawlik. Modelling of a Fuzzy Controller with application to the Control of Biological Processes. *Fuzzy Sets and Systems*, 31:13-22, 1989.

[Kolodner, 1993] Janet Kolodner. *Case-Based Reasoning*. Morgan Kaufmann, 1993.

[Lapointe et al, 1989] J. Lapointe, B. Marcos, M. Veillette, G. Laflamme and M. Dumontier. Bioexpert – an Expert System for Wastewater Treatment Process Diagnosis. *Computers & Chemical Engineering*, 13(6):619-630, 1989.

[Maeda, 1989] Kazuo Maeda. A Knowledge-based system for the wastewater treatment plant. *Future Generation Computer Systems*, 5:29-32, North Holland, 1989.

[Novotny et al., 1990] V. Novotny, H. Jones, X. Feng and A. G. Capodaglio. Time Series Analysis Models of Activated Sludge Plants. *Water Science & Technology*, 23(4-6):1107-1116, 1990.

[Patry and Chapman, 1989] Gilles G. Patry and David Chapman (editors). *Dynamic Modelling and Expert Systems in Wastewater Engineering*. Chelsea, MI. Lewis Publishers, 1989.

[Plaza et al., 1993] Enric Plaza, Agnar Aamodt, Ashwin Ram, Walter Van de Velde and Maarten Van Someren. Integrated Learning Architectures. In *Procc. of the European Conference on Machine Learning (ECML-93)*, LNAI-667, pages 429-441, Springer-Verlag, 1993.

[Riesbeck and Schank, 1989] Christopher K. Riesbeck and Roger C. Schank. *Inside Case-Based Reasoning*. Lawrence Erlbaum Associates Publishers, 1989.

[Robusté, 1990] Jordi Robusté. Modelling and identification of the activated sludge process. Ph. D. Thesis. Dept. de Química. Universitat Autònoma de Barcelona, 1990. (In Catalan).

[Sànchez et al., 1994a] Miquel Sànchez, Ulises Cortés Joan de Gràcia, Javier Lafuente and Manel Poch. Concept Formation in WWTP by means of Classification Techniques: a Compared Study. August, 1994.

[Sànchez et al., 1994b] Miquel Sànchez, Ignasi R.-Roda, Javier Lafuente, Ulises Cortés and Manel Poch. DAI-DEPUR Architecture: Distributed Agents for Real-Time WWTP Supervision and Control. In *Procc. of the 2nd IFAC/IFIP/IMACS Int. Symp. on Artificial Intelligence in Real Time Control (AIRTC'94)*, pages 179-184, València, October, 1994.

[Schank and Slade, 1991] Roger C. Schank and Stephen B. Slade. The future of Artificial Intelligence: learning from experience. *Applied Artificial Intelligence*, 5:97-107. Hemisphere Publishing Corporation, 1991.

[Serra et al, 1993] Pau Serra, Miquel Sànchez, Javier Lafuente, Ulises Cortés and Manel Poch. ISCWAP: a knowledge-based system for supervising activated sludge processes. 1993.

[Serra et al., 1994] Pau Serra, Miquel Sànchez, Javier Lafuente, Ulises Cortés and Manel Poch. DEPUR: a knowledge based tool for wastewater treatment plants. *Engineering Applications of Artificial Intelligence*, 7(1):23-30, 1994.

[Steels, 1990] Luc Steels. Components of expertise. *AI Magazine*, 11 (2):28-49, 1990.

[Stephanopoulos and Stephanopoulos, 1986] George Stephanopoulos and Gregory Stephanopoulos. Artificial Intelligence in the Development and Design of Biochemical Processes. *Trends in Biotechnology*, pages 241-249, September, 1986.

[Stephanopoulos, 1990] G. Stephanopoulos. Artificial Intelligence in Process Engineering: Current State and Future Trends. *Computers & Chemical Engineering*, 14:1259-1270, 1990.

[Venkatasubramanian, 1994] Venkat Venkatasubramanian. Towards Integrated Process Supervision: Current Status and Future Directions. In *Proc. of 2nd IFAC Workshop on Computer Software Structures Integrating AI/KBS Systems in Process Control*, pages 9-21, Lund, August, 1994.

CLASSROOM CONNECTIONS

Integrating General Expert Knowledge and Specific Experimental Knowledge in Waste Water Treatment Plant

Multiple Choice

Pick the best answer.

1. **What environmental problem is addressed?**
   A. Waste water treatment.
   B. Reducing pollution.
   C. Improving water conditions for plants and aquatic animals.
   D. Reacting to changes in microorganisms to reduce pollution.
   E. All of the above.

2. **What AI has been used to build Linneo+?**
   A. Knowledge acquisition or extraction.
   B. Fuzzy logic.
   C. Case based reasoning.
   D. Hybrid AI – AI together with sensor monitoring and analysis, bioreactor modeling, control optimization.
   E. Multi-agent systems.
   F. All of the above.

3. **How would you describe the qualities and types of data found in the waste water treatment plant management problem?**
   A. Imprecise.
   B. Real experimental case data.
   C. Both online and archived sensor data.
   D. Data comes from measurements of turbines, pumps, control panels, recirculation flows, temperature digesters.
   E. Big data is collected 24/7 and there is no real time analysis.
   F. A – D.
   G. All of the above.

4. **How is machine learning used in Linneo+**
   A. Using dynamic learning from past proposed solutions and its efficiency.
   B. To update the Case library.
   C. Using classification techniques to semi-automatically acquire new knowledge.
   D. Using deep neural nets to provide an explanation for inspections.
   E. A, B and C.
   F. All of the above.

True or False

Please decide if each of the statements below are True or False.

5. Sewage treatment and water treatment plants do not need sensor monitoring.

6. Cases denote a working situation of the plant that are previously experienced situations, that have been automatically captured and learned so that they can be reused in the solving of future situations.

7. The results of classification with Linneo+ provide intensive and extensive description of the generated classes (situations) and a fuzzy membership matrix that relates observations (data) to generated classes.

8. Linneo+ discovered that there are four subtypes of normal situations (usually, not considered by the human experts) and revealed that about 20% of the variables provided by the plant's operators were not relevant for the characterization of situations.

9. The system can be interactive with human operators, for example when asking for an explanation of its conclusions and analyses.

Answers can be found at the end of the book.

Chapter 4

Planning with Agents in Intelligent Data Management for Forestry

Daniel Charlebois

University of Ottawa, Canada

Stan Matwin

University of Ottawa, Canada

David G. Goodenough

Pacific Forestry Centre, Natural Resources Canada, Canada

1 INTRODUCTION

Data repositories useful for understanding the current state of the biosphere and the trends in vegetation over large areas are becoming available. Use and analysis of this data can lead to better, sustainable utilization of resources. The largest vegetative component on the surface of the earth is forestry. Natural coniferous forests provide 73% of the global industrial log supply. Global demand for wood fiber will require that an additional 77 million m³ of timber be harvested annually. The increased demand can not be satisfied, and a shortage of industrial wood is expected in the future. Plantation forests supply less than 10% of the world's industrial wood [Cartwright 1994]. Consequently old growth forests will continue to be the principal source of timber for three or more decades.

More than 40% of Canada's marketable timber can be found in British Columbia, often on rugged, mountainous terrain. In 1992 over 60% of the coastal lumber production was exported, accounting for 34% of the world's exports of coniferous lumber. Forest exploitation is and will remain an important economic sector in British Columbia. In 1991, the B.C. forest industry had 8.6% of B.C. jobs and provided 11% of B.C.'s GDP.

2 TECHNICAL CHALLENGES

The combination of environmental and economic concerns calls for highly sophisticated, timely and focused forest management practices. Moreover, the variability in terrain, climate and forest conditions and the introduction of the Forest Practices Code [BCGov 1992] make forest management complex, requiring sophisticated management information systems and decision support tools.

The problem with the access, use and analysis of the forest data is its diversity and complexity. This diversity is reflected in a variety of formats, media and granularity of data. The problem is compounded by the complexity and heterogeneity of the computing environments in which the data resides, as well as the multitude of software tools which are needed to extract the required information from the data. In forestry, for example, the advanced information systems integrate forest cover descriptions, topographic maps, remote sensing and application knowledge. Remote sensing data is essential for monitoring large areas. The volume of the incoming data is huge; it is anticipated that the rate of data acquisition for the nation will reach one terabyte per day by the year

2000. Data management systems for resources will need to make intelligent selections of the data in order to respond to users' goals, reduce complexity, and be more adaptable.

3 OUR SYSTEM

A project was begun in 1991 to develop a System of Experts for Intelligent Data Management (SEIDAM) for forest and environmental monitoring. The SEIDAM Project is conducted under the Applied Information Systems Research Program of NASA. The partners in the project include the Pacific Forestry Centre (PFC), the B.C. Ministry of Forests (BCMOF), the B.C. Ministry of Environment, Lands and Parks (BCMELP), the Royal Institute of Technology (KTH) of Sweden, the EECs Joint Research Centre (JRC) at Ispra, and MacDonald Dettweiler Associates.

One of the main problems that the SEIDAM system must tackle is the update of forest cover maps stored in digital form in geographical information systems (GIS) by processing remotely sensed imagery in order to detect changes in the state of the forest. The example below outlines some of the details of the processing involved to perform this task.

In order to manage forests efficiently, decision makers need fast access to up-to-date information about the forests. These decision makers may frame queries to their staff to be answered. For example, a decision maker might ask: What is the spatial distribution of Douglas fir in the Greater Victoria Watershed area? Below, we discuss the current practices in answering such a query.

The name Greater Victoria Watershed corresponds to six 1:20,000 maps or geographic information files (GIS). There are topographic GIS files, forest cover GIS files, soils, hydrology, geographic names, transportation, etc. The user would normally choose which GIS files to begin with and would specify the time for which this question is being answered, such as for July 1994. The GIS files may need processing to be transformed to a common map projection and datum, and to be joined together to form a seamless GIS cover for the Greater Victoria Watershed. The topographic data would need to be transformed from elevation points irregularly distributed to a regular grid having the appropriate spatial resolution for the query. These processes are usually performed in a GIS such as ESRI ARC/ Ingres. The user would need

to design the attribute database for the various GIS files and ensure the linkage between the graphical elements and the relational attributes. The GIS files would likely give the spatial distribution of Douglas fir for some older date, such as 1988.

In order to know the current state of the forest cover, the user could take satellite remote sensing imagery, such as Thematic Mapper from Landsat, integrate this imagery with a raster version of the topographic files, analyze the TM imagery for forest cover changes, and update the GIS forest cover files with these changes. To accomplish these tasks the user would need to run several processes in an image analysis system. The updating of the GIS files would be completed in a GIS. New clear cuts need to be identified and included in the forest cover GIS file in order to provide the user with the current state of the forest. It is important that the user is presented with visualizations of the remote sensing imagery and the GIS files. These visualizations are created as a result of processing. They help the user understand the spatial analysis and the accuracy assessment of each step. The answer to the original query would be presented as a visual product and an updated GIS file.

The process described here can be viewed as a navigation through data and software repositories. Navigation is performed under time and cost constraints. Navigation in this context is a knowledge-based problem solving exercise. Knowledge pertains to obtaining a solution to a query from solutions to its parts. For example, the above query would require expertise in forestry, topographic mapping, remote sensing image analysis, GIS operation, data base design, and visual representations.

The work presented here introduces the use of software agents (also known as apprentices [Mitchell 1994; Mitchell 1985] and softbots [Etzioni 1994], systems that unobtrusively observe the manner in which they are used, adapt to the tasks for which they are used, as well as learn from the circumstances of their use to perform the individual tasks listed above. These agents can each give a description of the task they perform in the form of a STRIPS-like [Fikes 1971] planning operator. These operators are then used by a problem-solving system that integrates the use of search based planning [Genesereth 1987], case-based reasoning [Carbonell 1986; Hammond 1989], derivational analogy [Carbonell 1986; Veloso 1992] and machine learning. These agents are acquired through the use of a training interface that allows domain experts to describe how each task is performed. The experts are therefore not required to hand code the agents since they are automatically generated by the training interface.

REFERENCES

[BCGov 1992] BCGov, Guidelines to Maintain Biological Diversity in Coastal Forests, 1992, B.C. Ministry of Forests and B.C. Ministry of Environment, Lands and Parks.

[Carbonell 1986] Carbonell, J.G., Derivational analogy: A theory of reconstructive problem solving and expertise acquisition, in *Machine Learning: An Artificial Intelligence Approach*, R.S. Michalski, J.G. Carbonell, and T.M. Mitchell, 1986, Morgan Kaufman.

[Cartwright 1994] Cartwright, D., Wilson, B. and Ennis, R., British Columbia Forest Products Industry, Editor, 1994, Pacific Forestry Centre.

[Etzioni 1994] Etzioni, O. and Weld, D., A Softbot-Based Interface to the Internet, *Communications of the ACM,* 1994, 37(7), pp. 72-79.

[Fikes 1971] Fikes, R.E., Hart, P.E. and Nilsson, N.J., STRIPS: A New Approach to the Application of Theorem Proving to Problem Solving, *Artificial Intelligence,* 1971, 2, pp. 189-208.

[Genesereth 1987] Genesereth, M.R. and Nilsson, N.J., *Logical Foundations of Artificial Intelligence,* 1987, Los Altos, CA, Morgan Kaufmann.

[Hammond 1989] Hammond, K.J., *Case-Based Planning: Viewing Planning as Memory Task*, 1989, Boston MA, Academic Press.

[Mitchell 1994] Mitchell, T., Caruana, R., Freitag, D., McDermott, J. and Zabowski, D., Experience with a learning personal assistant, *Communications of the ACM,* 1994, 37(7), pp. 80-91.

[Mitchell 1985] Mitchell, T., Mahadevan, S. and Steinberg, L., LEAP: A learning apprentice for VLSI design, in *Ninth IJCAI*, 1985.

[Veloso 1992] Veloso, M., *Learning by Analogical Reasoning in General Problem Solving,* Editor, 1992, Carnegie Mellon University.

CLASSROOM CONNECTIONS

Planning with Agents in Intelligent Data Management for Forestry

Multiple Choice

Pick the best answer.

1. **What is the environmental problem addressed by this chapter?**
   A. Detecting changes in forest cover from satellite and remote images.
   B. Supporting decision makers.
   C. Forestry management for the toothpick industry.
   D. Keeping forest cover maps updated from many sources and organizations.
   E. Supporting users who integrate information from multiple disciplines including forestry, topographic. mapping, image analysis, data base designs and visualization of data.
   F. A, B and D, E.

2. **What AI technologies are used for this project?**
   A. Windows 10.
   B. Software agents.
   C. Knowledge representation.
   D. Hybrid AI – integrating standard AI methods of case based reasoning, machine learning, analogy with image processing and data base systems.
   E. B – D.
   F. All of the above.

3. **Why are forestry management tools important?**
   A. They help tell us the trends of vegetation over large areas.
   B. The largest vegetative component on the surface of the earth is forest.
   C. Demand for wood products is greater than supply.
   D. We need to find a breadcrumb trail through the forest.
   E. B and C.
   F. A, B and C.

True or False

Please decide if each of the statements below are True or False.

4. The problem with the access, use and analysis of forest data is its diversity (variety of formats, media and granularity) and complexity (multitude of computing environments and software tools).

5. To make good decisions about forests we must have tools to allow us to quickly see changes such as recent clear cuts.

6. Software agents adapt and learn by example how to perform tasks from the user and then later can give an explanation of all decisions and activities.

7. The learn by example interface allows software agents to be automatically created.

Answers can be found at the end of the book.

Chapter 5

Water Pollution Prediction

Water Pollution Prediction with Evolutionary Neural Trees

Byoung-Tak Zhang
German National Research Center for Computer Science (GMD), Germany

Peter Ohm
German National Research Center for Computer Science (GMD), Germany

Heinz Mühlenbein
German National Research Center for Computer Science (GMD), Germany

ABSTRACT

An evolutionary learning method for modeling and prediction of complex systems is described and applied to an environmental system. The method is based on tree-structured neural networks whose node type, weight, size and topology are dynamically adapted by genetic algorithms. Since the genetic algorithm used for training does not require error derivatives, a wide range of neural models can be identified. The application of this method to the prediction of water pollution shows comparable results to those achieved by well-engineered, conventional system-identification methods.

1 INTRODUCTION

Modeling and predicting the behaviors of many environmental or ecological systems is difficult because these systems are often complex. They are generally characterized by a large number of variables, parameters, interactions, and limited amounts of collected data.

In this paper we present an evolutionary method for learning such models. Although several genetic algorithms [1] have been proposed for constructing neural networks (see, for example, [2] and [8] for a review of recent developments), our method is different from them in that we use a tree representation of the neural network, called neural trees. Unlike most conventional neural models, neural trees employ different types of neurons in a single network. The set of different types is defined by the application domain, and the specific type of each unit is determined during the evolutionary learning process. Any arbitrary units can be employed since the training algorithm we use, *i.e.*, the breeder genetic algorithm [7], makes no assumptions as to the differentiability of the activation function.

The structure and size of the network is also automatically adapted during the evolutionary learning process. With sigma and pi units, for example, the method can build a higher-order functional structure of partially connected polynomial units, resembling but different from the architecture constructed by the Group Method of Data Handling (GMDH) [5] and its descendants. The explicit use of product neurons has been very useful for solving problems which are difficult for multilayer perceptrons [4, 11].

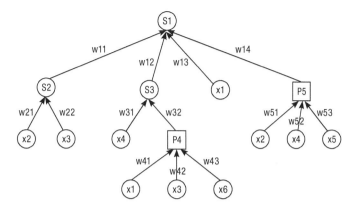

Figure 1. Tree representation of a sigma-pi neural network with six inputs and one output. Each unit has a local receptive field.

In section 2 we briefly describe the tree encoding scheme and the genetic algorithm for evolving problem-specific neural trees. Section 3 reports the application results on the prediction of an environmental system. Implications of current work are discussed in section 4.

2 EVOLUTIONARY NEURAL TREES

A neural tree consists of a number of artificial neurons connected with weights in a tree structure. The leaves of the tree are elements of the terminal set X of n variables, $X = \{x_1, x_2, ..., x_n\}$. The root node of the tree is called the output unit. All the nodes except the input units are non-terminal units. Each non-terminal node i is characterized by the unit type u_i, the squashing function f_i, the receptive field $R(i)$ and the weight vector $\mathbf{w_i}$. $R(i)$ is the index set of incoming units to unit i and can be different from unit to unit.

In the experiments described in the next section, we use sigma (S) and pi (P) units, i.e., $u_i \in \{S, P\}$, mixed into the same network. The sigma units compute the weighted sum of the input values y_j from other units, $\sum_{j \in R(i)} w_{ij}y_j$, and the pi units compute the product of their weighted inputs, $\prod_{j \in R(i)} w_{ij}y_j$. Each squashing function is either a sigmoid function, $f(x) = \frac{1}{1+e^{-x}}$, or a threshold function, $f(x) = +1$ if $x > 0$ and $f(x) = -1$ otherwise.

An instance of the sigma-pi neural tree is shown in Figure 1. Notice that although the set of neuron types and external inputs is finite, any arbitrarily large trees can be generated from them. This encoding scheme can represent any feed forward network with local receptive fields and direct connections between non-neighboring layers (see [9] for more details) and thus extends the tree representation used in [6]. This is contrasted with the more commonly used perceptron architecture of fully connected feedforward networks.

For the construction of neural models, we maintain a population A consisting of M individuals of variable size. Each individual A_i is a neural network represented as neural trees. The initial population $A(0)$ is created at random. In each generation g, the fitness values $F_i(g)$ of networks are evaluated and the upper $r\%$ are selected to be in the mating pool $B(g)$. The next generation $A(g + 1)$ of M individuals is then created by exchanging subtrees and thereby adapting the size and shape of the network. Mutation changes the node type and the index of incoming units. The best individual is always retained in the next generation so that the population performance does not decrease as generation goes on (elitist strategy).

Between generations the network weights are adapted by a stochastic hill-climbing search. This search method is based on the breeder genetic algorithm [7], in which the step size Δw is determined with a random value $\varepsilon \in [0, 1]$:

$$\Delta w = R \cdot 2^{-\varepsilon \cdot K}, \qquad (1)$$

where R and K are constants specifying the range and slope of the exponential curve. This method proved very robust for a wide range of parameter-optimization problems.

The fitness F_i of the individuals A_i is defined as

$$F_i = F(D|A_i) = \frac{E(D|A_i)}{m \cdot N} + \frac{C(A_i)}{N \cdot C_{max}} \qquad (2)$$

where m is the number of outputs, and N is the

number of training examples. The first term expresses the error penalty $E(D|A_i)$ for the training set. The second term penalizes the complexity $C(A_i)$ of the network. This evaluation measure prefers simple networks to complex ones and turned out to be important for achieving good generalization [9, 11].

3 PREDICTING AN ENVIRONMENTAL TIME SERIES

In recent years, system identification and time-series prediction have received much attention as promising application areas of neural networks. The task we have studied involves an environmental system in the Sangamon River, Illinois [3]. Our objective here is to predict nitrate levels a week ahead in the watersheds of the river from the previous values. The original study in the literature [3] also aims at giving some indication of the biochemical and physical relationships among the variables and of the controllability of the system.

The training data is based on the nitrate-nitrogen levels during the period from January 1, 1970, to December 31, 1971, graphed in Figure 2 (left). The sampling interval is one week. The training set is generated from this series using a time lag of 4. The initial population of the genetic

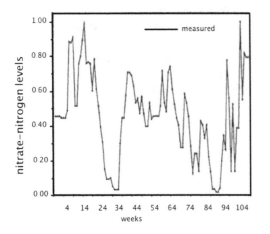 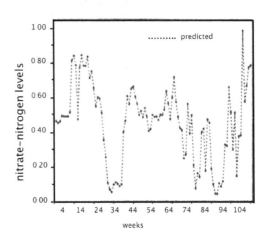

Figure 2. Performance for the training data: (left) measured, (right) one-step ahead prediction.

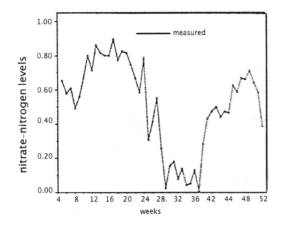 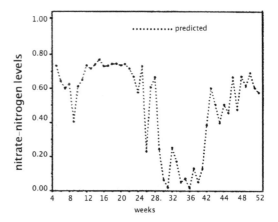

Figure 3. Performance for the unseen data: (left) measured, (right) one-step ahead prediction.

algorithm was created by randomly generating neural trees with a branching factor up to four and maximum depth of four also. 50% of the units were randomly chosen as sigma units and the rest as pi units. During evolution, however, sigma units usually survived more often than the pi units did. Using the weight interval of [-10,+10], the best solutions after 300 generations contained on average 10 hidden units in three layers.

An example of one-step ahead prediction performance for the training data is shown in Figure 2 (right) whose mean square error is 0.0104. To test the predictive accuracy of the neural tree models constructed by the evolutionary algorithm, unseen data for the same watershed for 1972 was used. The measured and predicted outputs for this test data are plotted in Figure 3. As can be seen in the figure, the nitrate levels for the following week was predicted relatively well, considering the sparseness of the training data. This result is as good as that obtained by the well-engineered GMDH algorithm [3].

4 CONCLUDING REMARKS

Most existing evolutionary methods for neural-network optimization represent the network as a linear string or matrix of fixed size whose connectivity and weights are changed in isolation. In contrast, our method is based on a tree-structured representation of the network, which allows dynamic adaptation of the neuron type, weight, and topology in a natural way using genetic operators.

The neural tree representation takes advantage of both the direct encoding scheme (little effort in decoding) and the indirect encoding scheme (easy to build modular structures) and is able to generate a very general class of feed-forward networks of partially connected heterogeneous neurons. One primary difficulty with this approach is that the network size may become very large without any improvement in generalization performance. The use of complexity penalty in fitness evaluation was very useful for solving this problem, as was indicated by the relatively good generalization performance in the water pollution experiments.

In contrast to conventional learning algorithms for neural networks, the evolutionary learning method described in this paper makes relatively few assumptions as to the architecture space in which the models for data are constructed. This method is especially effective in identifying the important variables and structures of the systems whose functional structures are unknown or ill-defined. Examples of the most promising application areas of the evolutionary neural trees include prediction, monitoring and diagnosis of complex systems, such as environmental processes.

REFERENCES

[1] T. Bäck and H.-P. Schwefel, An overview of evolutionary algorithms for parameter optimization, *Evolutionary Computation*, 1(1):1-23, 1993.

[2] K. Balakrishnan and V. Honavar, Evolutionary design of neural architectures, CS-TR-95-01, AI Lab, Dept. of Computer Science, Iowa State University, January 1995.

[3] J. J. Duffy and M. A. Franklin, A learning identification algorithm and its application to an environmental system, *IEEE Trans. on Sys. Man and Cyb.*, 5(2):226-240, 1975.

[4] C. L. Giles and T. Maxwell, Learning, invariance, and generalization in high order neural networks, *Applied Optics,* 26(23):4972-4978, 1987.

[5] A. G. Ivakhnenko, Polynomial theory of complex systems, *IEEE Trans. on Sys. Man, and Cyb.*, 1(4):364-378, 1971.

[6] J. R. Koza, *Genetic Programming: On the Programming of Computers by Means of Natural Selection*. MIT Press, 1992.

[7] H. Mühlenbein and D. Schierkamp-Voosen, Predictive models for the breeder genetic algorithm I: Continuous parameter optimization, *Evolutionary Computation,* 1(1):25-49, 1993.

[8] J. D. Schaffer. D. Whitley, and L. J. Eshelman, "Combinations of genetic algorithms and neural networks: A survey of the state of the art," in *Proc. Int. Workshop on Combinations of Genetic Algorithms and Neural Networks,* IEEE, 1992, pp. 1-37.

[9] B. T. Zhang and H. Mühlenbein, Evolving optimal neural networks using genetic algorithms with Occam's razor, *Complex Systems,* 7(3):199-220, 1993.

[10] B. T. Zhang and H. Mühlenbein, "Synthesis of sigma-pi neural networks by the breeder genetic programming," in *Proc. ICEC-94,* IEEE World Congress on Computational Intelligence, IEEE Computer Society Press, 1994, pp. 318-323.

[11] B. T. Zhang, Effects of Occam's razor in evolving sigma-pi neural networks, in *Lecture Notes in Computer Science 866,* Springer-Verlag, 1994, pp. 462-471.

CLASSROOM CONNECTIONS

Water Pollution Prediction with Evolutionary Neural Trees

Multiple Choice
Pick the best answer.

1. What environmental problem is addressed in this chapter?
   A. Predicting water pollution from nitrate-nitrogen imbalance.
   B. Creating tools to automatically predict water pollution from time series data.
   C. Discovering features and patterns in time series data about unknown systems.
   D. All of the above.

2. What are the advantages to using evolutionary algorithms to create predictive modeling systems on time series data?
   A. When prior knowledge or features of a complex system are not available, an evolutionary neural algorithm reveals the key features or patterns and the relations among features.
   B. They have good accuracy with time series data in general.
   C. The structure and size of the network is automatically adapted by the algorithm.
   D. All of the above.

3. What is the problem of excess nitrate-nitrogen in water?
   A. Excess nitrogen can hurt our food supply because it leads to hypoxic conditions (lack of oxygen) that hurt living creatures such as young cows, human infants or fish who depend on that oxygen (mass fish kills).
   B. Extreme algae growth and blocked light.
   C. It is not removed by sewage treatment.
   D. All of the above.

4. What are the sources of nitrate-nitrogen in water?
   A. Directly from manure and farm fertilizer runoff.
   B. Sewage runoff after storms or floods.
   C. Indirectly from atmosphere via combustion (coal, gasoline).
   D. Rocks.
   E. A – C.

True or False
Please decide if each of the statements below are True or False.

5. Modeling and predicting behaviors of ecological systems can be difficult because these systems are often complex.

6. Using evolutionary learning methods, the AI system automatically generates neural trees that predict behavior and answer questions about complex environmental systems.

7. Using evolutionary learning methods for time series data we remove the need for labelled data.

8. Automatically generating neural tree systems is helpful when predicting or monitoring an environmental system using vast amounts of time series data because they can identify important new patterns of previously unknown or ill defined system relationships.

9. Genetic programming involves a computer programming structure, such as a neural network or tree that can help look up family history.

Answers can be found at the end of the book.

Chapter 6

Toxic Algae Blooms

A Qualitative Modeling Approach to Algal Bloom Prediction

Ulrich Heller
Technical University of Munich, Germany

Peter Struss
Technical University of Munich, Germany

François Guerrin
INRA Toulouse, France

Waldir Roque
Federal University of Rio Grande do Sul, Brazil

ABSTRACT

Some problems typical for modeling ecological systems were encountered in the initial phase of a project that is concerned with the Rio Guaíba in Southern Brazil. This paper presents first results in modeling the phenomenon of algal bloom in a qualitative process-oriented modeling language. We addressed two problems. First, the spatial distribution of parameters and processes has to be taken into account, which leads us to locate processes in or between compartments, the elements of a topological partitioning of the area. Second, the various processes involved act with speeds of different orders of magnitude (*e.g.* chemical reactions vs. changes in fish population) which requires techniques of time-scale abstraction.

1   INTRODUCTION

Knowledge-based systems supporting analysis and decision making in the environmental domain require a representation of our knowledge about the involved processes. Because of the very nature of these processes, our knowledge about them, and the information available, this is a great challenge for qualitative modeling.

In a collaboration between researchers from Brazil, Germany and France, development of model-based systems has been started that are targeted to support decision making concerning environmental problems of the Rio Guaíba

in Southern Brazil. In this project, we started modeling the phenomena of the algal bloom. This paper presents some preliminary results of this work, a process-oriented description of some of the essential mechanisms contributing to algal bloom.

In particular, two problems have to be addressed that are typical for modeling ecological systems. First, the spatial distribution of parameters and processes has to be taken into account, which leads us to locate processes in or between compartments, the elements of a topological partitioning of the area. Second, the various processes involved act with speeds of different orders of magnitude (*e.g.* chemical reactions vs. changes in fish population), which requires techniques of time-scale abstraction.

In the following sections, we give a brief description of the Rio Guaíba and the environmental issues raised, with a focus on the algal bloom phenomenon, which will be further analyzed in section 3. Section 4 presents our approach to modeling the interactions involved in this phenomenon in a process-oriented language, QPC (4.1), the handling of compartments and their interaction (4.2), and the application of time-scale abstraction in the composition of a scenario model (4.3). Finally, we discuss some open issues and tasks for future work.

2 THE RIO GUAÍBA AND THE ALGAL BLOOM PHENOMENON

The Rio Guaíba passes the city of Porto Alegre, the capital of the southernmost state of Brazil. Calling it a river is just a convention, since its bays broaden up to 40 Km, while it stretches in its entire length only some 100 Km, thus partially behaving like a lake. Nevertheless, the flow in the center, called the navigation channel, reaches a speed of more than 1000 m³/s, which is caused by the Rio Jacui, the main affluent of the Rio Guaíba. Further complicated by the wind conditions and the connection to a large lagoon (Lagoa dos Patos), that is coupled with the ocean, the hydrodynamics within the water body is rather complex, and some phenomena like the temporary inversion of the flow, the so-called "reflux", are still not satisfactorily examined.

There are multiple sources of pollution, mostly city sewage of more than 1.2 million inhabitants and some industrial waste water of chemical plants and factories nearby. This adds to the organic pollution of the four affluent rivers, which drain industrial and agricultural regions. Because of the threat for the drinking water supply for the city and the increasing and severe dangers for the health of people swimming in bays near the city, the municipal department of water and sewage (DMAE) has been monitoring various parameters of the ecosystem in a number of locations over a period of more than 15 years.

However, the administration is mostly concerned with the suitability of the river for drinking water treatment, and therefore concentrates on a subset of chemical constituents and the important

number of fecal coliform bacteria stemming from household sewage, which establishes the main danger of diseases by contact with or drinking of the water.

Only recently, the general impact on the ecosystem has been studied, and, alarmed by the repeated occurence of local algal blooms, the city department started to probe and monitor the different species of algae in the phytoplankton and also in the sediment layers.

An algal bloom is a significant and steep increase in total algal biomass, while at the same time one species of algae becomes significantly predominant. The number of organisms per liter, which is about 1000 under oligo- and mesotrophic conditions (*i.e.* very low or average level of nutrients, respectively) can increase up to 1 million organisms/liter during the bloom. Typically, the single predominant species covers more than 95 percent of the biomass.

In the Rio Guaíba, such phenomena have been observed in various locations with slow flow speeds, low water levels and the hydrodynamic conditions for the accumulation of nutrients. The occurences typically lasted between 4 and 10 days and were limited to a spatial extent of about one square kilometer. All observed incidents happened in the summer, when high temperatures coincide with low water levels. Typically blue-green algae like *Anacystis* or diatoms like *Cyclotella* or *Melosira* have been found to dominate the blooms.

One of the locations of particular interest, where algal blooms have occurred frequently, is the bay of Praia do Lami, situated some 30 Km south of the city center of Porto Alegre. The area is still sparsely populated, but according to plans of the municipal administration, infrastructure including water supply and a sewage collecting pipe system will be built to enable the expansion of the residential areas down the river.

Up to now the bay is one of the few shore regions where swimming and other aquatic recreational activities are still possible. The area is therefore attractive to well-off inhabitants as well as illegal settlers. This imposes a serious problem, for the slums grow incontrollably and with few possibilities of restricting the discharge of waste into the river. In addition, there is a large number of visitors in the summer.

In recent years several occurences of extensive phytoplankton growth, part of which escalated to real algal blooms, have been recorded in the southern part of the bay. Among the undesirable effects of this phenomenon there is clogging of the filters during collection of water for treatment and unpleasant influences on taste and odor of the treated water, which cannot be removed with reasonable effort. Up to now there have been no real dangers like toxic substances released by algae.

However, the occurrence of algal blooms is an alarming indicator of instabilities in the ecosystem and its complex equilibrium mechanisms. Among the long-term effects of such disturbances is the reduction of the variety of species in the ecosystem. From the study of smaller water basins with complete eutrophication (*i.e.* the state of excessive accumulation of nutrients) the dangerous consequences are known.

It is important to develop and apply preventive measures for both immediate and long-term inhibition of algal blooms, as well as to react to the actual occurences immediately (*e.g.* by cutting off the pumps in the vicinity). Knowledge-based computer support for these tasks requires models of the involved processes as a basis for analysis, monitoring, and prediction of causes and effects. The following section describes the most important ones among these processes.

3 ALGAL BLOOM – CAUSES AND EFFECTS

Among the factors that are certain to influence phytoplankton growth, light conditions, water temperature and the availability of nutrients are the most important ones (see [Palmer 62], [Guerrin *et al.* 94]).

The following influences can be determined (compare Figure 2):

- Phyto-growth: the most important nutrients are nitrogen and phosphorus. The best available forms are ammonia (NH_4), nitrate (NO_3) and ortho-phosphate (PO_4). The consumption of nutrients by phytoplankton is dependent on temperature and on the N:P ratio. A value around 9:1 yields optimal growth. If significantly different from that value, the less available nutrient acts as the so-called "limiting factor" for the phytoplankton growth.

- Nitrification: The forms of the nutrients are changed by the activity of microorganisms, for example *nitrosomona* (which change ammonia to nitrite) and *nitro-bacter* (which transform nitrite into nitrate), the process as a whole

being called nitrification. The process is highly temperature dependent.

- Advection and dispersion: The actual concentration of these substances in a specific location is influenced by the hydrodynamics, which transport matter by advection (*i.e.* by means of the flow of water) and turbulative dispersion (*i.e.* assimilation of spatial concentration differences by means of turbulative mixing).

- Photosynthesis: The algal blooms in turn change the carbon-dioxide concentration by extensive photosynthesis, possibly even leading to CO_2 depletion.

- Acidity reaction: The decrease in CO_2 causes the pH to rise.

- Dissociation: This will cause the ammoniacal equilibrium ($NH_4 + OH \leftrightarrow NH_3O + H_2O$) to shift towards free ammonia (NH_3).

- Intoxication: There is the danger of toxic effects on fish and aquatic fauna by high concentrations of free ammonia.

- Predation and Respiration: The fish represent another important community in the aquatic ecosystem, interacting both directly with the phytoplankton and influencing the chemical system.

Presently we ignore the light conditions (which limit the algal growth to a layer near the surface of the water body and are affected by the algal bloom through a sharp increase in turbidity) and the oxygen equilibrium (influenced by respiration and photosynthesis as well).

4 MODELING

4.1 QUALITATIVE MODELING

As indicated by this verbal description, the expert knowledge in the hydro-ecological domain and particularly in the case of algal blooms is imprecise and of qualitative nature. For instance, the energy balance and the exact influence coefficients are usually not known, but rather general tendencies and limiting cases are used to reason about ecosystems.

To adequately represent this knowledge, a qualitative modeling approach is chosen, since

- the conclusions that can be drawn without precise quantitative knowledge are obtained with tractable effort and in a transparent way, so that intuitive explications about the inferences leading to the conclusion can be given to the user.

- the communication with the user is facilitated by a modeling language containing intuitive conceptual entities (*e.g.* processes), instead of requiring familiarity with complex formalisms and coding.

- even where quantitative calculations are necessary, they should be integrated into a conceptual and qualitative framework to check for their applicability in advance and to continuously verify their validity during the calculations, which both are inferences beyond the scope of classical mathematical methods.

- the model should predict the possible behaviors of the ecosystem in terms of alarming and dangerous events related to bloom occurrence, *i.e.* the expected output are statements of possibilities rather than quantities that still have to be interpreted qualitatively. Our approach provides models enabling the direct inference of such assertions.

- to account for the lack of exact knowledge about some relationships and interactions, we can use qualitative expressions of proportionality and influence, thus avoiding unreliable tentative descriptions and gaining the property of completeness (relative to the model), since the inferences will be valid for all instances of mathematical relationships. For example the relation I+(A,B) states that B positively influences A, *i.e.* the derivative of A will increase with B (all other influences assumed constant). The inferences that can be made without knowing the precise form of the dependency between A and B (typically a partial differential equation) will therefore be valid for all covered dependencies.

We refer to the process ontology of [Forbus 84], describing the system with a set of state variables and processes acting on them. A modeling assumption is that all changes of the state variables are caused by the effects of processes. An implementation of such a process-oriented modeling language is the Qualitative Process Compiler QPC ([Crawford *et al.* 90]). The model specification consists of a domain ontology, a process library, a scenario description and initial conditions. The ontology introduces the classes of entities (like the chemical constituents taken into account), the quantity types (like concentrations and values), relations and predicates. The process library consists of generic process descriptions (such as Figure 1). The scenario description specifies the entities present in the specific situation to be analyzed and states some properties in terms of relations and predicates. The initial conditions assert initial parameter values.

From this specification, a constraint model is obtained which can be executed by the qualitative simulation system QSIM ([Kuipers 86], [Kuipers 94]):

Process:	Nitrification
Individuals:	location (type: compartments)
	ammonia (type: ammonia-instance)
	temperature (type: temperature-instance)
Conditions:	Bacteria-present (location)
Operating-conditions:	Concentration (ammonia, location) > 0
Quantity-types:	rate
Relations:	rate = Value (temperature, location)
	* Concentration (ammonia, location)
	I+ (Concentration (ammonia, location), rate)
	I- (Concentration (nitrate, location), rate)

Figure 1. A sample process description: the nitrification process.

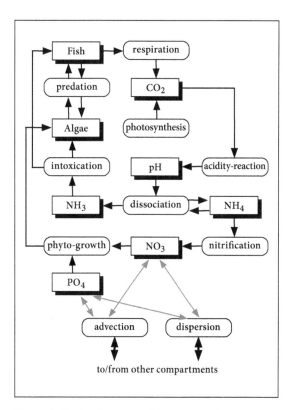

Figure 2. The basic process influence graph.

The processes will be instantiated for each set of entities specified in the *individuals* slot, satisfying additionally *conditions*. In each system state the *operating-conditions* determine whether the process is active, *i.e.* its relations and influences are in effect. The *quantity-types* are introduced as variables local to the process, used in the calculations of the effects in the *relations* slot. The influences I+, I- have been described above.

Figure 2 presents a graph of the influences of the modeled generic processes, with black arrows indicating positive influences and gray ones indicating negative influences.

4.2 SPATIAL DISTINCTIONS

Algal blooms are spatially limited phenomena, and in reasoning about them one of the important questions is "Where will they occur?", instead of simply predicting the possibility of a bloom anywhere in the modeled system.

Furthermore, a number of chemical as well as physical parameters show a distinctive spatial distribution, thus providing qualitatively different conditions for processes taking place at a local scale like chemical reactions or nutrient consumption. Therefore, reasoning about the involved processes will have to take spatial distinctions into account. These will be influenced by the advective flow of matter and the dispersive assimilation of constituent concentrations.

We adopt the notion of "hydrodynamic regimes", a terminology used by experts while reasoning informally, referring to regions with (almost) homogeneous flow characteristics, which result in similar parameter values and consequently similar conditions for local processes. We introduce a more general class of entities called compartments for a spatial partitioning of the system. We use them similarly as in compartmental modeling ([Ironi, Stefanelli 94]).

In the first step, only the surface area of the aquatic ecosystem is decomposed into compartments, whose parameter values will be treated as homogeneous. We ignore the third dimension and leave a partitioning into different horizontal layers for further development, concentrating implicitly on a layer with typically good conditions for algal growth. For the time being, the decomposition into compartments is determined by the modeler and fixed during simulation.

Process:	Advection
Individuals:	constituent (type: constituents)
	source (type: compartments)
	destination (type: compartments)
Conditions:	Distributed (constituent)
	Neighbor (source, destination)
Operating-conditions:	Flow (source, destination) > 0
Quantity-types:	loss-absolute, loss-relative, gain-relative
Relations:	loss-absolute = Flow (source, destination) *Concentration (constituent, source)
	loss-relative = loss-absolute / Volume (source) ; gain-absolute = loss-absolute
	gain-relative = loss-absolute / Volume (destination)
	I+ (Concentration (constituent, source), loss-relative)
	I- (Concentration (constituent, destination), gain-relative)

Figure 3. Example process advection.

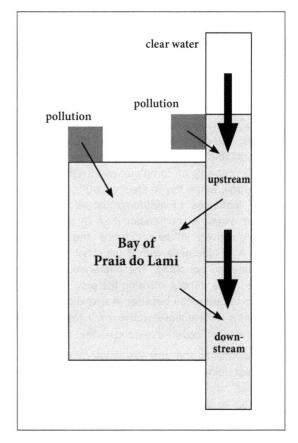

Figure 4. A simple compartmental structure of the scenario of Praia do Lami.

We model the exchange of any constituent, such as nitrate (and similarly the assimilation of physical parameter values) between neighboring compartments by generic processes "advection" (see Figure 3) and "dispersion". Advective transport of constituents is caused by the (directed) flow of water, whose speed becomes a variable for each pair of compartments in the neighboring relation. Also, the turbulative dispersion, resulting in the decrease of concentration gradients is calculated by combining the turbulence parameter of each compartment.

One of the important settings for the simulation is the Praia do Lami, which is tentatively modeled as a single compartment. Two additional compartments represent the upstream and the downstream part of the river. Similar constructions are used to give boundary conditions like the incoming pollution from the smaller affluents.

4.3 TIME-SCALES

In a complex ecosystem like the Rio Guaba, there exist processes acting at very different time-scales. Chemical reactions for example will take place and eventually establish an equilibrium between the participating reactants very much faster than a fish population number will react to changed conditions.

If the processes relevant for some reasoning task span a wide range of time-scales, this imposes difficulties. Qualitative simulation may produce spurious solutions, which could be pruned by information about the relative time-scale. For instance, after increasing the concentration of free ammonia, the chemical reaction ionizing free ammonia, resulting in a diminished danger of intoxication of a fish population by free ammonia, comes into effect. The predictive engine could generate a behavior under the assumption that additional free ammonia is absorbed by fish more rapidly than transformed by the chemical mechanisms, thus maybe leading to severe intoxication of the animals, even though in reality the ammonia would be neutralized within parts of a second.

One possibility to avoid these problems is the technique of time-scale abstraction (as described in [Kuipers 87], [Kuipers 94], [Struss 93]). For a specific time-scale of interest, all very much faster processes will be transformed into functional relationships, and much slower ones will be treated as constant. As a second desirable effect, the

model actually used for prediction will be much smaller and the reasoning will significantly gain efficiency.

The intention is to abstract the fastest equilibrium mechanisms (like chemical reactions) into functional relationships to facilitate long-term forecasts. By equilibrium mechanism, we denote a group of processes acting together to establish equilibrium. Since the exchange processes between the compartments are located at an intermediate time-scale (between chemical reactions and population developments), they can be used as a kind of reference time-scale. There is a correlation between the spatial partitioning and the different time-scales: The mechanisms with short response times (in relation to the global distribution mechanisms) can be seen as acting *inside* the single compartments, establishing a kind of dynamic equilibrium there, which will be shifted by the medium-term processes, the effects of which appear as if acting *between* the compartments. In a second step the system could derive a global equilibrium established by the exchange processes and the transformation acting on a comparable time-scale. The processes very much slower could either influence the compartment parameters, *e.g.* flow speeds, or even *change the spatial decomposition*.

We will give an example for a medium-term equilibrium for the nitrate concentration in a simplified scenario consisting of the upstream, the downstream and the bay compartment, without external pollution. We choose the processes of advection (with two instances of interest, the $advection_{up,bay}$ and the $advection_{bay,down}$) and the above mentioned nitrification of ammonia accomplished by bacteria (*nitro-bacter* and *nitrosomona*) approximately in the time-scale of hours, therefore matching the speed with which concentration changes propagate through the river by means of advection. The relevant influences on the state variable $nitrate_{bay}$ are the rate of the local nitrification process, which we denote $rate_{bay}$, and the loss ($loss\text{-}rel_{bay,down}$), respectively gain ($gain_{up,bay}$), by means of advection.

The equilibrium equation is obtained by setting the sum of the influences zero. Under the additional assumption that influences combine linearly and the two advection processes even equally, we obtain:

$$gain - rel_{up,bay} + k \cdot rate_{bay} - loss\text{-}rel_{bay,down} = 0$$

which expands to

$$\frac{flow_{up,bay} \cdot nitrate_{up}}{volume_{bay}} + k \cdot temp_{bay} \cdot ammonia_{bay} =$$

$$= \frac{flow_{bay,down} \cdot nitrate_{bay}}{volume_{bay}}$$

and under the (reasonable) assumption that the sum of the inflows equals the sum of the outflows of a compartment, in our case $flow_{up,bay} = flow_{bay,down}$ =: $flow_{bay}$, the equation can be solved for

$$nitrate_{bay} = nitrate_{up} +$$

$$+ k \cdot \frac{volume_{bay}}{flow_{bay}} \cdot temp_{bay} \cdot ammonia_{bay}$$

therefore determining the nitrate concentration in the bay by the nitrate concentration upstream and the ammonia concentration in the bay, which can be calculated by a similar equilibrium equation. The obtained equilibrium can be coded into constraints replacing the original dynamic modeling of the relationship. For long-term forecasts, the model will become smaller and more manageable in that way.

5   OPEN ISSUES AND FUTURE WORK

As of now, the algal bloom model has been implemented in QPC and will be evaluated and further developed based on the qualitative simulation results. Further calibration and validation will be carried out using the data available from DMAE. We do not expect the purely qualitative model to unambiguously predict or rule out the occurrence of algal bloom. For a detailed analysis it has to be extended by a semi-quantitative level, for instance based on interval mathematics.

The current model is based on some simplifications that will have to be dropped in the future. First, some influences are presently ignored, for instance the oxygen equilibrium. Second, the compartments introduced so far do not reflect distinctions along the vertical axis. However, the influence of light, air temperature and wind primarily affects the surface layer, giving rise to important variations with depth, and, hence, a three-dimensional compartmental structure will be more adequate.

Third, the current compartmental structure is fixed. Ultimately, a dynamic structure will be regarded, *e.g.* when changing conditions lead to significant parameter differences within a single compartment, the simulator should be able to split the compartment later. This raises the issue of how to determine the partitioning into compartments. The rationale behind this decomposition of a continuous system is to identify areas of strong, or fast, interactions, that interact with each other only in a weak, or slow, fashion. In our domain, this is closely related to direction and speed of flow, but other influences can be present. Rather than being defined beforehand, an appropriate compartmental structure could be detected automatically as a result of executing the qualitative model and/or interpretation of data.

Also, the transformation of models under time-scale abstraction should be performed automatically taking into account the respective purpose of using the model.

The modeling efforts described are a first step in the development of the ΣIGMA system ([Guerrin *et al.* 95]), a proposed framework for environmental decision support systems, that aims at integrating model building, situation assessment, simulation, diagnosis, and action planning. Sharing models across the various tasks will impose further requirements on the structure and content of the models.

ACKNOWLEDGMENTS

This work has been supported in part by the Brazilian research council (CNPq) and the German ministry of research and technology (project QUALIDADE). We benefitted from discussions with Paulo Marcos Amaral Alves, Elenara Correa Lersch and Maria Mercedes Bendati from the research department of DMAE.

REFERENCES

[Crawford *et al.* 90] Crawford J., Farquhar A., Kuipers B., *QPC: A Compiler from Physical Models into Qualitative Differential Equations.* In: Proceedings of AAAI-90.

[Forbus 84] Forbus K., *Qualitative Process Theory.* In: Artificial Intelligence 24(1984): 85-168

[Guerrin *et al.* 94] Guerrin F., Bousson K., Steyer J.-P, Trave-Massuyes L., *Qualitative reasoning methods for CELSS modeling*. In: Advances in Space Research, 14(11), 307-312, 1994.

[Guerrin *et al.* 95] Guerrin F., Heller U., Roque W., Struss S., *∑IGMA – um sistema integrado de gerenciamento do meio ambiente*. ECOS journal, DMAE Publications, Porto Alegre, 1995.

[Ironi, Stefanelli 94] Ironi L., Stefanelli M., *QCMF: a tool for generating qualitative models from compartmental structures*. In: Working notes of QR-94.

[Kuipers 86] Kuipers B., *Qualitative Simulation.* In: Artificial Intelligence 29(1986):289-338.

[Kuipers 87]
Kuipers B., *Abstraction by Time-Scale in Qualitative Simulation*. In: Proceedings of AAAI-87.

[Kuipers 94] Kuipers B., *Qualitative Reasoning – Modeling and Simulation with Incomplete Knowledge*. MIT Press, 1994.

[Palmer 62] Palmer C., *Algae in water supplies.* U.S. Department of Health, Education and Welfare, Public Health Service, Washington, 1962.

[Struss 93] Struss P., *On Temporal Abstraction in Qualitative Physics*. In: Working notes of QR-93.

CLASSROOM CONNECTIONS

A Qualitative Modeling Approach to Algal Bloom Prediction

Multiple Choice

Pick the best answer.

1. **Why do we need to predict algae blooms?**
   A. Predicting algae blooms helps us find where they come from.
   B. It helps document the events and conditions that cause them.
   C. Algae blooms clog water filters in sewage treatment plants and in our water supply.
   D. Species can die from toxins and lack of oxygen.
   E. All of the above.

2. **What kinds of information are used to manually predict algae blooms?**
   A. Satellite and Remote sensing.
   B. Meterological.
   C. Water quality – agricultural runoff, sewage contamination, etc.
   D. Maps of water bodies and their interconnections.
   E. Kayak rentals.
   F. A – D.

3. **What AI methods are helpful in automatically predicting algae blooms?**
   A. Pattern recognition.
   B. Qualitative and Conceptual Models of water bodies and flow, algae formation and influences.
   C. Distributed AI helps monitor wider areas.
   D. Siri.
   E. A – C.

True or False

Please decide if each of the statements below are True or False.

4. A model of a body of water can be topologically divided into elements.

5. Active water processes occur with different speeds and magnitudes that change over time.

6. In an algae bloom, a single predominant algae species covers more than 95 percent of the algae biomass.

7. Knowledge of hydro-ecology is imprecise and qualitative in nature.

8. It is important for an AI system to explain its decisions and recommendations.

9. Limiting cases are useless for AI reasoning about ecosystems.

Answers can be found at the end of the book.

Chapter 7

Recycling and Resources

The Green Browser:
A Proposal of Green Information Sharing and Life Cycle Design Tool

Yasushi Umeda
University of Tokyo, Japan

Tetsuo Tomiyama
University of Tokyo, Japan

Takashi Kiriyama
University of Tokyo, Japan

Yasunori Baba
University of Tokyo, Japan

ABSTRACT

The environmental issue is, without doubt, one of the most important and critical issues to solve urgently. In this paper, we propose the *Green Browser* which enables stakeholders (*e.g.*, employees, shareholders, consumers, regulators, NGO, etc.) to have access to environmental information. Through information-sharing and the promotion of public discussion, raising green literacy and ensued market selection are expected to produce effective pressure for corporate and public decision bearing positively on green production and environmental protection. First, we propose a representational scheme called *green life cycle model* which organizes corporate information for the Green Browser. For the purpose of supporting design for life cycle of green products *(green life cycle design)*, the scheme is built to illustrate a product's potential impacts from the raw material stage through use and eventual disposal or recycling. Firms are encouraged to process their firm-specific information based on the scheme. Second, we discuss how the Green Browser can support information sharing to enable stakeholders to obtain the detailed picture of products. We propose the coupling of the Green Browser with the Internet for the sharing of green life cycle models and relevant data resources.

1 INTRODUCTION

The environmental issue is, without doubt, one of the most important and critical issues to solve urgently. However, the following characteristics of the environmental issue make it quite difficult to deal with:

- It is impossible to solve the issue only by using technologies. Rather, collaboration among technology, policy, and economy is essential. In this sense, a multidisciplinary research project is important to tackle the issue.

- The environmental issue includes a wide variety of problems, ranging from global problems such as the greenhouse effect to local problems such as the disposal of hazardous materials. Moreover, the issue is so complicated that relationships and trade-offs among these problems cannot be defined universally. As a result, we do not have a universal estimation method. For example, even if one can optimize the recycling process of a car from the viewpoint of material consumption, this process might be worse in terms of the greenhouse effect.

How can AI contribute to this issue? Can it help introduce environmental concerns into corporate, policy, and decision-making processes?

One option is to develop a tool for environmental decision-making. A tool that clarifies trade-offs among strategic targets such as growth, industrial competitiveness, and environmental impact is thought to enhance the ability of reasoning of decision-makers, especially in the conventional centralized (command-and-control) system. However, once the tool explores the complex problem of gaining global sustainability, negative outcomes may result when the tool carries an incomplete or wrong model of cause and effect.

One alternative is to develop the *Green Browser* enabling stakeholders (*e.g.*, employees, shareholders, consumers, regulators, NGO, etc.) to have access to environmental information. Through information-sharing and the promotion of public discussion, raising green literacy and ensued market selection are expected to produce effective pressure for corporate and public decisions bearing positively on green production and environmental protection.

There have been already some networks about environmental information such as EcoNet[1], and EnviroWeb[2]. While we are planning to join these networks, our research focuses mainly on the manufacturing industry and aims at developing a methodology for supporting designers to design green products by using these networks.

This research proposes a representational scheme called *green life cycle* model which organizes corporate information for the Green Browser. For the purpose of supporting design for life cycle of green products (*green life cycle design*), the scheme is built to illustrate a product's potential impacts from the raw material stage

through use and eventual disposal or recycling. Firms are encouraged to process their firm-specific information based on the scheme. Then, stakeholders can obtain the detailed picture of products by browsing information with the Green Browser in the Internet space. We call it *green information sharing*.

In sections 2 and 3, we discuss requirements and our approach for the life cycle design support and the green information sharing, respectively. We sketch the ongoing implementation of the Green Browser in Section 4. Section 5 concludes this paper.

2   GREEN LIFE CYCLE DESIGN

Designers should design a product and its life cycle system so as to meet the requirements of environmental friendness over the life cycle of the product. Many researchers so far have pointed out the importance of design for reusing and recycling products effectively (*e.g.*, [1, 2, 6]). Namely, reuse and recycling of products are ineffective and expensive unless they are purposely designed. For instance, design for disassembly and appropriate modular design are indispensable for economical disassembling and efficient reuse, respectively. Namely, in order to develop a green product, environmental requirements throughout the life cycle of the product should be examined at the design stage. Table 1 shows some examples of requirements related to "greenness" in each life cycle process. As shown in this table, many requirements in each process are related to design. For example, in order to avoid producing hazardous waste in the manufacturing process, designers and manufacturing engineers should collaborate for designing the product so as to be manufactured in such a manner. Therefore, not only the product but also its appropriate life cycle system (*e.g.*, manufacturing, operation support, maintenance, recycling, and disposal) should be designed at the design stage. We call this *green life cycle design*. The concurrent engineering [3] is a hopeful approach to support the green life cycle design.

However, as we pointed out in Section 1, since the environmental issue is very complex, vague, and hardly well-evaluated, one of the most important needs for aiding the life cycle design is to support the designer to define the problem structure of the

---

[1] http://www.econet.apc.org/lcv/score100/econet_info.html

[2] http://www.gnn.com/gnn/wic/env.13.html

PROCESS	REQUIREMENTS	
	DESIGN RELATED	OTHERS
Manufacturing	no hazardous waste, least amount of material	low energy consumption
Operation	maintainability, long life, no hazardous wastes, low energy consumption	
Reuse and Recycling	reusable components, easy disassembling, recyclable material	no hazardous waste, low energy consumption
Disposal	no hazardous waste, least waste	

Table 1. Examples of Requirements in Each Life Cycle Process.

product life cycle at an early stage of design. This process includes picking out environmental and non-environmental requirements which the product should satisfy, clarifying the relations among these requirements, especially trade-offs, and selecting evaluation methods for the requirements.

In order to support this process, the Green Browser is designed to help a team of designers to form a consensus about "greenness" of the product. The Green Browser supports them to put together environmental requirements for the product into a model and thus to visualize trade-offs among them. The Green Browser is designed based on the following concepts:

1. Information generation
   While the green information sharing is important as described in Section 1, issues for it include by whom and how such green information is created. We believe that the created information about the life cycle of a product should be shared during and after the design. Therefore, the result of design should represent relations between the product and the environment over the life cycle clearly and explicitly.

   Here, two types of collaboration should be considered for supporting the information generation. One is collaboration in a process such as collaborative design work, and the other is collaboration among different processes. For example, in the latter case, for executing design for disassembly, designers should collaborate with recycling engineers and be supplied basic data from the engineers.

2. Process modeling
   Environmental factors must be examined in

each of the life stages such as raw materials, manufacturing the parts, assembly, shipping, duty time, reuse and recycling, and disposal. This means that the Green Browser should present the product information of different life stages. Furthermore, the planning of the production and the recycling process will be an important technical approach towards the environmental issue.

3. Qualitative representation
   Although impacts on the environment are important to be presented, it is not always possible to quantitatively evaluate them, as we pointed out in Section 1. For modeling such impacts, we use qualitative representations (*e.g.*, [5]).

In order to support the life cycle design with these concepts, we here propose a representational scheme called *green life cycle model*. Figures 1 and 2 show the representational scheme of the green life cycle model and an example, respectively. The model of a product consists of three sub-models which are linked to each other; namely, a strategy model, a process model, and object models.

2.1 STRATEGY MODEL

The strategy model represents how requirements for the product affect the achievement of overall goals of the development. The designers describe the following information in the strategy model.

- *Requirements and goals*
  Requirements include environmental requirements such as "recyclability" and "no emission of hazardous materials" as well as general requirements such as "inexpensiveness"

and "high speed." We call the most abstract requirements such as "competitiveness" and "greenness" goals.

- *Relations among requirements*
  The designer will find out relations among the defined requirements. For instance, a goal of greenness is positively affected by least materials, which is again achieved by selecting a recyclable material. For the same product, improving functionality will positively affect competitiveness. These two goals of greenness and competitiveness, however, may contradict in respect to materials because the selection of a recyclable material may reduce the functionality. Such positive, negative, and trade-off relations among requirements are represented with nodes and links as shown in Figure 1. Among these relations, it is the most important for designing green products to specify the trade-off relations explicitly.

- *Weighing and evaluation criteria*
  We assume that the designer can describe the importance of each requirement as

weight and evaluation criteria for concrete requirements. These kinds of information are put in each requirement node and will be used for evaluation of the product.

- *Pointers to the process and the object models*
  Each requirement should be related to some portion of the life cycle process and/or object models of the product. By using these pointers, the designer can organize existing tools and methodologies. This feature enables the designers to create green products and evaluate their whole life cycle.

2.2 PROCESS MODEL

The process model represents the life cycle of the product. It depends on the life stage how product requirements impact the environment. For instance, design for disassembly reduces impact in the recycling process but may increase complexity in the manufacturing process. Links from the strategy model show on which stage of the life cycle the impacts of the requirements are considered.

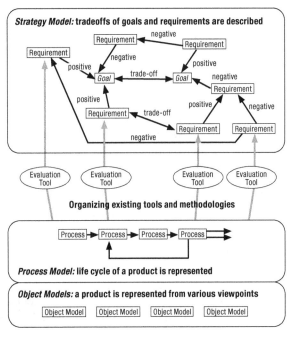

Figure 1. Scheme of the Green Life Cycle Model.

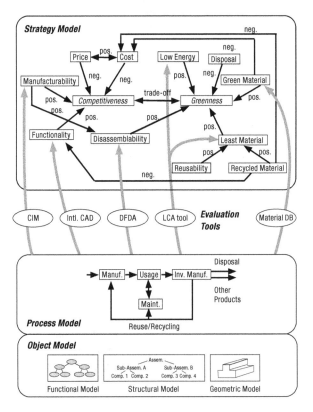

Figure 2. Example of the Green Life Cycle Model.

2.3 OBJECT MODEL

The object models represent the product from various viewpoints. Examples of the object models include functional model, geometric model, and structural model. These modelers of various viewpoints are being integrated into a framework called Knowledge Intensive Engineering Framework [4], which is currently developed by the authors. One of the features of the *Knowledge Intensive Engineering Framework* is to integrate various kinds of modelers including traditional modelers such as FEM modelers by providing a common knowledge base of ontology and relating concepts manipulated in each modeler to this ontology base.

3 GREEN INFORMATION SHARING

We believe that the basic information about "greenness" of product must be included in the green life cycle model and shared among stakeholders using the Green Browser (see Figure 3). We designed the green information sharing facility of the Green Browser based on the following concepts:

1. Linkage to external data sources
   Recent advances of the computer network give support to the effort of tackling the environmental issue. For example, as EcoNet and EnviroWeb provide, on the WWW one may find data of interest including life-cycle assessments, surveys, research papers, and reports. Such data resources may provide information relevant to the product. The Green Browser is designed so that the designer can obtain relevant data using it. Links to external data sources are associated with requirements in the strategy model. By selecting a requirement, the user can learn background information or relevant products associated with the data. For a team of designers, the browser allows to retrieve relevant data that have been linked up by other members.

2. Model sharing
   To obtain a consensus about the concept of the product, it is important to learn the views of other designers. The browser is planned to be a common workspace for making a consensus in which the designers collaborate

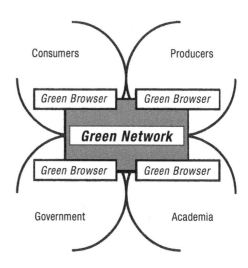

Figure 3. Green Information Sharing.

to construct a common green life cycle model of the product. The model represents explicitly different viewpoints of the designers in the strategy model; namely, while the strategy model representing difference is shared among the designers, the process and object models related to the strategy model might differ according to the difference of viewpoints.

It is supposed to happen that the same requirement is found in the strategy models of different products. For instance, for many products the requirement of least material is considered as a possible way to improve the greenness. So the requirements considered for one product might be used again for another product. For this reason we plan to collect strategy models of products, to extract requirements from them, and to put out a list of requirements on the network. Each requirement in the list has links back to the strategy model it was extracted from. This will allow the user to retrieve relevant strategy models as references.

4 IMPLEMENTATION

Currently, we are developing the Green Browser by mainly focusing on the strategy model and green information sharing. The system is being implemented in X-windows environment. Links to external data sources and tools are written in URLs (Universal Resource Locators) as practiced in the WWW. The Green Browser runs as a client of WWW, so that data requested by the user are obtained from remote servers in HTML. The Green Browser will be published with successful examples of life cycle design. The case of automobile is planned to be the example.

5 CONCLUSION

In this paper, we have proposed the *Green Browser* which supports green life cycle design and green information sharing. For supporting the *green life cycle* design, we have proposed the green life cycle model which consists of the strategy model, the process model, and the object models. In order to design green products, it is essential to support the designers to define the problem structure from the viewpoint of greenness. The green information sharing of the system encourages to share transparently the information about greenness of a product among designers, customers, regulators, NGO, and other stakeholders. We believe that, through information-sharing, green literacy is raised. It is expected that the green life cycle design support enables the designers to find out an answer for the green literacy of engineering.

Future work includes:

- continuing to develop of the Green Browser by integrating various modelers, evaluation tools, knowledge and data bases through the network,

- applying the system to many kinds of products in order to collect basic data, and

- providing the system as a public software for facilitating the green information sharing.

REFERENCES

[1] G. Boothroyd and L. Alting. Design for assembly and disassembly. In *Annals of the CIRP'92*. volume 41/2, pp. 1-12, Berne, Stuttgart, 1992. CIRP, Technische Rundschau.

[2] J. Ertel. Option of reusing electronic equipment. In K. Feldmann, editor, *RECY'94 (Second International Seminar on Life Cycle Engineering)*, pp. 234-237, Nuremberg, Germany, 1994. FAPS (Institute for Manufacturing Automation and Production Systems), University of Erlangen, Germany, and CIRP.

[3] G Sohlenius. Concurrent engineering. In *Annals of the CIRP '92*, volume 41/2, pp. 645-655. 1992.

[4] T. Tomiyama, T. Kiriyama, and Y. Umeda. Toward knowledge intensive engineering. In K. Fuchi and T. Yokoi, editors, *Knowledge Building and Knowledge Sharing*, pp. 308-316. Ohmusha and IOS Press, Tokyo, Osaka, and Kyoto, Amsterdam, Oxford, and Washington, 1994.

[5] D. Weld and J. de Kleer, editors. *Readings in Qualitative Reasoning about Physical Systems*. Morgan-Kaufmann, San Mateo, CA, 1989.

[6] R. Zust, R. Wagner, and B. Schumacher. Approach to the identification and quantification of environmental effects during product life. In *Annals of the CIRP'92*, volume 41/1, pp. 473-476. Berne, Stuttgart, 1992. CIRP, Technische Rundschau.

CLASSROOM CONNECTIONS

The Green Browser: A Proposal of Green Information Sharing and Life Cycle Design

Multiple Choice

Pick the best answer.

1. What is the purpose of the Green Browser?

A. To help foster collaboration of all parties during product life cycle design.

B. To support information sharing, public discussion and increase awareness.

C. To increase connection between the public and corporate decisions.

D. To increase awareness of use of plastic and other materials before mass production.

E. All of the above.

2. What kind of knowledge and data does it work with?

A. Environmental information about consumer products.

B. Life cycles of corporate products including raw materials, recycle and disposal.

C. Models of knowledge, strategies, goals and requirements.

D. Television commercials that sell plants.

E. A - C.

3. How can this kind of system support sustainability or clean environment goals?

A. Corporate board members can evaluate products from a green perspective.

B. The computerized product life cycle model now includes costs of disposal and transport.

C. The public can easily compare product environment information to help decision making.

D. Robots can sort through recycling bins.

E. A – C.

4. How can AI systems and users benefit from Green Browser-like systems?

A. Machine learning can use the green product life cycle descriptions as examples or data in order to learn how to generate sustainable product designs.

B. Corporations that share green product life cycle designs help educate designers and consumers.

C. By providing a standard computer model of product information for AI systems.

D. Users will find environmental product information easier.

E. All of the above.

True or False

Please decide if each of the statements below are True or False.

5. Consumer products need designs that meet environmental regulations through the entire life cycle of the product.

6. Green life cycle product design does not include product recycling or disposal of hazardous waste.

7. In the Green Browser project, product designs are documented and searchable on their environmental qualities.

8. Companies voluntarily care about the environment and share green product info with consumers.

9. Recycling of materials is an important part of product life cycle usually ignored in consumer electronics.

Answers can be found at the end of the book.

Chapter 8

Arguments in Decision Making

Support for Argumentation in Natural Resource Management

Mandy Haggith
University of Edinburgh, Scotland, UK

ABSTRACT

Natural resource and environmental management decisions often require that many people's point of view are taken into consideration, including scientific experts from different disciplines and local stakeholders with different goals and priorities. When there is disagreement, we require ways to explore the reasons for the different viewpoints and to seek out areas of consensus which can be built upon. This paper presents a meta-level argumentation framework for exploring multiple knowledge bases in which conflicting opinions about environmental change are expressed. A formal meta-language is defined for articulating the relationships between, and arguments for, propositions in knowledge bases independently of their particular object-level representation. A prototype system has been implemented to evaluate the usefulness of this framework and to assess its computational feasibility. The results so far are promising.

1   INTRODUCTION

1.1 INTRODUCTION AND MOTIVATION

When decisions are made which involve changes to natural resources such as oceans, forests or the atmosphere, the interests of various stakeholders need to be taken into account. Participative methodologies for natural resource development (*e.g.*: [Jiggins & Zeeuw 92]) are proving popular and successful and it is now accepted that wiser and more sustainable managment decisions can result from weighing up the views of all relevant parties. These parties include land-owners, residents, environmental pressure groups, wildlife biologists and other scientists, governmental bodies and industries. Industries are currently under increasing pressure to carry out environmental impact assessments of their proposed development plans and environmental audits of their activities,

and to integrate these into their decision making processes. However, ecosystems are highly complex phenomena and often a range of relevant specialists will produce conflicting predictions of the effects of environmental changes. In addition, conflicts can arise due to differing interests or goals, for example, conservation of particular wildlife habitats versus economic development. Conflicts can also result from the use of different terminologies by people from different disciplines – such conflicts are sometimes hard to untangle as both agreement and disagreement can be shrouded by differing language use. It is also important to note that environmental decision making does not happen in a social vacuum, so even if all parties agree on what the effect of a change will be, there may still be disagreement between people with different socio-economic value systems, as to whether these changes are a good or a bad thing.

As the environmental decision making process becomes more complex, computer support for it becomes desirable. As in other policy making areas, (*e.g.*: [Conklin & Begeman 88]), computer support can provide reliable records of various viewpoints, flexibility to record them in various places and at various times and to integrate them incrementally, and with the recent advances in network technology, computers can also provide open access to multiple viewpoints in an impartial manner.

Formal representation of the links or relationships between different viewpoints (*e.g.*: justification, disagreement, etc.) can enable more intelligent computer support to be provided. In particular, *argumentation* can be supported, for example, by defining search routines which will seek out all corroborating evidence for a proposition, or which will generate counter-arguments on demand on the basis of the formal relations. Only a very simple level of formality is required for this kind of argumentation support. This paper presents one such formalism.

Single, consistent knowledge bases are incapable of fulfilling the needs of situations such as those described above. Instead we require systems containing multiple knowledge bases, each of which can represent a particular viewpoint on a problem. We then need mechanisms for identifying, exploring and evaluating conflicts within and between knowledge bases. The overall aim of the research described in this paper is to construct such a knowledge-based system. The role of the user should be less like a novice asking a question of an expert who knows the answer, and more like a responsible decision-maker who calls, and chairs, a meeting of various relevant experts or interested parties. These agents can each argue for various positions, and the debate can be managed so that relevant counter-arguments are presented at the appropriate times. By interacting with the system in this way, the human user becomes better informed and more aware of the nature of the choices she has to make in order to make a wise decision.

It is important to make clear that this paper is *not* advocating systems which advise users how to make environmental decisions. The argumentation system described here does not carry out conflict resolution. It does not even suggest compromises. Conflicts are treated as opportunities for exploration, rather than problems. The purpose of the system is to assist users to explore the fullest possible range and diversity of opinion on the environmental aspects involved in their decisions. It shows where there are areas of consensus, which topics are particularly controversial and which positions are strongly entrenched. But it is ultimately up to the user to act as the human *locus of responsibility* (as explained in [Whitby 88]) in resolving conflicts, imposing value-judgements and coming to a decision.

1.2 RELATED WORK

The first area of related research concerns *argumentation*. There have been few attempts to capture arguments in KBS applied to natural resources, though [Robertson *et al.* 91] use arguments to aid in the construction of ecological simulation models, and [Robertson & Goldsborough 94] discuss representation of arguments for national park site selection in Prolog.

Most argumentation research is carried out in the legal domain. There is considerable interest in systems such as IBIS (Issue Based Information System) which allow legal regulations to be navigated around, and redrafted, using high-level relations between sections of text which indicate, for example, that one regulation subsumes another. Some examples are [Conklin & Begeman 88] and [Casson & Stone 92]. An important limitation of this work is its informality – the relations are not logically constrained, nor intended to have a particular formal interpretation, which provides the systems with great flexibility, but limits the amount of reasoning which can be automated using these relations. A similar criticism applies to other, linguistic, approaches to the mark-up of texts, notably the Rhetorical Structure Theory of [Mann *et al.* 89], Within the domain of law there is other work of a more formal nature, such as the resource-bounded argumentation strategies of [Loui *et al.* 93] and the representation of legal arguments as logic programs by [Kowalski & Sergot 90] and [Sartor 93], who addresses the problem of conflict between laws. Earlier work on formal argumentation in law includes [Toulmin 56].

Toulmin's ideas have been used as a basis of argumentation work in other domains, such as medicine. The algorithmic decision procedures of the early medical expert systems are giving way to a more expressive approach of supporting the formation of arguments for different diagnoses, and weighing up the alternatives in a qualitative manner. Examples are [Fox & Krause 92], [Fox *et al.* 92], [Krause *et al.* 93]. In this work, and that of

[Sartor 93], conflicts can be *resolved* by providing orderings of either propositions or argument structures. In this paper no attempt at all is made to resolve disagreements – the role of the computer here is to store and articulate disagreements rather than to impose consistency. A similar ideological stance towards inconsistency can be found in [Rescher & Brandom 79] and in [Gabbay & Hunter 91], [Gabbay & Hunter 93a]. This work is being applied in practice to supporting distributed software engineering by [Finkelstein *et al.* 93].

The second body of related work concerns inconsistency in logic. In order to explain why a meta-level framework is considered a useful way to study disagreement, we need to look more closely at this issue. The reason that inconsistency is usually perceived as a problem is because most knowledge based systems are founded in classical logic. In classical logic, the postulate called 'Ex Falsio Quod Libet' states that *any* proposition follows from a contradiction or falsity. Thus if we allow inconsistencies in knowledge bases, we effectively have 'logical chaos', as all statements are deducible. However, if we really want our knowledge bases to reflect the differing opinions of multiple experts, they will inevitably contain inconsistent statements.

There are several possible ways out of this impasse. The first is to allow the knowledge base to contain inconsistencies but to limit the set of possible inference rules in the system, and in particular to ban Ex Falsio Quod Libet. This is the *paraconsistent* approach of [Da Costa 74]. For an excellent survey of paraconsistency see [Priest *et al.* 89].

A second approach is again to construct inconsistent knowledge bases but to limit the set of propositions which inference rules can be applied to. This is the *restricted access* approach of [Gabbay & Hunter 93b].

A third approach is the *meta-level* approach adopted here and also used in the field of truth maintenance systems [Doyle 79], [de Kleer 86], in some work on belief revision [Gardenfors 23], [Doyle 92], [Galliers 89] and in [Gabbay & Hunter 93a] (which is rare in not insisting that the purpose of the enterprise is to restore consistency to a belief set.) In the meta-level approach, no attempt is made to create a single knowledge base in which inconsistency is handled, and reasoned *with* in the object-level logic, but rather, the inconsistencies between knowledge bases are reasoned *about* at the meta-level. The meta-level approach has

a significant benefit, which is that it allows us to abstract away from any particular object-level knowledge representation formalism or set of inference techniques. A meta-level framework for reasoning about differences of opinion, and for reasoning about the arguments which are used to support those opinions, can be applied to any object-level knowledge representation system, or indeed to systems involving hybrid representations. It is thus general purpose. More significantly still, it provides the first stage of a methodology for reasoning about multiple knowledge-based systems which may come from different sources, and each use their own representation language.

2 THE META-LEVEL FRAMEWORK

In this section, the formal language for reasoning about propositions and arguments is summarized. For full details see [Haggith 95].

2.1 META-LEVEL OBJECTS

There are three categories of meta-level objects which the language describes:

1. *Proposition Names* (Ai....Aj, Bi....Bj, denote proposition names)

2. *Arguments* (P <= {Qi....Qj}, where P is the conclusion of the argument and the Qi is set of premises, or alternatively, further arguments. Hence, arguments are recursive structures.)

3. *Sets* ({, }, ∪ (union), and ∈ (member) are the standard set symbols)

The language also uses some relation names (disagree, etc.) plus brackets and commas, together with &, v, ->, not, and the quantifiers, ie: the usual logical symbols.

2.2 TERMS AND FORMULAE

The terms of the language are names of any of the three object types. The *well formed formulae* (wffs) of the language are statements of relations and other wffs constructed in the usual way using the logical connectives. There are four primitive relations in the language, as follows:

a. *equivalent*(P, Q) : P and Q are names of propositions which mean the same, in terms of some function for transforming propositions in one object-level language into propositions in another language, or in terms of an object-level equivalence relation, or according to the opinion of some person marking up text.

b. *disagree*(P, Q) : P and Q are the names of propositions which disagree or express a conflict, according to some object-level notion such as negation, or temporal inconsistency, or according to the opinion of some person marking up text.

c. *elaboration*(P, S) : P is a proposition name and S is a set of names of propositions which elaborate or embellish upon P, according to multiple instantiations at the object level, or according to the opinion of some person marking up text.

d. *justification*(P, S) : P is a proposition name and S is a set of names of propositions which are a justification of P according to some object-level justification procedure such as modus ponens, abduction, or some other justification such as source or evidence, in the opinion of some person marking up text.

2.3 CATEGORIES OF ARGUMENT

It will be useful to give some definitions of types of arguments. An *actual* argument is one in which the <= connective represents justification, a *hybrid* argument is one in which it represents either justification or elaboration, and a *complete* argument is one in which every proposition in the argument is supported, either by other propositions or by the empty set, which indicates that it is a leaf node in the argument, ie: self evident, or an assumption.

Definition:
If P is a proposition name, S is a set of proposition names and *justification(P, S)*, then P <= S is an *actual* argument.

If P, Q are proposition names and P <= S, Q <= R are actual arguments, and S = S1U{Q}, then P <= S1 {Q <= R} is an *actual* argument.

Definition:
If P is a proposition name, S is a set of proposition names and *justification(P, S)*, or *elaboration(P, S)* or S ={E} *and equivalent* (P, E), then P <= S is a *hybrid* argument.

If P, Q are proposition names and P <= S, Q <= R are hybrid arguments, and S = S1U {Q}, then P <= S1 U {Q <= R} is a *hybrid* argument.

Definition:
An argument is complete iff its set of premises is empty, or all members of the set of premises are themselves complete arguments.

2.4 EXAMPLE

For the purposes of illustration, here is a simplified example based on [Dryzek 83] concerning the views of various parties in Alaska about the granting of state leases to drill for oil off the Alaskan coastline. Three parties are represented:

P: government bodies and industries interested in encouraging self-sufficiency in US oil production (Dryzek dubs these interests the 'Petroleum Club');

I: the indigenous Inuit population which is internally divided about oil production, particularly on the issue of employment; and

G: the 'Green Alliance' of environmental pressure groups and government bodies concerned with conservation of natural resources and concerned by the harm caused by oil production.

First the propositions representing the opinions are given, then the relations and arguments for each individual group, followed by some relations and arguments from multiple viewpoints.

THE PETROLEUM CLUB
P1 : A lease for oil production should be granted.
P2 : An adequate environmental impact statement has been produced.
P3 : Maximum rate of production of oil should be attained.
P4 : The lease for oil production will increase rate of production.
P5 : Oil production provides state revenue.
P6 : Oil production increases employment.
P7 : Oil companies share profits with the state.
P8: Profits from oil production and employment are taxable.
justification(P1, {P2, P3, P4}).
justification(P3, {P5}).
elaboration(P5, {P6, P7, P8}).
A1 : P1 <= {P2, P4, P3 <={P5 <={P6, P7, P8}}})

THE INUIT PEOPLE

I1 : A lease for oil production should not be granted.

I2 : Oil production is damaging to indigenous culture.

I3 : Oil production reduces work in fishing and hunting.

I4 : Oil production damages fish and whale stocks.

I5 : Oil production produces work in the oil and service industries.

justfication(I1, {I2}).

justification(I2, {I3, I5}).

justification(I3, {I4}).

A2: I1 <= {I2 <= {I3 <= { I4}, I5}}

THE GREEN ALLIANCE

GI : A lease for oil production should not be granted.

G2 : The environmental impact statement is not satisfactory.

G3 : Oil production causes pollution and disturbance.

G4 : Oil production reduces populations of fish and marine mammals.

G5 : Pollution kills fish and mammals.

G6 : Disturbance causes migration of animal populations.

justification(G1, {G2}).

justification(G2, {G4}).

elaboration(G4, {G3, G5, G6}).

A3 : G1 <= {G2 <= {G4 <= {G3, G5, G6}}}

INTER-AGENT RELATIONS

disagree(P1, I1).

disagree(P2, G2).

equivalent(G1, I1).

equivalent(I4, G4).

justification(P6, {I5}). (Note the support of the Inuit for the petroleum club's argument)

disagree(I3, P6). (Note the disagreement too)

MULTI-AGENT HYBRID ARGUMENTS

A4 : I1 <= {I2 <= {I3 <= { I4 <= {G4<= {G3, G5, G6}}}, I5}}

A5 :P1 <= {P2, P4, P3 <={P5 <={P6 <= {I5}, P7, P8}}})

2.5 META-LEVEL RULES

It is useful to state some properties of the four relations which constrain their possible applicability. These provide tests which can indicate which relations in an object-level language are suitable candidates for abstraction to the meta-level. Here are some examples :

1. *disagree(P, Q) -> disagree(Q, P)*
   (*i.e.*: disagreement is symmetrical)

2. *equivalent(P, Q) -> equivalent (Q, P)*
   (*i.e.*: equivalence is symmetrical)

3. *disagree(P, Q)-> not(equivalent(P,Q))*

4. *equivalent(P, Q) -> not(disagree(P, Q))*
   (*i.e.*: disagreement and equivalence are mutually exclusive)

5. *(disagree(P, Q) & equivalent(Q, R)) -> disagree(P, R)*
   (*i.e.*: disagreement is 'contagious' within equivalence sets)

6. *(equivalent(P, Q) & elaboration(P, S)) -> elaboration(Q, S)*
   (*i.e.*: elaborations apply to all members of equivalence sets)

7. *elaboration(P, S) -> (Q$\in$S, not(disagree(P, Q)))*
   (*i.e.*: elaborations must not disagree with the statement they elaborate on)

8. *justification(P, S) -> (Q$\in$S, not(disagree(P, Q)))*
   (*i.e.*: justifications for a statement must not disagree with it).

3 USING THE META-LANGUAGE TO EXPLORE THE ARGUMENTS

3.1 IMPLEMENTATION

This section sketches an implementation of the meta-level framework as described in section 2. A simple prototype has been constructed in Prolog to allow the following four basic facilities:

1. Creation of meta-level objects.

2. Mark-up of relations between them.

3. Exploration of conflicts.

4. Construction of higher-order argumentation structures.

The first two facilities are very simple in the Prolog implementation, so a hypertext tool has also been constructed (using HyperCard [Goodman 90]) which allows a piece of text to be edited and segmented into propositions, and allows relations between propositions and sets of propositions to be marked-up and written to a file which can be read by the Prolog system. In addition, a Prolog tool has been implemented for automatically marking up a limited form of knowledge base, represented in logic. Mark-up can be automated in two ways – either dynamically, by adjusting inference rules so that inference steps are recorded as justifications at the meta-level, contradictions are recorded as disagreements, etc. *whilst inference proceeds*, or alternatively, proofs or explanations of inference can be parsed to generate the same information, *after inference is complete*. Implementations of both approaches exist, though the latter is clearly more elegant as it does not require any adaption of object-level inference systems. Facilities (3) and (4) are described in more detail below.

3.2 CONFLICT EXPLORATION

In order to define a system for allowing a user to interact with the objects in the framework, the concept of a *conflict set* is useful. This set is a subset of all the proposition names, and it is used to represent those propositions which a user is currently interested in. Typically it will contain at least two propositions which are in disagreement, plus other statements equivalent to, or elaborating on those statements. It can also contain justifications for the propositions which may then generate further points of disagreement. The conflict set can be thought of as a window on the controversies within the knowledge base which can move around according to the relations between propositions. Conflict exploration results from altering the conflict set, by either *expanding* it to include new propositions related to those already in the conflict set, or *focusing* it to eliminate those propositions which are not interesting or which have been sufficiently explored. There are various different ways in which expansion and focussing can occur in the implementation. Full details are given in a longer version of this paper [Haggith 95]. Here it is sufficient to point out that this facility exists to enable a user to browse and explore the contents of the meta-level. Although the current interface is simple, the basic idea of a set expanding and contracting is clear and seems fairly intuitive. It avoids the restriction that a user feels when only viewing a single statement in a knowledge base. It is a useful technique for revealing the connectivity implicit in a knowledge base, and allowing the user to simulate the 'flow' of an argument or debate.

3.3 SYNTHESIS OF ARGUMENTATION STRUCTURES

The previous section described how the four basic relations could be used, interactively, to allow navigation around, or exploration of, marked-up knowledge bases containing conflicts. Another use of the framework involves automated construction of more sophisticated, or higher-order, meta-level relations defined in terms of the four primitive ones. Some examples follow to give a feel for what this would involve. They have all been implemented. The first and the last examples were chosen because they are each a primitive relation in other peoples' work on argumentation. The first, rebuttal, is a primitive in some current work on dialectical reasoning by Morten Elvang-Goransson. The last is from Sartor's work on representation of legal arguments. Details of other argumentation constructs can be found in [Haggith 95].

A. Rebuttal

In [Elvang-Goransson *et al.* 93], *rebuttal* is defined as a relation between arguments whose conclusions disagree. (Strictly speaking they say that the truth of the conclusion of one must imply the falsity of the conclusion of the other, but this is just one of many possible object-level interpretations of disagreement at the meta-level. The definition of rebuttal in terms of meta-level disagreement, has, I would claim, greater generality than their definition in terms of object-level implication and negation). The meta-level definition is as follows. (NB: in the following definitions, *argument (A, P, S)* is true if $A = P <= S$)

Definition:
rebuttal(P) is the set of arguments, *A,* such that
disagreement (P, Q) & argument(A, Q, _)
In other words, the rebuttal of a proposition P is the set of arguments for any propositions which disagree with P. Thus the Petroleum Club's argument that the oil production lease should be granted rebuts, and is rebutted by, the Green Alliance's argument that it should not.

B. Corroboration

The corroboration for a proposition is defined as the set of arguments for propositions equivalent to it. In the example, the Inuit's claim that oil damages fish and whale stocks is corroborated by the Green Alliance's argument about reduction in wildlife populations.

Definition:

corroboration(P) is the set of arguments, A, such that *equivalent (P, Q) argument(A, Q, _).*

C. Enlargement

The enlargement of P is the set of arguments for all elaborations of P. Again, in the example, the Inuit statement that the oil industry produces jobs in oil and services is part of the enlargement of the claim that oil production brings in state revenue.

Definition:

enlargement(P) is the set of arguments, A, such that *elaboration (P, S) & member(E, S) & argument (A, E, _).*

D. Counter-argument

This final structure is the richest of all, and is closely related to the definition given by [Sartor 93], in which a counter-argument to a proposition P is defined as an argument for the 'complement' (negation) of any proposition used anywhere in an argument for P. We could interpret this in two ways, either strictly, if we restrict the arguments to *actual* arguments (those involving only justifications) or more flexibly, using *hybrid* arguments (in which the argument steps may be justifications, equivalences or elaborations).

Definition:

counterargument(P, A) iff A ∈ rebuttal(P)
or *argument(P, B, Premisses) & member(Q, Premisses) & counterargument(Q, A).*

This is a recursive extension of the rebuttal definition. The two hybrid multi-viewpoint arguments (A4 and A5) given at the end of the example in section 3.1 are counterarguments to each other's conclusions, on the flexible interpretation. These structures provide a much broader view of the patterns of reasoning possible within a knowledge base, and provide a rich, coherently organised source of information relevant to any particular proposition. The current implementation can construct all of these sets for any proposition in its knowledge base.

These argumentation structures can provide a user with detailed comparisons between knowledge bases, detailed in that they provide, for each individual proposition, an analysis of how it relates to other propositions in the knowledge bases. The rebuttal and counterargument sets provide a detailed analysis of *conflicts*, so that

those propositions (such as the claim that leases for oil production should be granted) with large sets are highly controversial. Propositions with large corroboration sets are points of *consensus*. Large argument sets and big enlargements are indications of highly *cohesive* knowledge bases. Likewise small argument sets or small enlargements indicate *fragmentary* knowledge. These structures can provide evaluations of the overall 'shape' of knowledge bases, either during their construction or to guide a user in exploration of sets of completed knowledge bases.

4 CONCLUSIONS AND FUTURE DIRECTIONS

A meta-level framework has been described for representing relations, particularly conflicts and arguments, in and between multiple knowledge bases. An indication has been given of how the meta-level language can be used either interactively, to help in exploration of conflicting knowledge bases, or automatically, to construct and reason about more complicated relationships between them. An implementation of these ideas has been described to illustrate these two applications. This prototype is extremely encouraging as it has proved simple to implement (thus suggesting that the framework is computationally feasible) and successful in representing some examples from the resource management domain (thus suggesting that the ideas are useful).

There are several possibilities for enriching the meta-level framework (making it less abstract) such as explicitly representing the object-level reasoning techniques (*e.g.*: modus ponens) or the agents whose knowledge is being used, as meta-level objects. This would produce a much more fine-grained analysis which could be useful in evaluating, for example, *why* agents disagree.

This framework can be used both for bottom-up *abstraction* of existing object-level knowledge bases (via a process known as mark-up) or as top-down *specifications* of possible object-level knowledge bases (which could be created by a form of instantiation). It will be informative to assess each of these alternatives to see which is most useful. A crucial question is whether it is possible to automate the mark-up process, and if so, what the constraints on this are. Some preliminary work shows that this is possible for logic-based knowledge bases, but further investigation is needed here. This is an important issue as it will decide whether the framework is helpful in addressing problems with integrating existing 'legacy' knowledge bases into multiple KBSs. In the resource management domain, however, relatively few such legacy knowledge bases exist, so it is equally important to evaluate whether the framework supports the building of new knowledge based systems. No firm conclusions about the framework can be drawn until it has been evaluated under conditions of realistic complexity. Work is currently underway to assess the system's ability to provide support for the argumentation process involved in Environmental Impact Assessment, and for construction of knowledge based systems to support environmental management decision-making.

REFERENCES

[Casson & Stone 92] Casson, A. and Stone, D., An Expertext System for Building Standards, *Proceedings of Workshop on Computers and Building Standards,* Montreal, 1992.

[Conklin & Begeman 88] Conklin, J. and Begeman, M.L. gIBIS : A Hypertext Tool for Exploratory Policy Discussion, *ACM Transactions on Office Information Systems,* Vol. 6, No. 4, October 1988.

[Da Costa 74] Da Costa, N.C.A., On the theory of Inconsistent Formal Systems. *Notre Dame Journal of Formal Logic*, Vol. 15, No 4, pp 497-510, 1974.

[de Kleer 86] de Kleer, J., An Assumption Based TMS. *Artificial Intelligence,* Vol. 28, 1986.

[Doyle 79] Doyle, J., A Truth Maintenance System. *Artificial Intelligence*, Vol. 12, 1979.

[Doyle 92] Doyle, J., Reason Maintenance and Belief Revision : Foundations Versus Coherence Theories, Gardenförs, P. (ed.), *Belief Revision,* Cambridge University Press, 1992.

[Dryzek 83] Dryzek, J., Conflict and Choice in Resource Management : The Case of Alaska. Westview Press, 1983.

[Elvang-Goransson *et al.* 93] Morten Elvang-Goransson, Paul Krause and John Fox, Dialectical Reasoning with Inconsistent Information, *Proceedings of Uncertainty in AI,* 1993.

[Finkelstein *et al.* 93] Finkelstein, A., Gabbay, D., Hunter, A., Kramer, J., and Nuseibeh, B., Inconsistency Handling in Multi-Perspective Specifications, *Proceedings of Fourth European Software Engineering Conference* (ESEC 93), Springer-Verlag, 1993.

[Fox & Krause 92] John Fox and Paul Krause, Qualitative Frameworks for Decision Support : Lessons From Medicine. *The Knowledge Engineering Review,* Vol 7:1, 1992, pp 19-23.

[Fox *et al.* 92] John Fox, Paul Krause, Simon Ambler. Arguments, Contradictions and Practical Reasoning, *Proceedings of ECAI 92,* 1992.

[Gabbay & Hunter 91] Gabbay, D. and Hunter, A. Making Inconsistency Respectable : A Logical Framework for Inconsistency in Reasoning, Part 1 – A Position Paper, P. Jorrand & J. Kelemen (eds.), *Fundamentals of Artificial Intelligence Research.* Lecture Notes in Computer Science 535, Springer Verlag, 1991.

[Gabbay & Hunter 93a] Gabbay, D. and Hunter, A. Making Inconsistency Respectable : Part 2 – Meta-level Handling of Inconsistency, *Proceedings of ECSQUARU conference 1993, Lecture Notes in Computer Science,* 747, Springer Verlag, 1993.

[Galliers 89] Galliers, J.R., A Theoretical Framework for Computer Models of Coorperative Dialogue, *Acknowledging Muti-Agent Conflict,* Cambridge University Computer Lab, Technical Report No. 172, 1989.

[Gardenförs 92] Gardenförs, P., Belief Revision. Cambridge University Press, 1992.

[Goodman 90] Goodman, D., The Complete HyperCard Handbook, Bantam Books, 1990.

[Haggith 95] Haggith, M., A Meta-level Framework for Exploring Conflicts in Multiple Knowledge Bases, *Proceedings of AISB-95,* Sheffield, April 1995.

[Jiggins & Zeeuw 92] Participatory Technology Development in Practice : Process and Methods. In Reijntjes, C., Haverkort, B. and Waters-Bayer, A. (eds.), *Farming for the Future : An Introduction to Low-external-input and Sustainable Agriculture,* Macmillan Education, 1992.

[Krause *et al.* 93] Krause, P., Ambler, S., Elvang-Goransson, M. and Fox, J., A Logic of Argumentation for Uncertain Reasoning. *Computational Intelligence,* November 1993.

[Kowalski & Sergot 90] Kowalski, R.A. and Sergot, M.J., The Use of Logical Models in Legal Problem Solving, *Ratio Juris*, Vol. 3, No. 2. 1990.

[Loui *et al.* 93] Loui, R.P., Norman, J., Olson, J. and Merrill, A. A Design for Reasoning with Policies, Precedents and Rationales, *Proceedings of the Fourth International Conference on Artificial Intelligence and Law,* Amsterdam, The Netherlands, June 1993.

[Mann *et al.* 89] Mann, W.C., Matthiessen, C.M.I.M. and Thompson, S.A., Rhetorical Structure Theory and Text Analysis, *ISI Research Report ISI/RR-89-242,* University of Southern California, 1989.

[Priest *et al.* 89] Priest, G., Routley, R. and Norman, J. (eds.), Paraconsistent Logic : Essays on the Inconsistent. Philosophia Verlag, 1989.

[Rescher & Brandom 79] Rescher. N. and Brandom, R, The Logic of Inconsistency. *American Philosophical Quarterly Library of Philosophy, Vol. 5,* Basil Blackwell, Oxford, 1979.

[Robertson *el al.* 91] Robertson, D., Bundy, A., Muetzelfeldt, R., Haggith, M., and Uschold, M., Eco-Logic : *Logic Based Approaches to Ecological Modeling*, MIT Press, 1991.

[Robertson & Goldsborough 94] Robertson, D. and Goldsborough, D., Representing the Structure of Reserve Selection Arguments Using Logic Programs, Unpublished paper.

[Sartor 93] Sartor, G., A Simple Computational Model for Nonmonotonic and Adversarial Legal Reasoning, *Proceedings of the Fourth International Conference on Artificial Intelligence and Law,* Amsterdam, The Netherlands, June 1993.

[Toulmin 56] S. Toulmin, The Uses of Argument, Cambridge University Press, 1956.

[Whitby 88] Blay Whitby, Artificial Intelligence: A Handbook of Professionalism, Ellis Horwood Ltd., 1988.

CLASSROOM CONNECTIONS

Support for Argumentation in Natural Resource Management

Multiple Choice
Pick the best answer.

1. **What environmental problem does this system address?**
   A. Making decisions about natural resources such as oceans, forests and atmosphere from multiple points of view and expertise.
   B. Helping specialists find solutions to conflicts.
   C. Documenting explanations of decisions and arguments that include multiple kinds of goals such as conservation of wildlife or economic development.
   D. Untangling conflicting terminology from different disciplines for joint decision making.
   E. All of the above.
   F. None of the above.

2. **How is AI used to help with this kind of decision making?**
   A. Automatically recording and explaining decision making.
   B. Meta-analysis of arguments.
   C. Automatic exploration of alternative decisions.
   D. Automatic exploration of conflicts.
   E. All of the above.

3. **What concepts does the AI system work with?**
   A. Counter-arguments.
   B. Argument structure.
   C. Agreement and disagreement.

   D. Justifications and assumptions.
   E. Corroboration.
   F. All of the above.
   G. A and C.

True or False
Please decide if each of the statements below are True or False.

4. When decisions are made which involve changes to natural resources such as oceans, forests or the atmosphere, the interests of various stakeholders need to be taken into account.

5. It is now accepted that wiser and more sustainable management decisions can result from weighing up the views of all relevant parties.

6. Environmental decision making does not happen in a social vacuum, so even if all parties agree on what the effect of a change will be, there may still be disagreement between people with different socio-economic value systems, as to whether these changes are a good or a bad thing.

7. The purpose of the system is to assist users to explore the fullest possible range and diversity of opinion on the environmental aspects involved in their decisions.

8. Corporations and environmental groups often agree on oil drilling locations.

Answers can be found at the end of the book.

Chapter 9

Underground Nuclear Testing

An Intelligent Assistant for Nuclear Test Ban Treaty Verification

Cindy L. Mason
NASA Ames Research Center, USA

ABSTRACT

This paper presents an intelligent assistant that classifies and filters seismic data from Norway's regional seismic array, NORESS, for underground nuclear weapons test ban treaty verification. Verification of a Comprehensive Test Ban Treaty or a Low Yield Threshold Test Ban Treaty inspires development of enhanced seismic verification technology with lower detection levels and improved noise reduction signal extraction algorithms. However, lowering the detection threshold causes an exponential increase in the number of events detected. As each event must be analyzed to determine if it contains a clandestine nuclear test, the analysis and classification task overwhelms human seismic verification specialists. The Seismic Event Analyzer Project in the Treaty Verification Research Group at Lawrence Livermore National Laboratory (LLNL) is concerned with the development of technologies for the automatic processing of seismic monitoring data. The overall system is hybrid – it contains hardware and many kinds of software, such as advanced signal processing algorithms. Here we discuss one element of that larger system, an intelligent software agent, SEA.

Three important aspects of the intelligent software assistant SEA are (1) it reduces the workload of the human analyst by filtering and classifying the large volume of continuously arriving data, presenting interpretations of "interesting" events for human review (2) the user interface permits interactive or human-agent analysis and (3) it emulates the common sense problem solving behavior and explanation capability of the human seismic analyst by using a multi-context Assumption Based Truth Maintenance System.

1   INTRODUCTION

The ultimate goal of treaty verification data processing research is to understand the issues building a system to detect and locate events, discriminate between earthquakes and other seismic sources, and estimate yields of underground nuclear explosions. Here we focus on the seismic location problem, which may be used, in part, to classify the seismic event we are witnessing, and to provide information that constrains theories on possible evasive measures. The most reliable means available to verify compliance with treaties regulating underground nuclear weapons testing is seismic monitoring [1], [2]. However, monitoring for a Comprehensive Test Ban Treaty (CTBT) or Low Yield Test Ban Treaty (LYTBT) increases the requirements on current verification technology.

To evade treaty provisions, nuclear tests would be designed to produce weak seismic signals. These low signal to noise ratio (SNR) events can be hidden in background noise or occur in conjunction with other seismic events. To address this problem sensor technologies offering lower detection levels and improved SNR must be used. However, lowering the detection threshold increases the number of

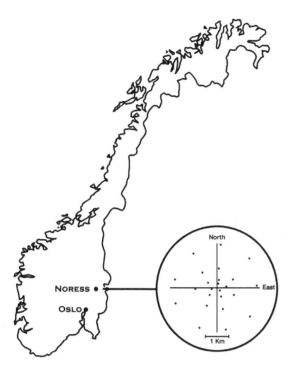

Figure 1. Norwegian experimental seismic array station, NORESS.

events which must be examined. Our experience indicates up to 20,000 events a year may need to be analyzed from Norway's experimental seismic array, NORESS, as shown in Figure 1. Such events include earthquakes and chemical explosions as well as possible nuclear explosions. Each event must be analyzed to determine if it contained a clandestine nuclear test. There are few specialists available for this type of interpretation problem. Therefore, reliable verification of a CTBT or LYTBT will require an automated system to help analyze and classify seismic events. Such a system, called SEA (Seismic Event Analyzer), is described in the remainder of this paper.

The following section gives an overview of the treaty verification research system at LLNL and motivates our intelligent systems approach to the problem of seismic interpretation. The next two sections examine the common sense problem solving strategy used by seismologists and relate this strategy to belief revision. We show three example events, including a scheduled test event. Subsequently, SEA's knowledge representation and common sense reasoning schemes are presented. Finally, we describe our user interface, SEA's explanation facility, and some of our implementation experiences, and answer the question, "Does it work?"

2 SYSTEM OVERVIEW

SEA analyzes seismic data from the Norwegian experimental seismic array station, NORESS[3]. Figure 1 shows the array geometry, located in eastern Norway, about 100 Km north of Oslo. SEA presently interprets data from 25 sensors deployed in four concentric rings, the largest being about 3 Km in diameter.

As shown in Figure 2, we receive seismic data from Norway via satellite and archive it onto an optical disk. It is then processed by an event detection program which examines the raw sensor data for a possible seismic event. The event detector program generates an event file for each seismic event detected and processed by hardware and sends it via Ethernet to the UNIX workstation where the software assistant performs the event analysis. SEA stores the results of the analysis, including detailed records of its decision making process, in a disk file. This setup gives the human specialist an option to review the analyses either as they are generated by the assistant or at a later time.

During the review process, the seismic analyst can query SEA's explanation facility, view the waveforms before and after applications of signal processing, and view the information comprising an interpretation. The human analyst can interactively add new information and direct the intelligent agent system to make additional analysis, modify existing ones, or develop an analysis manually (*i.e.* without the aid of the assistant) to produce a "second opinion." This philosophy makes maximum use of AI automation while leaving the final decision to the human analyst. SEA's classification and analysis knowledge was obtained by observing and interviewing seismologists and verification analysts who work with NORESS[3] and is comprised of general seismological knowledge as well as knowledge specific to the NORESS array.

Previous attempts to automate the task of seismic data analysis using traditional programming techniques rely almost entirely on the algorithmic use of signal processing. Human analysts outperform these programs by using their common sense knowledge about regional propagation characteristics and patterns in the signal or noise to judiciously apply signal processing while forming an interpretation. The human analyst also considers non-geologic common sense such as the shooting schedule of mines and the breaking up of river ice in the spring. A common sense knowledge approach to building

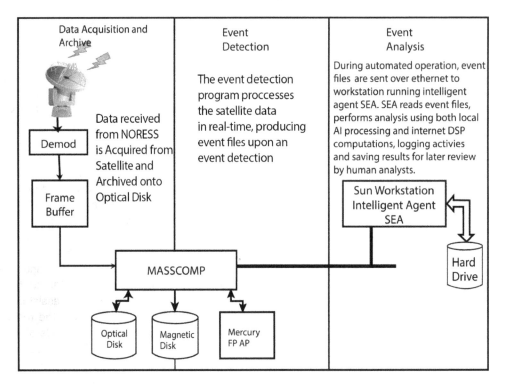

Figure 2. Architecture and Data Flow of the Interpretation System.

a software agent assistant directly supports the representation of knowledge and drives the signal processing in a pattern-driven fashion in the same fashion as the human analyst.

3   SEISMIC MONITORING

The goal of hypothesizing an interpretation of the seismic data is to create an analysis about the number and location of events that would generate the signals present in a seismogram. To understand how this is done, it helps to visualize what happens during a seismic event. As a seismic event releases energy, it sets up a number of characteristic waves, or phases, which propagate along various paths through the earth (see Figure 3). Because these waves don't travel the same distance and propagate at the same velocity, they arrive at the seismic sensor at different times. Longitudinal waves (called P for primus) arrive first, followed by transverse waves (S for secundus) and then surface waves (named after their discoverers Rayleigh and Love) (see Figure 4). It is this difference in arrival time which enables a seismologist to estimate the distance of an event. The further apart the phases

are, the farther they had to travel to reach the station. Direction is determined using a number of phase characteristics calculated with signal processing tools. The location of a seismic source is then estimated using distance and direction.

However, formation of a hypothesis is further complicated when signals from multiple overlapping events arrive at the station. Not all phases from the events will arrive, and those that do arrive can be of poor quality. In order to form an interpretation, the seismologist needs to identify phase type and associate phases as belonging to

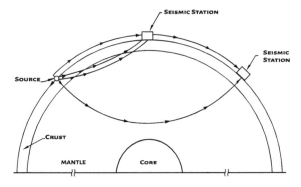

Figure 3. Seismic waves separate and take distinct paths through the earth.

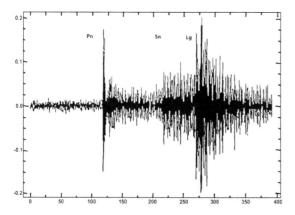

Figure 4. This seismogram recorded at the NORESS seismic array in Norway was produced by a mining explosion in the former Soviet Union. Three distinct wave arrivals are shown: (1) a compressional wave (Pn) that propagated deep into the crust, (2) a following shear wave (Sn) that also propagated deep into the crust, and (3) a type of surface wave (Lg) immediately following.

the same event. Furthermore, the events that are of most interest have a low signal to noise ratio. In essence, a human creates an event analysis by hypothesizing with common sense assumptions and testing the implications of those assumptions. Figure 5 shows the overall process used by the analyst to understand a seismic event. In general, the process is one of sequentially building a series of partial hypotheses, each an extension of one before it.

Each partial hypothesis is checked for semantic consistency and discarded if shown to be inconsistent. Because we reason with common sense, we do not rely on 'logical' but semantic consistency about whether concepts 'make sense' together, if they create semantic conflict.

Initially a core set of signal processing routines is applied to the seismic data. This yields information that is used to make an initial set of partial interpretations. These form the basis for additional signal processing to be done that will be used to extend the partial interpretation.

This cycle continues until a partial interpretation is disproved or extended to a full interpretation. A full interpretation that has not been disproved constitutes a valid interpretation of the seismic data.

4 TRUTH MAINTENANCE SYSTEM

The process whereby a human analyst builds up a partial analysis and determines its validity can be formally described by hypothesis-and-test with a belief revision system with common sense assumption contexts. A partial hypothesis (analysis) is disproved if the belief in it leads to a semantic contradiction. For example, it is known that a Pn phase must have a velocity of greater than 6 Km/sec. Suppose that it is believed that a phase

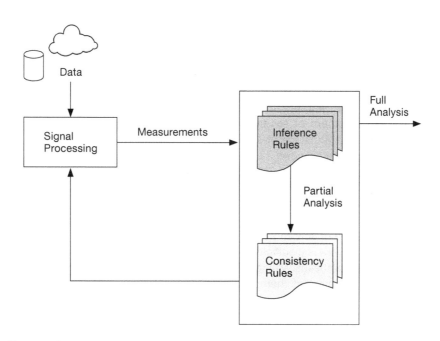

Figure 5. General interpretation process used by seismologist in analyzing a seismic event.

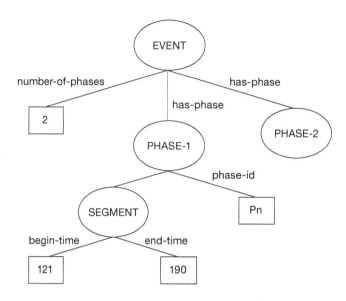

Figure 6. The Semantic Network indicates the EVENT has 2 PHASES. PHASE-1 is shown.

is Pn in a partial hypothesis and that gives rise to a reasoning chain resulting in the fact that the phase has a velocity less that 6 Km/sec. Then it must be the case that the belief is incorrect and the partial hypothesis is "discarded". Truth Maintenance Systems (TMS) have been shown to handle this kind of belief revision by maintaining records about dependencies between facts and detecting logical contradictions among believed facts. SEA uses a method of TMS based on semantic consistency rather than logical consistency. It also parallelizes the process by using multiple belief contexts in parallel to pursue several common sense hypotheses about the data simultaneously with a modified Assumption Based Truth Maintenance System (ATMS)[5].

Typically, an ATMS is most appropriate in situations where there are a number of solution contexts and all must be found. In situations where there is only one solution or where only one must be found an ATMS is not as efficient as a TMS, DeKleer[5]. In theory, a single correct hypothesis or belief context exists for a detected seismic event. However, in practice multiple interpretations are unavoidable. In fact, analysts are unable to arrive at a single interpretation when there is insufficient information to exclude invalid hypotheses. Multiple valid hypotheses from SEA indicate that there is not enough information or knowledge to reject invalid hypotheses.

5 KNOWLEDGE REPRESENTATION SCHEME

5.1 SEMANTIC CONCEPT NETWORK

A semantic concept network formalism is used as the knowledge representation scheme for common sense analysis. As shown in Figure 6, links represent relations among concepts and are directed, going from a single concept node to another single concept node. There are two types of concept nodes: atomic nodes and non-atomic nodes. Non-atomic nodes represent seismological analysis concepts such as EVENT, PHASE, or SEGMENT. Atomic nodes represent a value, such as begin-time or number-of-phases, and only have links pointing into them. Values may be computed by a numerical algorithm on another machine.

For the purpose of accessing and processing the concept net in a common sense rule, we define a fact to be a < **node, link, node** > triple. A network is completely specified by the set of facts that it contains. Thus the net in Figure 6 consists of the facts

```
<EVENT,      number-of-phases,   2>
<EVENT,      has-phase,          PHASE-1>
<EVENT,      has-phase,          PHASE-2>
<PHASE-1,    has-segment,        SEGMENT>
<PHASE-1,    phase-id,           Pn>
<SEGMENT,    begin-time,         121>
<SEGMENT,    end-time,           190>
```

5.2 IF-THEN COMMON SENSE RULES

IF-THEN rules are the knowledge representation scheme used to encode the common sense analysis knowledge. Each common sense rule has the form

(rule-name pattern action)

During program execution, all the *pattern* portions of common sense rules are incrementally populated with concept nodes and relationship links of the semantic network to determine the common sense rules that will have their *action* portion executed. The action is executed locally or through a foreign function call invoking processes across a network. It is worth noting that we designed the code so external processes can be invoked from both the pattern and the action. This is the key to accessing numerical computations performed external to the software agent.

Consider a common sense rule to compute the velocity of a Pn phase using the semantic concept network illustrated in Figure 6.

```
(compute-velocity-for-Pn
      ((EVENT has-phase PHASE-1)
       (PHASE-1 phase-id Pn))
      (ASSERT (PHASE-1 velocity (compute-
       vel-using-beamform))))
```

The *pattern* portion of the common sense rule matches the facts describing an EVENT which has a PHASE whose phase-id is Pn. The action is to invoke a function (which may be written in LISP, C or FORTRAN) over the network to compute the phase's velocity using a signal processing technique, beamforming. Beamforming is computationally intensive so it is computed on another machine with greater CPU power. The computed value is then added into the network as the fact <PHASE-1, velocity, value> via the "ASSERT" function. The assumption context is also recorded.

6   COMMON SENSE ASSUMPTION BASED REASONER

The common sense assumption reasoning techniques of SEA are a hybrid of the efficiency of context management found in Stallman and Sussman[6] and the parallel multi-context assumption based reasoning methods of

DeKleer[5]. The SEA system functions by creating a bread crumb trail of its own computations. It tags each decision/reasoning step and deduced/assumed fact with a complex record (justification) indicating the common sense rule and antecedent facts context used to create it and the assumption context(s) under which the fact is believed. It creates similar records when contradictions occur. This information is useful in providing an explanation facility for people as well as a trace of system operation for debugging. This same information determines the current state of beliefs at any point in time and in efficient algorithms for multi-context dependency-directed backtracking.

The ATMS is composed of an assumptions context database and common sense TMS rules. Control of rule firings is achieved in a forward chaining manner, using antecedent demons to monitor the facts data base and instantiation queues to control the order of rule firings.

6.1 THE ASSUMPTIONS DATA BASE

The Assumptions Data Base contains an assumption context represented as a set for each fact/concept in the Semantic Concept Network. The assumption set for a fact indicates the assumptions or contexts upon which its belief state ultimately depends (*i.e.* a fact is believed if its assumption set is believed). More formally, an assumption set is defined to be a subset of the known facts

$$F = \{f_1, f_2, ..., f_n\}$$

Thus, the set of all assumption sets is the power set of **F**. Any assumption set **A** is labelled either BELIEVED or DISBELIEVED. BELIEVED means that facts of **A** are semantically consistent with one another, *i.e.* they can all be believed at the same time. DISBELIEVED means that the facts of **A** are semantically inconsistent, *i.e.* they cannot all be believed at the same time. Let **A** and **B** be assumption sets with **A** ⊂ **B**. If **A** is DISBELIEVED then since *the subset of facts in **A** that cause it to be inconsistent or DISBELIEVED will also be in **B**, so **B*** must also be DISBELIEVED.

Each fact **f** has an assumption set **A(f)** associated with it. In essence, **f** is believed if **A(f)** is BELIEVED and is DISBELIEVED if **A(f)** is DISBELIEVED. The manner in which assumption contexts or sets are assigned to facts, their labels and possible subsequent relabelling provides the mechanism by which common sense assumption based reasoning or assumption based truth maintenance is realized. When a rule fires with the sets of antecedent facts $a_1, \cdots, a_n$ and the set of created facts $c_1, \cdots, c_m$. Each c_i, can be created by one of three actions each producing a different value for $A(c_i)$. The actions and the values for $A(c_i)$ are:

$$ASSERT(c_i) \longrightarrow A(c_i) \quad = \quad \bigsqcup_{j=1}^{n} A(a_j)$$

$$ASSUME(c_i) \longrightarrow A(c_i) \quad = \quad \bigsqcup_{j=1}^{n} A(a_j) \quad + \quad c$$

$$GIVEN(c_i) \longrightarrow A(c_i) \quad = \quad c$$

For example, consider the following inferences

$$\perp \quad \longrightarrow \quad GIVEN(a),\ GIVEN(b),\ GIVEN(c),$$
$$a \wedge b \quad \longrightarrow \quad ASSUME(d)$$
$$d \wedge c \quad \longrightarrow \quad ASSERT(e)$$

This gives rise to < *fact, assumption set* > pairs

```
                <e, { abcd }>
              /              \
        <d, {abd}>            \
        /       \              \
  <a, { a }> <b, { b }>     <c, { c }>
```

6.2 TRUTH MAINTENANCE RULES

The right hand side actions thus far have been concerned with computations that create facts. The system is monotonic in that facts are never deleted. Non-monotonic reasoning is achieved by changing the *label* value of an assumption set. This is accomplished through a special class of common sense rules concerning semantic consistency called TMS rules. TMS rules take the same form as common sense inference rules. In a TMS rule, pattern specifies a group of believed facts which constitute an inconsistency. If the pattern successfully matches against the semantic concept network, an inconsistency among facts has occurred and the action CONTRADICT is invoked to repair the Assumptions Data Base.

For example, if the common sense rule instantiation

$$a_1,\ a_2,\ \ldots,\ a_n \quad \longrightarrow \quad CONTRADICT$$

fires, then the assumption set $\bigsqcup_{j=1}^{n} A(a_j)$ is

marked DISBELIEVED. In the above example, suppose we now have

$$b \quad \wedge \quad c \quad \longrightarrow \quad CONTRADICT$$

The assumption context set **{b,c}** as well as any superset **{a, b, c, d}** are marked DISBELIEVED. Thus, the fact **e** that was BELIEVED is now DISBELIEVED. It no longer has the support of a set of consistent semantic concepts.

To illustrate this in the seismic analysis domain, suppose after computing the velocity for the phase in the "compute-velocity-for-Pn" rule, we realize the value contradicts the belief that the phase-id is Pn. Notice this is not a logical but a semantic inconsistency. The following common sense truth maintenance rule encodes the semantic inconsistency between the two facts.

```
(Pn-velocity-consistency
    (Believed (EVENT has-phase PHASE-1)
              (PHASE-1 phase-id Pn)
              (PHASE-1 velocity < 6.5))
    (CONTRADICT))
```

At this point, the semantic contexts or assumption sets for the facts involved are no longer BELIEVED. Any other facts dependent upon these contexts or assumptions become DISBELIEVED as well. Initially, all facts default to state *Unknown*, meaning they do not exist in the database yet and are NOT (*BELIEVED* or *DISBELIEVED*). A created fact will be *BELIEVED* until all its contexts or assumption sets become involved in a contradiction.

6.3 QUEUE-ORIENTED CONTROL AND EXPLANABILITY

Control of common sense rule firing is achieved using antecedent demons to monitor the facts database and instantiation queues to populate common sense inference and truth maintenance rules. Common sense rules are implemented as instantiation frames whose slots are variables waiting to be bound. Initially instantiations are unsatisfied and reside in the "unsatisfied" queue. Each time a fact is added to the data base, the antecedent demon tries to satisfy instantiation slots in memory using the fact as a variable binding. Once all slots are finally satisfied, the rule is triggered and can do one of two useful things: detect a contradiction or create new facts.

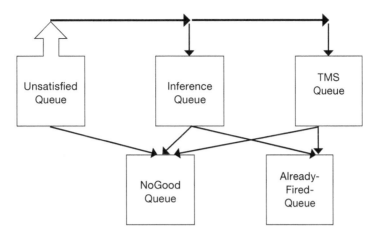

Figure 7. Instantiations frames migrate among queues during program execution.

Contradiction rule instantiations move to the "TMS-ready-to-fire" queue where they will all be executed in the current inference cycle. Common sense rule instantiations on the other hand move to the "INF-ready-to-fire" queue and may not fire immediately, since they are subject to prioritization. Inference instantiations are inserted into the queue in the order in which they are to fire, the top-most instantiation being the next to fire. This idea is illustrated in Figure 7.

Once a common sense rule has fired, the instantiation moves to the "already-fired" queue. Hence the queues provide a complete memory of how the common sense knowledge was applied in solving a particular problem instance. Together with the queue, the memory of all the contexts or assumption sets (both believed and disbelieved) helps create an explanation for the user.

6.4 BELIEF REVISION DURING PATTERN MATCHING

During the time an instantiation is waiting to be completely satisfied, the belief status of the previously bound variables may change. Hence after each submatch the belief status of the partial assumption set $\coprod_{j=1}^{k} A(a_j)$ is checked, where k is the number of submatches so far. If it is DISBELIEVED then $\coprod_{j=1}^{k} A(a_j)$ will be DISBELIEVED and the instantiation may be discarded and moved to the

"NO-GOOD-instantiation" queue. This prevents any further pattern matching on partially instantiated patterns that can never be a consistent con-

text. A similar circumstance can occur while a satisfied common sense inference pattern is waiting to be fired in the "INF-ready-to-fire" queue.

This inferencing technique will find all consistent interpretations and is independent of the order in which instantiations fire. However, the order has a profound effect on the amount of time required to find these interpretations. Recall that if assumption sets **A** and **B** are such that $\mathbf{A} \subset \mathbf{B}$ and **A** is DISBELIEVED then **B** is DISBELIEVED. Suppose $a_1, \ldots, a_n \longrightarrow c$ where c is ASSERTed or ASSUMEd and $\coprod_{j=1}^{n} A(a_j)$ is DISBELIEVED. Then A(c) must also be DISBELIEVED. In our hybrid system, **c** may invoke expensive numerical computations on other systems, and this work would be wasted if **A(c)** is DISBELIEVED.

Checking the belief state of the set $\coprod_{j=1}^{n} A(a_j)$ *before* the instantiation action is evaluated prevents useless work from taking place. If the set is DISBELIEVED the instantiation is discarded or moved to the other queue and **c** is never created. The failed NOGOOD instantiation queue serves the purpose of helping provide explanations to the user on decision making.

6.5 OBSERVATIONS

In general, there can be more than one possible interpretation generated for each event. This introduces the problem of assigning a confidence measurement of interpretations derived by the system. The usual approach taken in such systems is to provide confidence values to facts that are in turn derived from the rule and confidence values of antecedent facts (see for example, Shortliffe[7]).

In a common sense assumption based system a single fact may have multiple combinations of rules and antecedent facts, each inferring the fact or its negation. Therefore, the credibility of a single fact will depend on all rules and antecedent fact credibility. The nature of this dependability has not been addressed, although the analysis found in Ginsberg[8] may be applicable.

SEA uses a different approach in determining hypothesis credibility. In essence, the human strategy in evaluating an analysis is to apply all possible inferences about a hypothesis trying to find a reason to discard it as soon as possible. Although rules may vary in discrimination power, in general, with this strategy the more inferences made without encountering a contradiction, the more credible the hypothesis becomes. Therefore, the total number of inferences made on a hypothesis is a measure of the hypothesis' credibility.

A single contradiction is enough to cause work on a hypothesis to halt. It is often the case, however, that there are several contradictions that can be generated for a hypothesis because there are multiple contexts. Due to the multi-context support of the assumption based architecture it is possible to find some or all of these contradictions. A single fact can have several DISBELIEVED assumption sets. Even after inferencing has stopped for a hypothesis, assumption sets that support facts already in the interpretation can be marked DISBELIEVED. So the total number of contradictions associated with a hypothesis provides a measure of incredibility.

7   USER INTERACTIONS

SEA is designed to operate in two fundamental modes: automatic and interactive. When started in automatic mode SEA processes events in real-time without human intervention. From interactive mode, SEA can be used as an assistant for manually processing seismic data, or may be used by an analyst to review results processed during automated operation. The analyst reviews events processed in automated operation by running SEA in its interactive mode. In this mode, the display screen is divided into four windows:

1. *Editor Window* – The window editor of Emacs is used to run and communicate with SEA. Progress during event analysis, such as names of the common sense rules that execute, incoming high-level numerical or graphical results of remote signal processing systems, and debugging information, is displayed in this window. Common sense rules and system code may be edited and debugged in Emacs without having to exit SEA.

2. *Semantic Concept Network Display Window* – Once a signal has been classified, common sense concepts and analysis information related to the classification is graphically displayed in this window. The displayed information is organized in a relations/concept or hierarchical semantic fashion reflecting its structure in the semantic concept network. Users can interactively query information about a concept selecting it with the mouse.

3. *Scrolling Waveform Display Stack* – Three vertically stacked windows display results of signal processing as it occurs during sensor analysis. The window also displays results from human interactions to run algorithms such as plotting or signal processing. At any one time, three windows are displayed, but a window history stacking mechanism provides a scrolling chronological overview of signal processing activity during event analysis. A waveform is displayed by scrolling the top two windows down, and plotting the new waveform in the top window.

4. *FK Analysis Contour Display Window* – This window displays a contoured image of the surface resulting from frequency-wavenumber (FK) analysis. This analysis technique is used to determine the direction and velocity of a seismic phase, and the image displayed in this window provides feedback on the quality of the direction/velocity estimate.

The analyst's input to SEA's interactive interface is performed primarily by pointing and selecting with the workstation's mouse. Waveforms may be examined and selected with the mouse for analysis, information may be obtained about items in the semantic network by "clicking" the mouse in specific regions of the semantic network display, and several actions can be invoked through the use of menus.

At the beginning of an interactive session, SEA presents a menu of events that are available for review. When an event is selected from the menu, SEA reads the event's data with any results saved from automated processing. SEA processes the event in a manner identical to automatic mode, but it runs faster when results are available from a previous analysis.

Once processing completes, a menu of hypotheses displays with "CONSISTENT" beside a hypothesis if it is BELIEVED, or the word "INCONSISTENT" if it is DISBELIEVED. Selecting a hypothesis from the menu displays the event waveform with superimposed phase information on the waveform display stack, and associated info from the semantic network is displayed in the semantic concept network display window.

Furthermore, if the selected hypothesis is DISBELIEVED, the inconsistencies that caused the interpretation to be DISBELIEVED are also shown in the semantic network display window.

8 DOES IT WORK?

We have begun to perform extensive testing to determine if SEA will acceptably perform the task it was designed for, and to identify areas of further improvement in the processing strategy, knowledge representation, and user interface. Initial results obtained from testing during development and operating in real-time follow.

8.1 DEVELOPMENTAL TESTING

Archived data were used during development and refinement of common sense analysis to determine how closely the system followed the

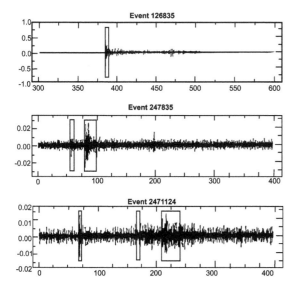

Figure 8. Events from the test data set include a Teleseismic P (top), an event from Southern Norway (middle), and an event from a mining explosion in the Leningrad region of the USSR (bottom). Events are labeled with an index relative to the beginning of the data file.

analyst's reasoning in estimating event locations, and how efficiently the system used time-intensive computations in the interpretation process. Several events from the archived data – exhibiting a variety of signal conditions and source locations – form the basis of a test set used to determine how changes in the rules affect the overall intelligent assistant's performance.

This off-line processing has enabled us to correct and tune the interpretation strategy employed by SEA. Our experience now shows that the system has evolved enough to analyze events and estimate source locations with a high degree of reliability. Some events from the test data set are shown in Figure 8. They illustrate the variety of events the system must be able to analyze.

The first event (1987 126 8 35) is from an announced underground nuclear test at the former USSR Semipalatinsk Test Site. The interpretation provided by SEA characterized the event as a teleseismic P phase (indicating a source distance near or greater than 2000 Km) with an estimated velocity of 16.5 Km/s and a bearing of 80 degrees Northeast. Our domain analyst interpreted the event using a different set of analysis tools and obtained a similar characterization with a velocity of 16.8 Km/s. Analysis of the second event (1986 247 8 35) by SEA characterized the event as a Pn/Lg combination, and estimated the location of the source at latitude 59.3 degrees north, longitude 9.6 degrees east (in Southern Norway). The location provided by the analyst was 59.2 degrees north, 9.4 degrees east. The final event (1986 247 11 24) was interpreted by the agent system as a Pn/Sn/Lg combination located at 61.1 degrees north, and 29.0 degrees east (in the Leningrad region). The analysts's interpretation concurs with SEA's, locating the event at 60.0 degrees north, and 29.6 degrees east.

8.2 REAL-TIME TESTING

To determine how SEA would perform in an operational environment, SEA was run nearly continuously for five days in on-line automated mode. While the automated system was interpreting real-time data, SEA's interactive facilities were used to review the automated mode's interpretations and arrive at final conclusions for each detection processed. During the evaluation period, the event detection process was triggered 84 times by the real-time data stream and sent the event detection to SEA for interpretation. A summary of the results of this evaluation is presented in Table 1.

Total number of events detected	84
False alarms	31
Events missed	2
Unacceptable interpretations	2
Acceptable interpretations	46

Table 1. Summary of real-time evaluation.

Over one third of the detections were attributed to false alarms which are typically caused by abnormalities such as errors introduced in data transmission, or are a result of surface waves produced by a seismic source local to the array such as a car or train. SEA has demonstrated the ability to reject most detections caused by data abnormalities. False alarms caused by local sources usually lack the phases necessary to locate the source, but when detected by SEA, are interpreted as single phase events. Since the number of false alarms increases significantly as the detection threshold is decreased, the proper handling of false alarms is important in prioritizing and filtering interpretations presented for review.

SEA clearly missed two events, both teleseismic P phases with low signal to noise ratios. We have since modified the processing that the agent system uses to detect such phases and are encouraged by the initial results. Five interpretations were not acceptable without refinement by the human expert, but in each case the interpretation that was provided was useful in drawing the final conclusions.

The remaining 46 interpretations SEA produced in automated mode were considered acceptable by our domain analyst. Distances of the events processed range from 50 to over 1000 Km, and a large number of directions were covered. Those events that were not teleseismic are shown by location in Figure 9. Areas with a large number of detections (indicated by clusters of *'s) suggest frequent seismic activity such as that produced by mining or construction.

Results observed from off-line developmental testing and real-time operation are very encouraging and tend to indicate that SEA does an acceptable job interpreting and locating seismic events using the NORESS array. More evaluation is planned for SEA, including a comparison of results obtained from other agencies using the NORESS array.

9   IMPLEMENTATION

SEA was originally prototyped as a neural network. We were unable to provide explanations to the human analysts or ourselves for its classification decisions, so it was decided to use a symbolic approach within the context of a human analyst. We used a Symbolics 3600 LISP Machine using ZETALISP, Flavors, and the Symbolics LISP Development Environment. The system was ported to the Sun Microsystems family of workstations under Common LISP for delivery. The Sun UNIX environment is based on the MIT X Window System, and the GNU Emacs editor. Several parts of the original system were rewritten in C or FORTRAN and are accessed from LISP through a foreign function interface. The agent system requires approximately twenty to twenty-five megabytes of virtual memory and performs well with eight to sixteen megabytes of physical memory. SEA

Module	Implementation Language
ATMS Inference Engine	LISP
Signal and Image Processing	C, FORTRAN, LISP
Graphics	LISP
File I/O, Network I/O	C, CSH
Seismic Specific Support	LISP
Site Specific Support	LISP
Common Sense Rules	LISP Based Production Rule Language

Table 2. SEA Component Modules and the Implementation Languages.

requires a floating point coprocessor for signal processing and has support for the Sun floating point accelerator. The major components of SEA are shown in Table 2.

10 SUMMARY

We have presented the SEA intelligent assistant for the task of sensor data analysis for test ban treaty verification. The assistant enabled us to mimic the problem-solving behavior of the human analyst on NORESS data. While the system is still undergoing further testing and development, our preliminary results indicate this is a viable approach to be used in reducing the analysts' workload necessary for seismic verification. Based on the single agent work, we are continuing the development of an agent architecture and problem-solving protocols for collaborative assistants to interpret data from a global network of seismic monitoring stations. [9]

ACKNOWLEDGEMENTS

This work was performed while the author was a University of California-Lawrence Livermore National Laboratory doctoral fellow. This project was funded by the Department of Energy for the Treaty Verification Research Program (what is now the Non-Proliferation Program) at Lawrence Livermore National Laboratory and by the University of California for graduate research support. We thank the seismologists, treaty verification experts, and engineers in the Earth Science and Engineering Research Departments for their continuous support throughout the project. In addition, we thank the United Nations GSE subcommittee in the Conference on Disarmament program. This work has been performed under the auspices of the U.S. Department of Energy by the Lawrence Livermore National Laboratory under Contract W-7405-Eng-48. Thanks also to the AI Group at NASA Ames and to the National Research Council.

REFERENCES

[1] Hannon, W.J., Seismic Verification of a Comprehensive Test Ban, *Science*, January:251-257, 1985.

[2] Richards, Paul, Progress in Seismic Verification of Test Ban Treaties, *IEEE Technology and Society Magazine*, 9(4):40-52, 1991.

[3] Breding, Dale R., First 1.5 Years With The Norwegian Regional Seismic Array, *Proceedings 1986 RSTN/NORESS Research Symposium*, 6-32, 1986.

[4] Doyle, J., A Truth Maintenance System, *Artificial Intelligence*, 12(3):231-272.

[5] deKleer, J., An Assumption Based TMS,"*Artificial Intelligence*, 28:197-224.

[6] Stallman, R., and Sussman, G., Forward Reasoning and Dependency-Directed-Backtracking in a System For Computer Aided Circuit Analysis, *Artificial Intelligence*, 9(2):135-196.

[7] Shortliffe, E. H., *Computer Based Medical Consultation: MYCIN*, American Elsevier, New York, 1976.

[8] Ginsberg, Matthew, Non-Monotonic Reasoning Using Demptster's Rule, *Proceeding of the National Conference on Artificial Intelligence*, Austin, Texas, 1:126-129, 1984.

[9] Mason, Cindy, Cooperative Seismic Data Interpretation for Nuclear Test Ban Treaty Verification, *International Journal of Applied Artificial Intelligence*, Summer, 1995.

CLASSROOM CONNECTIONS

An Intelligent Assistant for Nuclear Test Ban Treaty Verification

Multiple Choice

Pick the best answer.

1. What are the main problems of monitoring treaty regulations for a comprehensive nuclear test ban?

A. Every event must be examined no matter the size and this causes an impossible work load for people.

B. Global network of 24/7 streamed data many kinds of sensors and sensor configurations.

C. Many different kinds of knowledge are needed to understand the full meaning of the data.

D. Each data set has multiple possible interpretations.

E. People drink beer in the sensor hut.

F. A – D.

2. How does AI help with this problem?

A. AI software reduces the workload by filtering out 'interesting events' from massive piles of data.

B. It allows consistent application of analysis methods across different kinds of sensors and sensor locations.

C. AI software can work through an archive of data while people are sleeping.

D. It remembers and can explain its decisions for every event it examines, whether significant or not.

E. It can capture important and rare knowledge from a handful of specialists from around the world.

F. All of the above.

3. What AI techniques can be helpful for this problem?

A. Intelligent agents that filter massive data to find 'interesting' events for further investigation by human verification specialists.

B. Pattern directed application of resource intensive computations.

C. Hybrid systems - digital signal processing and cooperative intelligent agents.

D. Common sense knowledge, meta-knowledge and ontologies.

E. Explanation facility for AI decisions and conclusions.

F. All of the above.

True or False

Please decide if each of the statements below are True or False.

4. Countries sometimes try to hide their nuclear tests to make detection difficult.

5. Clusters of intelligent agents can be helpful in classifying global and regional networks of sensor data.

6. AI systems need to explain their behaviors, decisions and conclusions in a way that is easy for humans to follow.

7. Hybrid AI systems allow us to engage existing technologies like signal processing together with an AI system.

8. Common sense knowledge gives understanding to the meaning of data.

Answers can be found at the end of the book.

Part II
Data, Data, Everywhere

Chapter 10

Assembling Satellite Data

The COLLAGE/KHOROS Link: Planning for Image Processing Tasks

Amy L. Lansky
Recom Technologies/NASA Ames Research Center, USA

Mark Friedman
Recom Technologies/NASA Ames Research Center, USA

Lise Getoor
Recom Technologies/NASA Ames Research Center, USA

Scott Schmidler
Recom Technologies/NASA Ames Research Center, USA

Nick Short Jr.
NASA Goddard Space Flight Center, USA

ABSTRACT

This paper describes the application of the COLLAGE planner to the task of generating image processing plans for satellite remote sensing data. In particular, we focus on the linkage of COLLAGE to the KHOROS image processing system. Several obvious requirements presented themselves when we first confronted integrating COLLAGE and KHOROS: low-level connection tasks; representation translation tasks; the need to present users with a suitably coherent combined architecture. However, one overarching and pervasive issue became clear over time: how to represent and partition information in a way that fosters extensibility and flexibility. This is necessary for at least two reasons. First, KHOROS is an "open" system – its suite of image processing algorithms is constantly changing. Second, our combined architecture must be useable by a variety of users with different skill levels. These kinds of issues, of course, are common to many software engineering enterprises. Our experience with COLLAGE indicates that planning systems will also have to cope with them when they are used within operational environments.

1 DATA ANALYSIS PLANNING

The goal of this work is to apply domain independent planning methods to help scientists plan out their daily data analysis tasks. We are particularly interested in aiding Earth system scientists who study Earth's ecosystems using a mixture of remotely sensed data (satellite imagery) and ground-based data sets (*e.g.*, vegetation studies, soil maps, etc.). Although these scientists are most interested in developing theories or models, they usually find themselves spending the bulk of their time puzzling over low-level data selection and manipulation tasks. Such tasks make up the "busy work" of their science. In the era of EOS (NASA's Earth Observing System – a suite of satellites slated for launch in the next decade), scientists will have more data at their fingertips than ever before – an expected 1.2 terabytes/day. Fundamental innovations are required to keep the relatively small Earth science community from becoming swamped in the deluge.

For example, conducting even a relatively small study using one or two images can take weeks of a scientist's time. They may have to utilize two or three image processing or geographic information systems, each with its own set of algorithms, formatting requirements, and idiosyncracies regarding parameter usage. More often than not, each of these systems is resident on a different machine. To compound the problem further, a scientist must typically access several distinct databases to find the data they require.

Interestingly, similar problems are confronted by users of other types of software – *e.g.* graphic artists or users of other complex software tool kits. The heterogeneity and scope of such systems can create a logistical nightmare for their users. Although they may understand what they want to accomplish, users are awash in a sea of possible data, tools, and software routines. In the data analysis domain, scientists who can afford it hire technicians who specialize in data preparation. If they cannot, they muddle through, often using methods they are most familiar with rather than the ones that are most appropriate for their task.

In the context of software engineering and product design for such systems, there have been increasing efforts to create more integrated desktop environments to solve some of these problems. Indeed, the KHOROS image processing system we are working with is representative of one such effort [13]. Available for free over the Internet, KHOROS fosters an object-oriented approach to image processing. Users make use of and can augment a variety of toolboxes containing image processing algorithms. Algorithms can be selected from these toolboxes and combined to create visual image processing data flow diagrams (plans) using a GUI editor called **Cantata**. However, even with these tools, the expertise required to create such plans is substantial.

In the AI planning community, there have been growing efforts to automate parts of the data analysis process. For instance, several researchers in planning have begun to study how *data access* plans can be generated to aid users in finding the information they need [5, 16]. In contrast, our work focuses on aiding scientists in their use of the image processing and geographic information systems that sit on their desk. That is, given a high-level task description, the goal of our application is to decompose it into a partially ordered set of steps corresponding to transformation algorithms executable on a particular platform. Other planning work in this vein is being done by Short [4, 15], Chien [3], Matwin [11] , and Boddy [2].

The role of our planner can be viewed as much like that of a logistical assistant or technician [8], While a data analysis planner does not require deep knowledge about a particular scientific discipline, it *can* be usefully embued with information about: the steps making up typical data processing tasks; the available algorithms on various platforms; and what the requirements of these algorithms are – their parameter settings, their applicability to various data types, etc. Interestingly, this is also the kind of mundane (yet volatile) information that a scientist would rather not deal with. The net effect is that the planner fills a role that is desired and valued, which also increases the likelihood of its eventual acceptance and use.

Of course, to be truly useful, a data analysis planner cannot sit in a vacuum. Ideally, it should be connected to the platforms on which the algorithms will be executed; the plan can be downloaded into the input format of a particular platform and executed there. A data analysis planner should also be connected to a framework that expedites data selection. Given an integrated planning architecture of this kind, a variety of issues must be reckoned with: utility (*i.e.* breadth and depth capability); ease of use; and openness to the natural evolution of component systems. The rest of this paper describes our experiences in building an architecture of this kind. Section 2 describes the overall framework and problems we have faced.

Section 3 focuses on some of the larger issues that underly these problems.

2 COLLAGE/KHOROS LINK: CORE ISSUES

Figure 1 depicts the overall architecture of our integrated data analysis framework. In collaboration with a team from NASA's Goddard Space Flight Center, we are integrating the COLLAGE planner into Goddard's IIFS framework (the Intelligent Information Fusion System) – an object oriented framework for ingesting and storing remotely sensed data, generating derived products and information about that data, and aiding the user in data selection [14] (see Figure 2). Scientists using the IIFS can utilize the KHOROS image processing system to create desired data products. COLLAGE serves as a front-end to this framework to plan out exactly what KHOROS algorithms should be used to achieve a particular task.

Ultimately, it is also our intention to link other image processing and geographic information systems (GIS) into this framework, A GIS deals with map data in addition to image data, and in particular, enables correlation between these two types of data. The most likely GIS choice for incorporation into our framework is ARC/INFO [1]. Besides our collaboration with NASA Goddard and the IIFS, we also plan to link COLLAGE/KHOROS into another data access framework being built at the Lockheed AI Laboratory [16].

COLLAGE itself is a nontraditional domain independent planner with several unique features [6, 7, 8, 9]. Of these features, the most relevant to this application are COLLAGE's domain description language and planning methods, which are based on the use of *action-based constraints*. This approach contrasts rather sharply with the traditional planning representation and methodology that utilize STRIPS-based (*i.e.* state-based) reasoning [7]. In particular, all planning requirements are specified in terms of required forms of action instantiation, action-decomposition, temporal and causal relationships between actions, and "CSP-based" [10] binding requirements among action parameter variables.

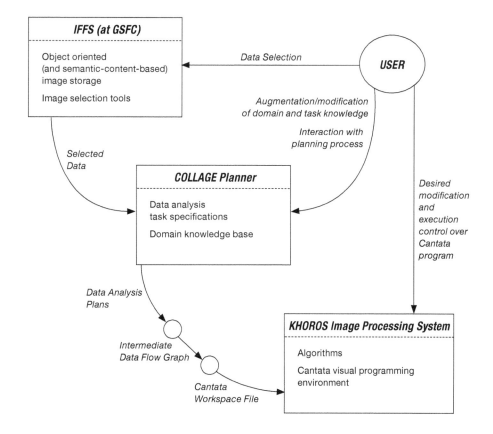

Figure 1. Integrated Planning Architecture for Data Analysis.

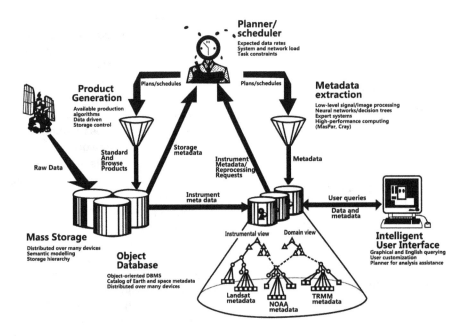

Figure 2. Intelligent Information Fusion System Architecture.

No explicit preconditions or goal states are used. For example, in the data analysis domain, planning requirements are specified by, first, requiring the addition of high-level "task" actions into the plan (via COLLAGE's **action** constraint form). These high-level actions are then incrementally decomposed (via COLLAGE's **decompose** constraint form) into lower level actions, and ultimately into actions which represent specific algorithm instantiations.

One important feature of COLLAGE's method of constraint satisfaction is that any constraint can be conditionalized upon the emerging form of the plan as well as information in a static *knowledge base* that incorporates domain-specific facts and functions. For example, depending on the form of the plan or scientific domain information, a high level action might be decomposed in one of several possible ways. The domain knowledge base facts and functions can also be used to functionally define the various binding requirements that are imposed on plan variables during the constraint satisfaction process.

Figure 3 depicts the overall COLLAGE architecture. Besides a constraint-based approach to planning, this Figure also shows another unique aspect of COLLAGE – its use of *localized* or partitioned reasoning spaces. In particular, the set of constraints that make up a problem/domain

description may be partitioned into sets called *regions*. Each regional reasoning space is focused on creating a regional plan that satisfies regional constraints. Regions may be interrelated in fairly arbitrary ways; *e.g.* they may form hierarchies or share subregions. The job of COLLAGE's localized search mechanism is to make sure that the overall "global" plan is consistent and satisfies all regional requirements. In general, the planning cost savings provided by localized search can help deal with the problem of scaling up to large domains [6]. In this application, however, where scale is less of an issue, localization provides a useful mechanism for structuring domain constraint information.

Once a COLLAGE plan has been generated for a particular data analysis task, it can be automatically translated for use by KHOROS. This is done via a two-step process. First, the plan is translated into an intermediate form, similar to a data flow graph. This form is then translated into a **Cantata** workspace file. **Cantata** is the visual programming environment for KHOROS. The workspace format serves as the storage representation for **Cantata**'s visual programs. After a COLLAGE-generated workspace file is loaded into **Cantata**, it can be directly modified or manipulated there and executed by KHOROS. Figure 5 depicts KHOROS's **Cantata** visual

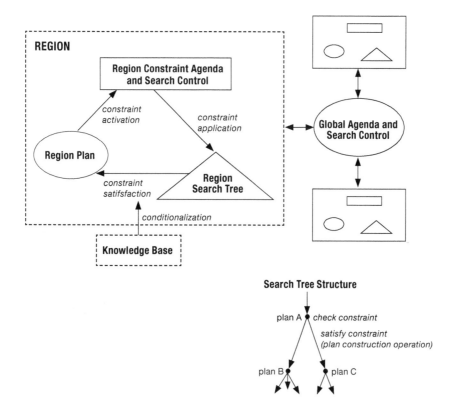

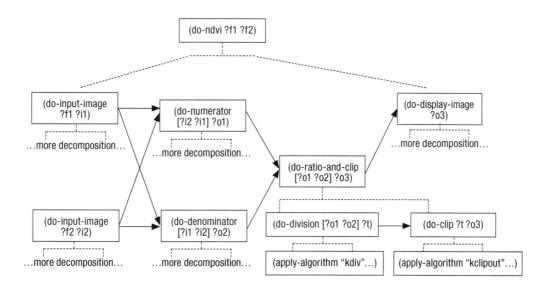

Figure 3. COLLAGE Architecture.

Figure 4. A simple plan fragment.

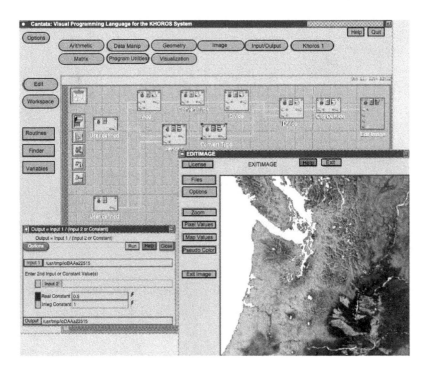

Figure 5. COLLAGE plan utilized in KHOROS/Cantata environment.

programming environment, loaded with a COLLAGE-generated plan, a fragment of which is depicted in Figure 4. This plan derives a vegetation index that quantifies biomass from images taken by the NOAA AVHRR instrument. The visual inset on the bottom-right shows the result of executing this plan on an image of the Pacific northwest. The more lightly colored areas depict areas of high concentrations of biomass. The inset on the lower-left shows an interaction menu for one of the plan steps and illustrates **Cantata**'s interface for modifying algorithmic parameters.

When we originally faced the task of linking COLLAGE to KHOROS (and the IIFS), we easily recognized several tasks that had to be accomplished:

Creating a low-level link between systems.

In a first crack at this problem, we have considered only the transfer of information from COLLAGE to KHOROS (rather than vice versa). This was achieved via translation to the workspace format. Ultimately, we will also consider how to send information back from **Cantata** to COLLAGE, in service of more reactive planning capabilities (*e.g.* reactions to plan-modifications made by the user using **Cantata**). This will probably be achieved via a reverse translation process that decodes workspace information into a form usable by COLLAGE.

As far as the translation process itself, this task required us to do reverse engineering on the workspace format, since it isn't documented nor meant for user viewing and editing. We also designed the intermediate data-flow-graph as a structure that was amenable to translation into the workspace format. Our hope is that this intermediate form will also ultimately serve as an "interlingua" between COLLAGE and other image processing and GIS systems. Finally, we also had to write our own mechanism for automatic graphical layout of the plan components, since this layout is normally provided manually by the **Cantata** user as they build their data flow plans.

Deciding upon a desired form for COLLAGE generated plans that is amenable to translation.

A natural corollary to this task was figuring out how to write domain specifications that could generate such plans — *i.e.* we had to come up with a "template" for writing task specifications for the data analysis domain.

The most problematic feature of this task was representing the parameters of the image processing algorithms and the data flow relationships between these parameters. Since the suite of available KHOROS algorithms is constantly in flux, we also wanted to have a single generic action-type that could be instantiated to represent the application of any type of algorithm, rather than a separate type for each algorithm. This action-type description is given below.

```
:action-type
    (apply-algorithm
     ?n_algname ?i_inputparams
     ?o_outputparams ?p_otherparams)
```

Notice how this representation identifies the algorithm name **?n** as a parameter. It also utilizes two distinguished input and output parameters **?i** and **?o**, which are bound to lists of input and output parameter variables that are used by the algorithm. In particular, the input parameters are received from other algorithms and the output parameters are sent to other algorithms – *i.e.* these parameters play a role in the data-flow diagram created for **Cantata**. The final parameter **?p** is another list of variables (algorithm parameters) that are also required by the algorithm but are not linked to other algorithms. To represent the data flow relationship between specific algorithm parameters, we used a combination of "CSP"-style relations between relevant variables (in particular, between **?i** and **?o** subvariables) and a special pipe relation between the apply-algorithm action instances.

Notice that while most planners only allow for action parameters that can be bound to simple atomic values, our representational choice for apply-algorithm required us to allow for action parameters that could be bound to indefinite lists of subvariables (*i.e.* lists of actual parameters passed for a particular algorithm). Indeed, because of the complexity of parameter information in this domain, we also needed to allow for other forms of structured parameter variables. Coupled with this was the required ability to impose and propagate binding requirements on these variables and their component parts.

For example, many of the parameters of our COLLAGE actions (as well as those ultimately passed down to KHOROS algorithms) are pointers to images, each associated with many features (*e.g.* time, location, and formatting information). Since the planning process requires reasoning about these features, it is most suitable to represent these "image" variables as a record of information, whose slots are filled by other variables. All of these variables and subvariables must be accessible to the binding propagation

facility. We recognized these needs early on in this effort, and focused several months of project time augmenting COLLAGE with these capabilities. The foreseen requirements of this domain were also the driving force behind our incorporation of a static domain knowledge base and planning capabilities that conditionalize the planning process of that knowledge.

Presenting users with a coherent view of a heterogenous system.

This problem is complicated by the fact that we forsee many different kinds of users for this framework, with different skill levels. For example the bulk of the users will be scientists who will only be interested in a very high-level view of both COLLAGE and the IIFS (basically, for selecting data and posing task goals); most of their interactions will be directly with KHOROS. At the other end of the spectrum are the COLLAGE and IIFS developers. In the middle are computationally sophisticated scientists who may develop new algorithms for incorporation into KHOROS as well as new task specifications for COLLAGE.

Our first crack at this problem was to utilize the same user-interface framework for both COLLAGE and the IIFS; we are currently developing TK-based [12] front ends for both systems (see Figure 6). We also plan to make the mode of interaction with TK similar to one that is utilized heavily in KHOROS – "forms-based" interaction. A scientist end-user will thus interact with **Cantata** and high- level TK-based views of COLLAGE and the IIFS in much the same way. More sophisticated users will interact at a deeper level with COLLAGE, but also via TK. We are currently working on a specification builder for COLLAGE that will utilize a TK-based GUI interface. This will replace the current mode of creating Lisp-based task specifications using a text editor. It will foster flexible structuring and configuration of specification information and enable sharing and reuse among various task applications.

Our most intensive work on this data analysis framework has been going on since the spring of 1994. Since then, we have found many of the tasks described above to be solvable. However, one basic issue has emerged as persistent and problematic: the inherent "openness" of the environment we are targetting. Thus, COLLAGE is facing problems common to most large, open software development environments.

For example, in the past six months, we have already reckoned with two new major releases

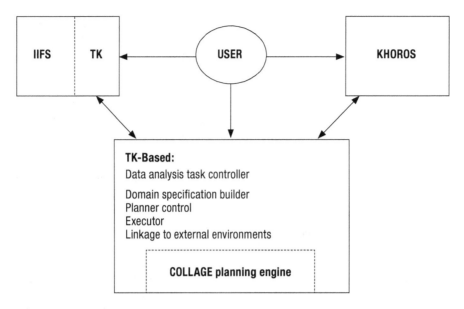

Figure 6. Creating a coherent user interaction environment.

of KHOROS. Each new release manifested a complete reorganization and, in one instance, a complete overhaul of the KHOROS algorithm suite. Even the workspace format changed. It is clear that our architecture must take into account the fact that KHOROS (and indeed any image processing or GIS system we link into) will remain a moving target. The same type of problem arises in the development of our constraint task specifications; *i.e.* the suite of tasks we wish to cover will always be changing or restructuring. We soon recognized the need to write and structure our task specifications so that certain portions could be shared and so that necessary changes (*e.g.* to accommodate algorithm modifications within KHOROS) didn't propagate wildly throughout the specification code. As in other software enterprises, we have found that the key to openness, reusability, flexibility, and modifiability is an appropriate use of structuring techniques – *i.e.*, the partitioning and abstraction of information in appropriate ways.

3 PLANNING IN OPEN ENVIRONMENTS

One way to view the "openness" problem and many of the other tasks described in the previous section is in terms of representation and language issues. There are several different "languages" at work in our framework: COLLAGE's domain specification language; COLLAGE's plan language or

representation (*i.e.* the form of generated plans); the intermediate data flow graph language; **Cantata**'s workspace format; and the user-interface "languages" presented by all three systems. Most of the discussion in the previous section dealt with language translation or expressiveness. System openness must be handled by focussing on language structuring, information hiding and layering, and reconfigurability.

Figure 7 depicts the ways we have handled these problems thus far. Quite early on in this project we recognized the need for a knowledge base of facts and functions distinct from COLLAGE's constraint-based task specifications. The knowledge base is used to conditionalize the application of constraints and to define functions used by variable binding requirements. By keeping the knowledge base distinct, the constraints used in the task specifications can be reused in different knowledge-base contexts. This obviously fosters reusablity.

However, it also serves the function of keeping different kinds of information and information of interest to different communities physically distinct. For example, information about Earth-science-specific datatypes, facts, and functions is understandable to scientist users and should be open to and modifiable by a broad range of those users. In contrast, the COLLAGE constraint specifications that specify how various tasks should be decomposed are of interest to a much smaller community. There are only a limited number of

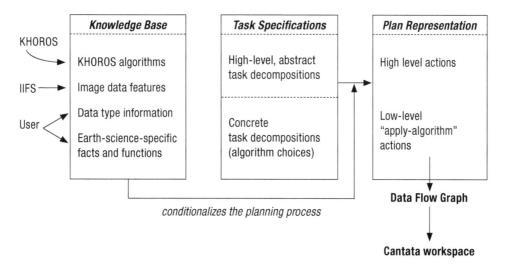

Figure 7. Structuring of information.

data-analysis task forms; once defined, these can be reused by all system users. And since learning the COLLAGE constraint language is more difficult than modifying some predicate-based facts in the knowledge base, we felt it was best to shield most scientists from this information by focussing most of their interaction on the knowledge base.

Of course, even within the knowledge base, there is useful partitioning of information. For example, it contains information about the available KHOROS algorithms as well as information about specific images obtained from the IIFS. Both kinds of information could profitably be downloaded automatically, which would in turn greatly enhance the overall system's ability to remain open to changes within KHOROS or the IIFS.

There are also natural levels of abstraction or partitioning apparent within the suite of constraints that make up the task specifications. These levels are also reflected within the plans themselves. During the planning process, the highest level task actions are decomposed into more detailed high-level task descriptions without any reference to specific algorithm choices. Indeed, there may be multiple levels of decomposition at work within this more abstract context. At the bottom level, however, the lowest level task descriptions bottom out in the choice of an algorithm that performs that task (see Figures 4 and 7).

Our task specifications directly reflect this partitioning into levels via use of COLLAGE's region mechanism. We have found that this partitioning

has numerous advantages. The most important is that only the lowest level constraints need be modified if the algorithms within KHOROS change. These low-level constraints can then be *reused* or *shared* between different high-level task contexts, which greatly alleviates the specification task. It also enables a broader range of users to write task specifications; scientists can easily write high-level task specifications while ignoring low-level platform-specific detail. The issues of flexibility, configurability, and information-hiding have also been the driving force behind our development of our new TK-based interface framework for COLLAGE. This framework will foster incremental development, reuse, and flexible configuration of the domain knowledge that COLLAGE utilizes, as well as linkages to the other systems.

4 CONCLUSION

This paper described the connection of the COLLAGE planner to the KHOROS image processing system and NASA Goddard's IIFS data framework. The initial problems we faced in this application included making low-level connections between the systems, expanding the expressivity of our planning language, and a host of translation tasks. The ongoing issues that now confront us deal more with the inherent openness and volatility of this framework. Our solution thus far has been to focus on underlying representation issues;

i.e., how system components and information should be compartmentalized, shared, expanded, and reconfigured. In the future, we expect that much more work will be needed to foster domain knowledge capture and to ensure user accessbility to this complex heterogenous system.

REFERENCES

[1] *ARC/INFO User's Guide,* Environmental Systems Research Institute, 380 New York Street, Redlands, California 92373.

[2] Boddy, M., White, J., Goldman, R., and Short, N., "Planning Applications in Image Analysis", 1994 NASA-GSFC Proceedings of Space Applications of AI, Greenbelt, MD, May 1994, pp. 17-28.

[3] Chien, S. "Using AI Planning Techniques to Automatically Generate Image Processing Procedures: A Preliminary Report," *Proceedings of the Second International Conference on AI Planning Systems,* Chicago, Illinois, pp. 219-224 (1994).

[4] Cromp, R. F. and Campbell, W. J. and Short, Jr., N. M., "An intelligent information fusion system for handling the archiving and querying of terabyte-sized spatial databases," *International Space Year Conference on Earth and Space Science Information Systems,* American Institute of Physics, 1992.

[5] Knoblock, C. and Y. Arens, "Cooperating Agents for Information Retrieval," in *Proceedings of the Second International Conference on Cooperative Information Systems*, University of Toronto Press (1994).

[6] Lansky, A. "Localized Planning with Diverse Plan Construction Methods," NASA Ames Research Center, Artificial Intelligence Research Branch, Technical Report FIA-94-05 (1994). Under review for AIJ.

[7] Lansky, A. "Action-Based Planning" in *Proceedings of the Second International Conference on Artificial Intelligence Planning Systems* (AIPS-94), Chicago, Illinois, pp. 110-115 (1994).

[8] Lansky, A. "A Data Analysis Assistant" in *Proceedings of the 1994 AAAI Stanford Spring Symposium on Software Agents*, Stanford University (1994). Also in *Proceedings of the Third International Symposium on Artificial Intelligence, Robotics, and Automation for Space* (I-SAIRAS 94), Pasadena, California, pp. 373-377 (1994).

[9] Lansky, A. and A. Philpot, "AI-Based Planning for Data Analysis Tasks," Proceedings of the Ninth Conference on Artificial Intelligence for Applications (CAIA-93), Orlando, Florida, pp. 390-398 (March 1993). Also appeared in *IEEE Expert Magazine,* Volume 9, Number 1, February 1994.

[10] Mackworth, A.K. "Consistency in Networks of Relations," *Artificial Intelligence,* Volume 8, pp. 99-118 (1977).

[11] Matwin, S., Charlebois, D., and Goodenough, D., "Machine Learning and Planning for Data Management in Forestry," *Workshop on AI Technologies for Environmental Applications,* 1994 National Conference on Artificial Intelligence, July 31–August 4, 1994, Seattle, WA, pp. 83-90.

[12] Ousterhout, J.K. *Tcl and the Tk Toolkit*, Addison Wesley Publishers (1994).

[13] Rasure, J.R. and C.S. Williams, "An Integrated Data Flow Visual Language and Software Development Environment," *Journal of Visual Languages and Computing*, Volume 2, pp. 217-246 (1991).

[14] Short, N. *et al.*, "AI Challenges within NASA's Mission to Planet Earth," Workshop on AI Technologies for Environmental Applications, 1994 National Conference on Artificial Intelligence, July 31-August 4, 1994, Seattle, WA, pp. 1-15.

[15] Short, N. and Wattawa, S.L., "The Second Generation Intelligent User Interface for the Crustal Dynamics Data Information System", *Telematics and Informatics,* Volume 5(3), pp. 253-268.

[16] Toomey, C.N., Simoudis, E., Johnson, R.W., and W.S. Mark, "Software Agents for the Dissemination of Remote Terrestrial Sensing Data," in *Proceedings of the Third International Symposium on Artificial Intelligence, Robotics, and Automation for Space (I-SAIRAS 94)*, Pasadena, California, pp. 19-22 (1994).

CLASSROOM CONNECTIONS

The COLLAGE/KHOROS Link: Planning for Image Processing Tasks

Multiple Choice

Pick the best answer.

1. **What is the environmental problem solved in this chapter?**
   A. Generating an image of earth with many satellite images.
   B. Automatically connecting images from different kinds of data representations.
   C. Providing access to integrated satellite image data for many kinds of people.
   D. Viewing middle earth.
   E. An AI driven application of graphical information systems.
   F. A – C and E.

2. **What AI technologies does the system use?**
   A. Planning and scheduling.
   B. Intelligent assistant that automates parts of the GIS analysis problem for users.
   C. Hybrid AI that connects an object oriented system for data with an AI planning system for GIS data analysis.
   D. Constraint satisfaction.
   E. Meta-knowledge.
   F. All of the above.

3. **What problems do earth systems scientists face when analyzing graphical images?**
   A. Integration of many different kinds of data at different scales and sizes.
   B. Finding and connecting meaning among multiple images sources and their data products.
   C. Keeping an analytics history of algorithms and comparing to current analysis methods.

   D. Explaining images and sharing their data products to many different communities.
   E. All of the above.
   F. Hobbits visiting middle earth.

True or False

Please decide if each of the statements below are True or False.

4. Earth system scientists study Earth's ecosystems using a mixture of remotely sensed data (satellite imagery) and ground based data (vegetation studies, soil maps, etc.).

5. The COLLAGE/KHOROS system helps earth scientists by assisting them with the 'busy work' of examining data from many different scales, sources, and types.

6. The system has an intelligent user interface that allows the scientist to link data sets with different algorithms.

7. The system uses metadata but not megadata.

8. The system is used for rocket launches at NASA.

Answers can be found at the end of the book.

Chapter 11

Forest Ecosystem Simulation

KnowledgeBased Land Information Manager and Simulator (KBLIMS)

For Forested Ecosystem Simulation Management

Vincent B. Robinson
University of Toronto, Canada

D. Scott Mackay
University of Toronto, Canada

ABSTRACT

Applications such as forest ecosystem modeling demand management of geographically-based information detailing complex interactions between climatic, topographic, hydrologic, pedological and ecological processes. The Knowledgebased Land Information Manager and Simulator (KBLIMS) is based on the notion of a query model which executes a set of user-defined queries. Each query is deductive so a user may define a simulation experiment by first identifying a set of objects as a spatial query, then specifying some action to be performed on these objects, such as a combined simulation query and aggregation query. The KBLIMS approach has led to a parsimonious coupling of geographic information system (GIS) and ecosystem simulation modeling. The user, *e.g.* an ecologist, need not explicitly parameterize and run simulation models. Typical use of the simulation system is managed by the knowledgebase using its metaknowledge, which allows for the integration of either tightly-coupled or loosely-coupled systems.

1 INTRODUCTION

Within the forest ecosystem modeling community there is much attention devoted to developing models for simulating carbon, water and energy flux processes at regional scales. One such effort is the Regional HydroEcological Simulation System (RHESSys) (Band et al 1993. RHESSys provides ecological modeling capability at the scale of watersheds. Because of the geographic elements around which RHESSys is organized, the use of geographic information systems (GIS) to support RHESSys simulation has been suggested (*e.g.* see Michener et al, 1994). However, GIS and simulation models such as RHESSys organize their information in fundamentally different ways. Objects in a GIS are typically in the form of primitives such as points, lines, polygons, or layers. Objects in a simulation model are defined in terms of system state, mass and energy fluxes, and interaction and dynamics of species or individuals. Management of these two different domains usually means that large, cumbersome files are developed and modeling is conducted in a rigid, almost batch-oriented approach. There is also usually little flexibility in what kinds of geographic queries can be asked the system(s). To bridge the conceptual gap between GIS objects and simulation objects we have designed a hybrid knowledgebase management system that transforms simple observations and relations in collected data into higher order concepts.

This paper describes the KnowledgeBased Land Information Manager and Simulator (KBLIMS), a knowledgebased geographic information system (GIS) approach to organizing both data and simulation models on the basis of distinct, identifiable landscape units such as watersheds. KBLIMS is based on the notion of a query model which executes a set of user-defined or system-defined queries. Each query is deductive so a user may define a simulation experiment by first identifying a set of objects as a spatial query, then specifying some action to be performed on these objects, such as a combined simulation query and aggregation query.

Simulation modelling of ecosystem processes, or information management of the physical characteristics of the landscape, over large areas, is hampered by the extreme variability of the land cover, topography and soils. As an example, the processes of evapotranspiration and photosynthetic productivity of a forest canopy are dependent on surface variables including soil properties, elevation, aspect, solar radiation, humidity, wind speed, and standing vegetation characteristics (*e.g.* species, leaf area index, biomass). In mountainous watersheds, each of these variables shows strong dependencies on landscape position such that different factors limit growth on ridges as opposed to valleys, or on north facing as opposed to south facing slopes. Depending on the community structure, soil properties or geomorphic context of a forest stand, it may be possible to ignore certain processes or emphasize others to simulate forest activity. Hence, general models that can accurately simulate forest processes over the full range of conditions encountered over a region are often not tractable. Choosing and structuring the proper simulation model for each of a potentially large number of landscape units is a tedious and error-prone task. Instead, our approach is based on encoding the basic ecosystem knowledge required to infer the state of the landscape unit, to decide and choose the proper strategy for simulation.

2 SYSTEM DESIGN METHODOLOGY

Knowledgebased Management

Terrain analysis and simulation modeling tasks require specialized tools that are generally separate from the information management facilities provided by a GIS. We assume that information systems are knowledge-intensive, as are the specialized tools needed to perform tasks such as terrain analysis and ecosystem simulation. Therefore, system components are viewed as types of knowledge which can be incorporated into a hybrid knowledgebased system. The knowledgebase is organized around a query model manager which distinguishes between three types of knowledge: (1) extensional and intensional predicates, (2) structural descriptions, and (3) procedures. (Mackay et al, 1994).

Terrain analysis and simulation modeling tools are viewed as procedural knowledge, as they embody specialized knowledge from their respective domains in the form of programs. Query models build concrete objects by combining predicates, procedures and abstract structural descriptions. Concrete objects are instantiated counterparts of their respective class descriptions. The transformation from object class descriptions to instantiated objects is accomplished using definitions of *Class description, isA relation, Query, Query model,* and *Object structure* discussed in Mackay et al (1994).

An object structure reflects the description given in the class schema. The target object structure is instantiated by: (1) retrieving all attribute descriptions from the isA graph, such as the attributes given in the topographic_object and hillslope class descriptions; (2) resolving any attribute cancellations such as replacing the attribute, (*e.g.*, elevation, feet), with the attribute; (3) generating a query model from retrieved descriptions; and (4) populating the object structure with the result.

It is often important to ecologists to retrieve aggregate totals for queries over a number of objects of the same class. To perform aggregation in queries we distinguish between atomic identifiers, and complex identifiers. Each instantiated object of a given class has a unique identifer. Complex identifiers, *e.g.* [1,2], are made up of unique atomic identifiers from some class and denote aggregates of objects from that class. Results of queries on objects with complex identifiers are obtained by applying the query over each of the objects represented by the atomic identifiers within the complex.

Methods provide access to the database but hide procedural aspects of queries. System-defined methods include models for asserting attributes, retracting attributes, retrieving attributes, and checking constraints on objects. Each method has an external interface that provides a declarative semantics for queries. The system takes a description for an object attribute and automatically generates an implementation query. This strategy forms a distinction between an implementation layer and class description layer. Layering permits changes in low-level procedures without changing the semantics of descriptions defined at a higher level.

Deductive rules are specialized kinds of methods which infer new facts. Deduction refers to the fact that inferences made during a previous transaction are available as explicit facts for subsequent transactions. Furthermore, a user may select, or browse, a set of objects without knowing specifically what kinds of questions to ask about these objects. The system retains retrieved objects and assists in asking more specific questions.

Terrain Analysis

Information used for discovering terrain objects is image and map based. The terrain analysis system translates layer-based geographic information into object-based geographic information. The layer-based model of geographic information represents spatially distributed attributes as a set of data layers each of which defines a distribution of a single attribute over a defined space. The object-based model combines generic spatial objects (points, lines, polygons), explicit spatial relations between objects (lines with left and right polygons) and attributes (*e.g.* area) into a single, unified data model.

Transformation from image data to symbolic elements is a three-step process: (1) extraction of drainage basins and their segmentation into hillslopes and stream links, (2) analysis of the hillslope and stream links, and (3) generation of objects. Terrain partitioning uses techniques described by Band (1989). This approach can adaptively scale terrain partitioning from a few, large hillslopes to many, small hillslopes for any given drainage basin by adjusting the constraints on pruning the drainage area transform. It is the scale flexibility that allows layer-to-object

transformation without significant loss of land surface heterogeneity meaningful to ecosystem simulation.

In KBLIMS, analysis of hillslopes and streams follows Lammers and Band (1990), with extensions to incorporate soils, remotely sensed imagery, and detailed topology (Band and Robinson 1992). Analysis includes geometric computations such as gradient, aspect, and junction angles, topological computations such as stream link connections, stream link to hillslope connections, and hillslope to hillslope connections, or locations of divides, and computation of hillslope distributional information for soil hydraulic properties and leaf area index. This information is incorporated into the *knowledgebase* (Mackay *et al.*, 1994).

Simulation System

The ecosystem simulation system is based on the Productivity and Hydrology Simulator (PHS) (Band and Robinson, 1992). PHS is derived from the model components of the Regional Hydro Ecological Simulation System (RHESSys) (Band *et al.*, 1993) which includes MTCLIM, FOREST-BGC and TOPMODEL. It is designed to simulate the distribution of forest carbon and water flux, and storage processes over a mountainous landscape. MTCLIM extrapolates daily meteorological observations from base stations using adiabatic lapse rates, orographic gradients, and topographic correction of solar radiation. FOREST-BGC is a stand level model of forest carbon, water and nutrient budgets. It computes daily carbon photosynthesis, respiration, evaporation, snowmelt and runoff production, using site conditions such as current stand characteristics, observed or computed daily meteorological data, and soil properties. In addition, daily and seasonal hydrologic flux processes such as snowmelt, interception, runoff and evapotranspiration are computed.

Integrating the Knowledge Base and Simulation System

Metaknowledge is used to integrate the simulation system and the knowledgebase. Metaknowledge provide a means of describing how the *knowledgebase* interfaces with the simulation system, including data structuring, procedural calls, and retrieval of results. Current versions of the simulation system are designed to operate both as a stand-alone system, as well as an integral part of the knowledgebase. System-defined metaknowledge provides a seamless view of integration of system components to the end-user, hence it is not visible at the user interface level. The simulation system operates on simulation objects, which are specialized kinds of objects, defined within the knowledgebase to integrate information from topography, remote sensing and soils domains.

3 IMPLEMENTATION AND TESTING

The KBLIMS knowledgebase is implemented in Prolog (BIM 1990), PHS is implemented using a combination of Prolog and C, and the terrain analysis package is in C. Users interact with KBLIMS through the Terrain Object Interface (TOI) that is a graphical database interface providing a graphical query facility, a hypertext-like browsing facility for object classes, and text and graphics windows for displaying results. The top level of TOI is accessed from a toolbar that has pull-down menus for displaying windows, accessing databases, editing class descriptions, and accessing application tools (Figure 1). The graphical query tool shows stream objects, stream-hillslope connectivity, and divides representing Turkey Lakes. There is a hierarchical organization to database queries, with the graphical tool providing rapid access to specific regions within a database, and hypertext to move about locally.

Graphical queries are facilitated through a transformation of topological relations between drainage basin objects into a graph. Links between objects are physically stored as binary relations but are recognized by TOI as graphical objects. A graphical object is queried using a mouse pointer. Each graphical object is classified as a given type (*e.g.* stream, divide, or stream-to-hillslope), each of which is isomorphic to a conceptual object class. Organizing around a relatively small number of binary topological relations provides access to all attributes and other spatial relations, while giving the end-user a simple, uncluttered graphical query tool. Since graphical queries are limited to graphical counterparts of binary topological relations, the association of object classes to these primitive object types allows for accessing any objects within the knowledgebase.

As a testbed of variable land surface and process representation requirements, we using the Turkey Lakes watershed in Ontario, Canada.

As an example of a watershed scale management problem, we used KBLIMS to determine how a specific catchment within the Turkey Lakes Watershed would respond to clearcutting. By observing discharge differences between a forested baserun simulation and clearcut simulation, inferences can be made about potential effects on water quality (*e.g.* nutrient loading to aquatic environments) in areas downstream of the cleared catchment. Figure 1 show the results of the simulation for the queried catchment. Results indicate that clearcutting, approximated by reducing leaf area index to 1.0, results in greater spring melt runoff and a sustained higher summer baseflow. We can infer that enhanced nutrient loading to the downstream wetland will be accompanied by enhanced anaerobic conditions, which means the nutrients may be lost or unavailable for extended periods of time early in the growing season. Other potential effects of clearcutting the catchment, such as compaction of soil, would further enhance runoff.

4 CONCLUDING COMMENTS

The approach taken in KBLIMS has led to a parsimonious coupling of GIS and ecosystem simulation modeling using object-oriented techniques that transform simple observations and relations into higher-order concepts based on structural, deductive and procedural knowledge. A terrain analysis system transforms layer-based information to object information for use by the system. The knowledgebase uses a layering strategy to hide implementation details from higher level descriptions. Layering allow changes in low level tools such as simulation models and terrain analysis tools without changing the semantics of the objects which are defined in terms of meaningful hillslope and forest stand units.

KBLIMS exploits the notion of a query model which executes a set of user-defined or system-defined queries. Each query is deductive so a user may define a simulation experiment by first identifying a set of objects as a spatial query, then specifying some action to be performed on these objects, such as a combined simulation query and aggregation query. The user, *e.g.* an ecologist, need not explicitly parameterize and run simulation models, although access to low level tools is provided. Typical use of the simulation system is managed by the knowledgebase using

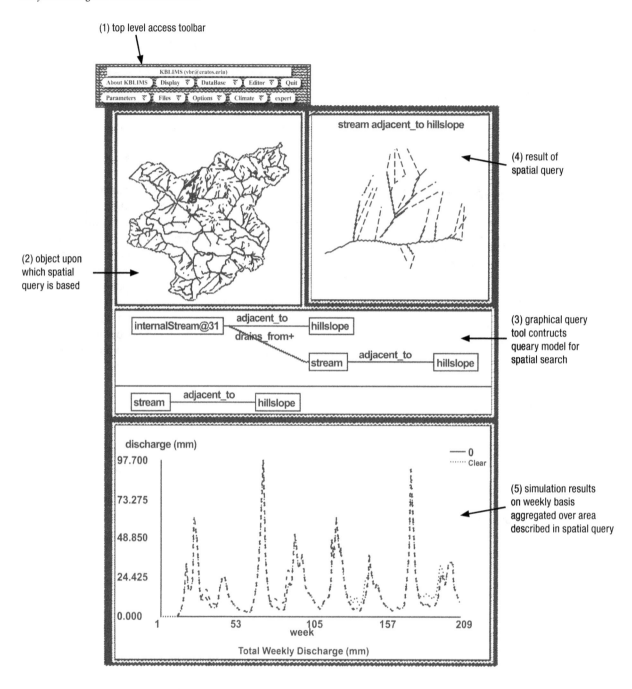

(1) top level access toolbar

(2) object upon which spatial query is based

(4) result of spatial query

(3) graphical query tool contructs queary model for spatial search

(5) simulation results on weekly basis aggregated over area described in spatial query

Figure 1. KBLIMS provides multiple windows for interaction with the system.

its metaknowledge. This allows for integration of either tightly-coupled or loosely-coupled systems designed to operate as integrated or standalone programs respectively, while maintaining a seamless view at the user interface level.

There is considerable benefit of the KBLIMS approach to support resource management and research where geographically-structured simulation modeling is important. The potential exists for a forest manager to sit down with the graphical interface and explore management scenarios in an efficient, effective manner. Land management researchers can also use a KBLIMS approach in developing and testing their models by using the information management tool to maintain a record of results tagged by a set of constraints for simulation. This approach provides fast, easy access to simulation resources and results without the substantial information management overhead of creating and maintaining cumbersome input files for simulation programs.

ACKNOWLEDGEMENTS

The work was partially supported by a grant from the Natural Sciences and Engineering Research Council (NSERC) of Canada, a NSERC Doctoral Fellowship and a Tri-Council EcoResearch Doctoral Fellowship.

REFERENCES

Band, L.E. 1989. A terrain-based watershed information system. *Hydrological Processes* (3): 151-162.

Band, L.E., Patterson, P., Nemani, R. and Running, S.W., 1993. Forest ecosystem processes at the watershed scale: Incorporating hillslope hydrology. *Agricultural and Forest Meteorology.*

Band, L.E. and Robinson, V.B., 1992. Development of an Intelligent Land Information System (ILIS) as Part of the System for Hierarchical Experts for Resource Inventories (SHERI) Program, Final Report, *Canada Centre for Remote Sensing.*

Beven, K.J. and Kirkby, M.J., 1979. A physically based, variable contributing model of basin hydrology. *Hydrological Sciences Bulletin* (24): 43-69.

BIM. 1990. Prolog by BIM, BIM, Kwikstraat, 4-3078 Everberg, Belgium.

Jenson, C.S., Clifford J., Gadia, S.K., Segev A., and Snodgrass, R.T., 1992. A glossary of temporal database concepts. *ACM Sigmod Record* 21 (3): 35-43.

Lammers, R.B. and Band, L.E., 1990. Automating object representation of drainage basins. *Computers and Geosciences* (16): 787-810.

Mackay, D.S., Robinson, V.B., and Band, L.E., 1994. A knowledge-based approach to the management of geographic information systems for simulation of forested ecosystems, in Michener, W.K., Brunt, J.W., and Stafford, S.G. (eds), *Environmental Information Management and Analysis: Ecosystem to Global Scales*, Taylor & Francis, London, pp. 511-534.

Michener, W.K., Brunt, J.W., and Stafford, S.G. (eds.), 1994. *Environmental Information Management and Analysis: Ecosystem to Global Scales*, Taylor & Francis, London.

Moore, I.D., Turner, A.K., Wilson, J.P., Jenson, S.K., and Band, L.E., 1991. GIS and land surface-subsurface process modeling, in Goodchild, M.F., Parks, B.O. and Steyaert, L.T. (eds.), *Environmental Modeling with GIS*, Oxford University Press, New York. pp. 196-230.

CLASSROOM CONNECTIONS

KBLIMS for Forested Ecosystem Simulation Management

Multiple Choice

Pick the best answer.

1. **What is the environmental problem addressed in this chapter on land management?**
   A. Developing models to answer a variety of queries about larger scale forested ecosystems that includes complex interactions among climatic, topographic, hydrologic, pedological and ecological processes simulating carbon, water and energy flux processes.
   B. Aggregating and combining GIS data and simulation models that organize their information in fundamentally different ways to answer user queries about forest ecosystems.
   C. Allowing flexibility in user queries about ecosystems from a variety of combinations and aggregations with differing scales and constraints over GIS data and simulation models.
   D. Bringing many kinds of sensed data together with numerous simulation models to create caring balanced policy and government decision making among many institutions.
   E. Finding water in the desert.
   F. A – D.

2. **In the KBLIMS for forested ecosystem simulation management, how does AI technology help with answering queries on larger regions of land?**
   A. By automating the tedious and time consuming process of aggregating numerous analysis results of smaller subregions AI makes it easier to answer multiple queries about larger regions under different constraints, scales and query perspectives.
   B. Knowledge abstraction and meta-knowledge create an ontology or 'universal language' across conceptually different systems to allow integration of information and provide explanation.
   C. Intelligent query answering gives the user answers based on deductions across multiple systems and disciplines.
   D. Hybrid AI provides a framework that allows integration and aggregation of multiple systems when answering user queries.
   E. Generally, by using AI we take the tediousness out of the repetitive tasks, create a language for information sharing concepts across different disciplines and allow greater flexibility in asking more different kinds of queries.
   F. All of the above.

3. What AI concepts does this system work with?

A. Hybrid AI.

B. Meta-knowledge and knowledge/concept representation.

C. Intelligent query answering.

D. Deduction.

E. All of the above.

F. None of the above.

True or False

Please decide if each of the statements below are True or False.

4. Objects in a GIS are typically in the form of primitives such as points, lines, polygons, or layers whereas Objects in a simulation model are defined in terms of system state, mass and energy fluxes, and interaction and dynamics of species or individuals.

5. Without AI, human interaction with GIS and simulation systems usually means large, cumbersome files are developed and modeling is done in a rigid, almost batch oriented approach.

6. KBLIMS exploits the notion of a query model which executes a set of user defined or system defined queries.

7. Terrain analysis and simulation modeling are often separate from GIS systems.

8. Because the specialized tools needed to perform tasks such as terrain analysis and ecosystem simulation are knowledge-intensive the KBLIMS system components are viewed as types of knowledge which can be incorporated into a hybrid knowledge based system.

9. Choosing and structuring the proper simulation model for each of a potentially large number of land units is a tedious, and error-prone task.

Answers can be found at the end of the book.

Chapter 12

Weather Bulletins

SCRIBE: An Interactive System for Compostion of Meteorological Forecasts

R. Verret, G. Babin,D. Vigneux, J. Marcoux, J. Boulais, R. Parent, S. Payer and **F. Petrucci**
Canadian Meteorological Centre, Canada

ABSTRACT

SCRIBE is an interactive system for composition of meteorological forecasts. It can generate plain language public forecast bulletins from weather element matrices available at a set of stations or sample points. The matrices are prepared at a three-hour time resolution. Upon reception of the matrices, the knowledge base system processes the data to extract the ideas or concepts hidden behind the digital guidances. The knowledge base system works through a domain space of rules to generate the concepts which are the results of a semantic numerical analysis of the weather element matrices content. The concepts follow standards of codification that provide a simpler way to display the content of the weather element matrices on the graphical interface for editing rather than displaying the raw numbers. Once the editing task is complete at the interface level, the modified concept file is quality controlled before being fed to the knowledge base system again to generate the plain language bulletin.

The knowledge base system uses approximately 600 rules to generate the concepts. It can produce more than 40 precipitation concepts (rain, rain heavy at times...), including three types of concepts applicable to thunderstorms (risk, possibility, a few) at up to three levels at the same time (ex.: rain and snow possibly mixed with ice pellets). It can also produce two types of concepts applicable to precipitation accumulation (liquid and frozen), six classes of probability of precipitation concepts, 13 sky cover concepts (11 stationary states and two evolving states), 14 classes of wind speed with eight directions, two types of visibility concepts (blowing snow and fog) and ten types of maximum/minimum temperature concepts.

The knowledge base system uses approximately 1000 rules to generate the plain language bulletins. Forward chaining is normally used to query the rules although backward chaining is also possible depending on the problem to be solved. The knowledge base system creates a basic sentence structure that can be matched into different structures representing different semantics expressing the same content, following a case base reasoning approach.

1   INTRODUCTION

The Canadian Meteorological Centre (CMC) has designed an interactive system for composition of meteorological forecasts called SCRIBE (Verret *et al.* 1993; Boulais *et al.* 1992). SCRIBE uses a set of objective weather element matrices that include sdirect model outputs and statistical products generated centrally at CMC at a number of stations or sample points. The matrices are transmitted to the Regional Weather Centres and Weather Service Offices where they are processed before being displayed on a user-friendly graphical interface. The system can generate plain language bilingual (English and French) forecasts either in an automatic or in a manual mode. The system provides the capability of editing the guidance.

A simplified diagram showing the structure of SCRIBE can be found in Figure 1. The weather element matrices at sample points are processed by the Space and Time Combination system to generate area forecast matrices which are then processed by the Concept Generator. This module will do a numerical synthesis of the matrices content. The output of the Concept Generator is displayed on the graphical interface for editing. The output of the interface is quality controlled before being fed to the Text Generator. The major components of the system will be briefly described in the following paragraphs.

2   WEATHER ELEMENT MATRICES

The weather element forecasts found in the matrices are available at 3-hour intervals. The matrices include the following parameters: the climatological maximum/minimum temperature; the statistical spot time temperature forecasts; the maximum/minimum temperature forecasts, calculated from the spot temperatures on a local time window; the climatological frequencies of precipitation over 6-h and 12-h periods; the statistical total cloud opacity forecasts; the statistical forecasts of probability of precipitation over 6- and 12-h periods at various thresholds; the model precipitation amount forecasts over 3-h intervals; the Showalter index; the vertical velocity at 850 hPa; the conditional precipitation type forecast; a companion to the precipitation type (used to forecast blowing snow and fog); the surface dew point depression; various thicknesses; the wind direction, the wind speed and wind gust; the Canadian UV Index (Burrows *et*

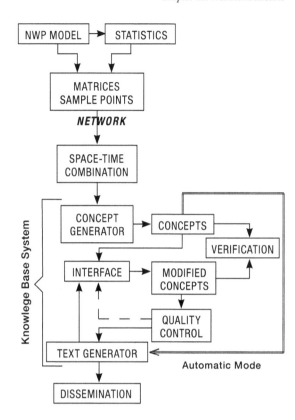

Figure 1. Simplified structural diagram of SCRIBE.

al., 1993); the model total clouds; the 6- and 12-h diagnostic probability of precipitation forecasts based on model precipitation amounts; the model surface temperatures; the model temperatures and dew point depression near the sigma level 0.97; the sea surface temperatures; the ice cover; the snow depth on the ground; the significant wave height forecasts; the freezing spray accumulation forecasts.

Two sets of matrices are prepared at each production cycle (00 and 12 UTC): one based on the Canadian Global model (operational version in May 1995: spectral, 119 waves with a triangular truncation, 21 sigma levels in the vertical) and one based on the Canadian Regional model (operational version in May 1995: finite elements, variable resolution grid with a 50 km horizontal resolution window over Canada, 25 sigma levels in the vertical). The Global model matrices cover a 72-hour period while those generated from the Regional model cover a 48-hour period. It is planned to expand the Global model matrices to 144 hours. A number of other parameters can be generated from the variables in the matrices, such as the drying index for example, used in the agricultural forecasts.

The statistical forecasts included in the matrices are based on Perfect Prog (PP) (Klein *et al.*, 1959) multiple linear regression equations. These forecasts are all operational at CMC (Verret, 1992). The conditional precipitation type forecasts are prepared using an algorithm that studies the vertical temperature profile as generated by the driving model (Bourgouin, 1992). All the remaining weather element forecasts in the matrices are direct model outputs. The model clouds, temperatures and probabilities of precipitation are used to supplement the statistical parameters when and where they are not available. There is no time interpolation in any of the forecasts included in the matrices, which means that SCRIBE has a true 3-hour time resolution.

The weather element matrices are prepared at 264 Canadian stations or sample points. The spatial resolution of the system needs improvement, and a doubling of the number of stations is foreseen in future versions of the system. The matrices are compressed and transmitted to each Regional Office on the Wide Area Network. The total amount of data transmitted on the network for the purpose of SCRIBE is about one megabyte per day, including both production cycles and both numerical models.

3   COMBINATION SYSTEM

The weather element matrices for each forecast area are generated locally from those available at the sample points within the area. This is done by forcing the combination of the matrices available at the stations (sample points) within the same forecast area. If there is only one sample point within the forecast area, the matrix at that point becomes the matrix for the whole area. The area forecast matrices will be in the same format as the original ones. A rule-based approach is taken to create the resulting matrices from those available at the different sample points.

The system then tries to combine together the area forecast matrices for neighboring regions. The approach taken follows Miller and Glahn (1985). The system scans in time each weather element in the different matrices potentially to be combined, and calculates the number of occurrences of no differences, small, medium and large differences. The thresholds used to define a small, medium or large difference are adjustable. The system will decide whether there is combination or not depending on adjustable preset thresholds on the number of differences. Directive lists are built in the system to control the way neighboring regions can be combined. The lists allow the users to specify that a particular region never combines and is always by itself, or that some regions are normally combined together but not with others. If the system decides that there is combination, it will produce a weather element matrix valid for the group of regions, in the same format as the original ones following a rule-based approach.

4   CONCEPT GENERATOR

The main task of the Concept Generator is to extract from the raw data the ideas or constructs that are hidden behind the digital weather element forecasts in the matrices. The concepts represent the meteorological events resulting from the numerical synthesis of the content of the matrices and are coded according to a specified standard. This codification standard is a context-free representation of the content of the weather element matrices based upon the Backus-Naur-Form (BNF) notation (Centre météorologique du Québec, 1992). The concepts always give the conditions at the beginning and at the end of the valid period of a particular event applicable to each weather element that can be displayed on the graphical interface. They also include the beginning and ending times of the validity period.

The inputs to the Concept Generator come from the weather element matrices, either at the sample points (stations) or after being processed by the Space and Time Combination system. It queries approximately 600 decision rules, each one having one or more conditions and actions. The concepts are generated for the complete period of interest, from 0 to 72 hours after initialization time. The concepts have a 3-hour time resolution, dictated by the weather element forecasts found in the matrices. All the processes to generate the concepts are based on a scanning in time of the weather element forecasts with cross-referencing between them. The Concept Generator uses the SCRIBE knowledge base system (Boulais, 1992) (see section 7).

The Concept Generator can produce more than 40 precipitation concepts (rain, rain heavy at times...) including 3 types of concepts applicable to thunderstorms (risk, possibility, a few) at up to 3 levels at the same time (ex.: rain and snow mixed with risk of freezing rain). It can also produce 2 types of concepts applicable to precipitation accumulation (liquid and frozen), 6 classes of probability of precipitation concepts, 13 sky cover concepts (11 stationary states and 2 evolving states), 14 classes of wind speed with 9 directions, 2 types of visibility concepts (blowing snow and fog), 10 types of temperature concepts (maximum, minimum, steady, inverse trends etc.) and one type of dew point temperature concepts. The Concept Generator can also produce concepts for the probability of 5 mm or more of precipitation from the raw data in the matrices.

5   INTERFACE

The interface is used to display and edit the concepts produced by the Concept Generator or to input manually new concepts into the system. It is also used to modify the proposed groupings of forecast regions generated by the Combination system, or create new groupings of regions. The forecasters use icons, simple dialogue menus and tool boxes to do the work at the interlace, and everything can be done with the mouse. The interface is also used to trigger the Quality Control module and the Text Generator.

A picture of the interface can be found at the end of the paper (Figure 3). The bar at the very top of the screen is used mainly to select the bulletins to be generated, to load the guidance, to display the forecast regions and to trigger the Text Generator. Tool boxes appropriate to each weather element are activated by clicking on buttons on the left-hand side of the screen. The actual working area occupies most of the screen, with a horizontal scrolling bar at the bottom. It is divided into sub-areas for each weather element from top to bottom: sky cover, precipitation, probability of precipitation (trace and 5 mm thresholds), temperatures and dew point, winds, visibility, precipitation accumulation and warnings. All the concepts displayed in the working area are completely editable. Although the concepts generated by SCRIBE are at a 3-hour time resolution, the interface allows the user to work at a one-hour time resolution, with the restriction that a concept cannot last less than three hours.

6   TEXT GENERATOR

The concepts, once modified at the interface, are fed into the Quality Control module. This module does a consistency check of each weather element over time, and a consistency check of the different weather elements against each other. Messages are displayed at the interface to signal the main inconsistencies that may be found in the modified concept file. The users have the choice to do the necessary corrections on the concepts or simply to by-pass the Quality Control system, and trigger the Text Generator.

The quality controlled concept file is preprocessed before going into the Text Generator as such, to make sure that there are no more than three concepts over a particular forecast period (normally a 12-hour period) for the clouds, precipitation and winds. The concepts will be generalized if they are too numerous. This preprocessing is applied only when generating the text for the public forecasts.

The Text Generator uses the SCRIBE knowledge base system (see section 7). The rules (more than 1000) in the knowledge base can be considered as the branches in a decisional tree. The design of the rules is largely based on Marcoux (1992) for precipitation and sky cover. Most of the rules are used for logical decisions, and only the terminal nodes of the branches in the tree determine the selection of the words in the lexicon to construct the sentences. The Text Generator will create a basic sentence structure that can be matched into different structures representing different semantics expressing the same content, following a case-based reasoning approach (see section 7). Grammar rules are also available to make sure that the text complies to the syntax both in English and French. The Text Generator can calculate some parameters such as the drying index to fill in the proper sentences. Figure 2 shows examples of texts generated with SCRIBE. It shows the flexibility of the system and its capability of generating different styles of wording. The number of possible sentences is almost limitless.

7   THE KNOWLEDGE BASE SYSTEM

The knowledge base system (SCRIBE/KBS) is used by both the Concept and the Text Generators. The three major functional constituents of the SCRIBE/KBS are the compiler to compile the rules, the inference engine to query the rules and the fact database management system. They work together to extract and manipulate the concepts embedded in the raw data, based on the knowledge represented by an ensemble of rules, and to solve the truth system particular to each meteorological situation. The compiler is used only once when the rules are modified or updated.

A rule is divided into three parts: preconditions, conditions and actions. Once compiled and coded, the rules are selectively queried by the inference engine. The inference engine uses a set of functions and/or the fact database management system to solve each rule that is being looked at. A rule will see its actions executed only if the pre-conditions and conditions are tested as true. The actions are used to create or modify the facts and to execute functions which modify the facts, generate products and/or redirect the inference engine. The fact database management system updates, adds or withdraws facts or information in the database. The facts are used to solve the rules or to realize the actions prescribed by the rules.

The case-based reasoning in SCRIBE is a four-step process used to correct and adjust the terms, syntax or content of a sentence or group of sentences in a meteorological forecast (Riesbeck *et al.*, 1989). The four steps involved are: a) the construction of a structured set of indices; b) retrieving a problematic forecast out of a set of forecasts; c) resolution of the matching rules; and d) resolution of the adaptation rules.

As the SCRIBE/KBS builds the plain language forecast, it also constructs a dynamic data structure outlining the semantic/syntactic concepts, as well as the terms used in its resolution process. According to the value of context variables, the forecasts are then retrieved as inputs for the matching and adaptation rules. The chosen structured set of indices is matched against a set of cases exemplified as a sequence of terms and semantic/syntactic concepts. When an actual match is made, adaptation rules are used to operate on the forecasts, which include a combination of the following three functions: a) substitution of terms or group of terms by some other constant term, constant group of terms or terms derived from the resolution of some other semantic/syntactic concept; b) insertion of terms or group of terms; or c) deletion of terms or group of terms. For example, the text « Today.. Rain ending this afternoon. Then cloudy with chance of a shower. » is containing in its structured set of indices the concept « possible precipitation ». If the context variables designate this text to be reorganized to include the actual probability of precipitation forecast, for example 70% chance of precipitation, the forecast is retrieved for handling by the matching and adaptation rules. A match is made between the semantic/syntax case « possible precipitation

» and the structured set of indices of the forecast per se. Adaptation rules then delete « chance of a » and all possible qualifiers on the occurrence of precipitation, find the associated probability of precipitation and reinsert, for example, « 70% chance of ». The new text then becomes: « Today.. Rain ending this afternoon. Then cloudy with 70% chance of a shower. ».

The main advantage of the SCRIBE/KBS is that it uses a predicate language. It is consequently possible to generate and modify the rules easily and rapidly. The SCRIBE/KBS has been coded in standard C.

8 VERIFICATION SYSTEM

The SCRIBE Verification system under development is based on the following framework. All available observations, synoptic, hourly and supplementary aviation observations are used to create a truth file at a set of stations. The truth file is basically a matrix that includes all observed weather elements with a time resolution of one hour, taking into account the special observations produced at non-standard times. The weather elements are cross-checked between themselves to validate the observations and thus create the truth, assumed to be the actual representation of the weather that really occurred. For instance, the temperature observations available at each hour are cross-referenced against the maximum/minimum temperatures reported in the synoptic observations, to establish the true maximum/minimum temperatures on a local time window and to identify inverse temperature trends. Similar treatment is done to assess occurrences of precipitation. The truth files are generated once a day at each station, for the past 24 hours. The truth files can be downloaded to the Regional Weather Centres for their own use.

On the other hand, a similar set of matrices are generated from the modified concept file (output of the interface) used to generate the plain language forecasts. The forecast and the truth matrices can then be compared and the validity and skill of the forecasts assessed.

The verification system is flexible enough to be used to verify specific events, or events that meet specific threshold criteria. It will be able to verify any weather element that can be forecast and observed. A graphical interface will be developed so that the verification system can be used efficiently.

```
MONTREAL.
TODAY..
PROBABILITY OF PRECIPITATION OF 5MM AND MORE 50 PERCENT
DRYING INDEX VERY LOW
AMOUNT OF HOURS OF SUNSHINE 3
SOUTHWEST WINDS 15 TO 30 KM/H BECOMING LIGHT AND VARIABLE THIS MORNING.
HIGH NEAR 24.


TONIGHT..
PROBABILITY OF PRECIPITATION OF 5MM AND MORE LESS THAN 5 PERCENT
LIGHT AND VARIABLE WINDS.
LOW NEAR 14.


WEDNESDAY..
PROBABILITY OF PRECIPITATION OF 5MM AND MORE LESS THAN 5 PERCENT
DRYING INDEX MODERATE 37
AMOUNT OF HOURS OF SUNSHINE 12
LIGHT AND VARIABLE WINDS.
HIGH NEAR 28.


-----------------------------------------------------------------------------------------


SOUTHWESTERN ONTARIO.
TODAY..FREQUENT CLOUDY PERIODS WITH A CHANCE OF SHOWERS THIS AFTERNOON. HIGH 24 TO 27.
TONIGHT..INCREASING CLOUDINESS NEAR MIDNIGHT WITH CHANCE OF SHOWERS. LOW 17 TO 20.
SATURDAY..CLOUDY WITH A FEW SHOWERS. HIGH NEAR 30.
PROBABILITY OF PRECIPITATION IN PERCENT..30 TODAY. 60 TONIGHT. 60 SATURDAY.
WINDS..VARIABLE 10 KM/H TODAY. VARIABLE 10 KM/H TONIGHT. VARIABLES 10 KM/H SATURDAY.
AVERAGE DEW POINT..22 TODAY. SATURDAY 19 INCREASING TO 25 IN THE AFTERNOON.
MOST LIKELY PRECIPITATION AMOUNT..NIL TODAY EXCEPT FOR TRACE TO 2 MM IN SHOWERS. 2 TO 5 MM
TONIGHT. 10 TO 15 MM SATURDAY.
DRYING INDEX..NEAR 20 OR LOW TODAY. ZERO OR NEAR ZERO IN SHOWERS SATURDAY.


-----------------------------------------------------------------------------------------


OKANAGAN VALLEY DISTRICT.
TODAY..MAINLY CLOUDY WITH A CHANCE OF SHOWERS.
TONIGHT..MAINLY CLOUDY WITH A CHANCE OF SHOWERS, CLEARING TOWARDS MORNING.
WEDNESDAY..SUNNY WITH CLOUDY PERIODS.
```

LOCATION	TODAY			TONIGHT		WEDNESDAY	
	HI	POP	UV	LOW	POP	HI	POP
VERNON	24	30	X.X	9	30	28	0
KELOWNA	23	30	X.X	9	30	28	0
PENTICTON	24	0	X.X	12	0	28	0
OSOYOOS	24	30	X.X	9	30	28	0
SUMMERLAND	24	30	X.X	9	30	28	0

Figure 2. Examples of text generated with SCRIBE. The first one is taken from an agricultural forecast bulletin for Quebec, the second one from a public/agricultural forecast bulletin for Ontario and the third one from a public forecast bulletin for British Columbia.

```
FPCN11 CYQX     Public forecast for Newfoundland
FPCN13 CYQX     Public forecast for Labrador
FPCN20 CYQX     Marine forecast for Newfoundland
FPCN21 CYQX     Marine forecast for Labrador
FPCN24 CYQX     Marine forecast for Newfoundland - NAVTEX
FPCN25 CYQX     Marine forecast for Labrador - NAVTEX
FPCN26 CYQX     Marine forecast for Belle-Isle Strait - NAVTEX
FPCN40 CYQX     Agricultural forecast for Newfoundland
FPCN11 CWHX     Public and agricultural forecast for Nova Scotia
FPCN13 CWHX     Public forecast for Isles de la Madeleine
FPCN15 CWHX     Public forecast for Prince Edward Island
FPCN22 CWHX     Marine forecast for the Maritimes
FPCN11 CWZF     Public and agricultural forecast for New Brunswick
FPCN11 CWUL     Public forecast for western Quebec
FPCN12 CWUL     Public forecast for northern Quebec
FPCN13 CWUL     Public forecast for central Quebec
FPCN14 CWUL     Public forecast for eastern Quebec
FPCN42 CWUL     Agricultural forecast for Quebec
WBCN07 CWUL     Public forecast for extreme northern Quebec
FPCN50 CWUL     Snow forecasts for Quebec
FPCN58 CWUL     Snow forecasts for Quebec (commercial version)
MET800 CWUL     Forest fire forecast for Quebec
FPCN11 CWOZ     Public forecast for eastern Ontario
FPCN40 CWOZ     Agricultural forecast for eastern Ontario
FPCN11 CWTO     Public forecast for southern Ontario
FPCN12 CWTO     Public forecast for northern Ontario
FPCN30 CWTO     Forest fire forecast for Ontario regions east of Nipigon
FPCN40 CWTO     Agricultural forecast for southern Ontario
FPCN11 CWWG     Public and agricultural forecast for southern Manitoba
FPCN13 CWWG     Public forecast for northwestern Ontario
FPCN16 CWWG     Public forecast for central and northern Manitoba
FPCN11 CWXE     Rural forecast for southern Saskatchewan
FPCN12 CWXE     Public forecast for northern Saskatchewan
FPCN13 CWXE     Urban forecast for southern Saskatchewan
FPCN11 CWEG     Public and agricultural forecast for southern Alberta
FPCN12 CWEG     Public and agricultural forecast for northern Alberta
FPCN15 CWEG     Public forecast for the Northwest Territories
FPCN16 CWEG     Public forecast for the Northwest Territories
FPCN17 CWEG     Public forecast for the Northwest Territories
FPCN18 CWEG     Public forecast for the Northwest Territories
FPCN19 CWEG     Public forecast for the Northwest Territories
WBCN23 CWEG     Forecast for the Northwest Territories - CBC North
FPCN11 CWLW     Public forecast for southwest interior of British Columbia
FPCN13 CWLW     Public forecast for the Columbia Districts of British Columbia
FPCN15 CWLW     Public forecast for the Kootenay Districts of British Columbia
FPCN16 CWLW     Public forecast for central interior of British Columbia
FPCN18 CWLW     Public forecast for the Peace River District of British Columbia
FPCN11 CWVR     Public forecast for coastal British Columbia
FPCN11 CYXY     Public forecast for western Yukon and northern British Columbia
FPCN12 CYXY     Public forecast for southeastern Yukon and northeastern British Columbia
FPCN60/61/62    City forecasts for the main cities across Canada
```

Table 1. List of products/bulletins that can be generated with SCRIBE (as of May 1, 1995).

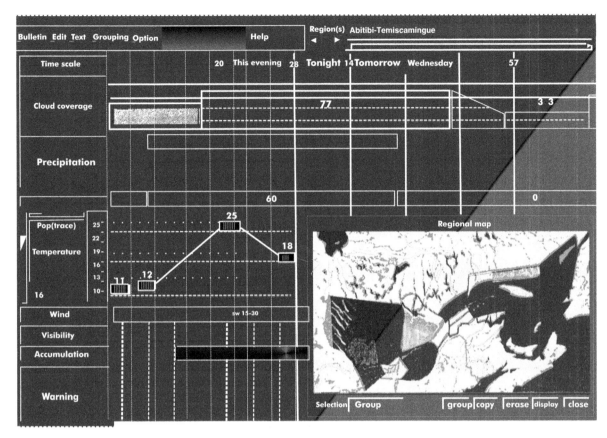

Figure 3. Picture of the SCRIBE graphical interface.

9 PRODUCT GENERATOR

Although the output of the interface goes into a text generator, it will be possible in the future to generate a whole suite of different products – either in textual, tabular or graphical formats – from the concepts database. Table 1 gives a list of the products (as of May 1, 1995) that can be generated with SCRIBE.

10 CONCLUSIONS

SCRIBE has been installed at all the Regional Weather Centres and Offices. It needs about ten megabytes of disk space, including a ten day archiving of the data. Once the weather element matrices are available, it can generate public and agricultural forecasts, in English and French, for 244 zones (forecast regions) in 26 bulletins across Canada, for days 1 to 3 in approximately 15 minutes real time on an HP9000-735 machine, in the automatic mode. The weather element matrices are produced on the mainframe frontal computer at CMC.

Considerable efforts are dedicated to include the recommendations of all Weather Centres in future updates of the system. In particular, tools will be developed to generate locally from the SCRIBE database several new products tailored to different users.

11 REFERENCES

Boulais J., 1992: A knowledge base system (SCRIBE/KBS) analyzing and synthesizing large amount of meteorological data. *Preprints 4th AES/ CMOS Workshop on Operational Meteorology,* Whistler, B.C., Sept 15-18, 1992, pp. 283-286.

Boulais J., G. Babin, D. Vigneux, M. Mondou, R. Parent and R. Verret, 1992: SCRIBE: an interactive system for composition of meteorological forecasts. *Preprints 4th AES/CMOS Workshop on Operational Meteorology,* Whistler, B.C., Sept 15-18, 1992, pp. 273-282.

Bourgouin P., 1992: Criteria for determining precipitation types. *4th AES/CMOS Workshop on Operational Meteorology*, Sept 15-18 1992, Whistler B.C., pp. 460-469.

Burrows W. R., L. J. Wilson and M. Vallée, 1993: A statistical forecast procedure for daily total ozone based on TOMS data. *Preprints 13th Conference on Weather Analysis and Forecasting*, Vienna, Virginia, Aug 2-6, 1993, pp. 331-334.

Centre météorologique du Québec, 1992: METEOCODE: Norme de codification. Version 2.2, révision 92-04-01, p. 42.

Klein W. H., B. M. Lewis and I. Enger, 1959: Objective prediction of five-day mean temperature during winter. *J. Meteor.,* 16, pp. 672-682.

Marcoux J., 1992: Liste des critères objectifs pour un générateur de prévisions météorologiques. Centre météorologique du Québec, p. 35.

Miller R. L. and H. R. Glahn, 1985: Techniques used in the computer worded forecast program for zones: interpolation and combination. *TDL Office Note* 85-5, NOAA, NWS, p. 22.

Riesbeck, C. K. and R. C. Schank, 1989: Inside case-based reasoning. Lawrence Erlbaum Associates Publishers, p. 423.

Verret, R., 1992: CMC operational statistical products. *Preprints 4th AES/CMOS Workshop on Operational Meteorology,* Whistler, B.C., Sept 15-18, 1992, pp. 119-128.

Verret, R., G. Babin, D. Vigneux, R. Parent and J. Marcoux, 1993: SCRIBE: an interactive system for composition of meteorological forecasts. *Preprints 13th Conference on Weather Analysis and Forecasting,* Vienna, Virginia, August 2-6, 1993, Amer. Met. Soc., pp. 213-216.

12   ACKNOWLEDGMENTS

The authors wish to acknowledge the participation in the project, either for their work or for their advice and recommendations, of the following people: D. Layton, J. Murtha and A. Macafee at the Maritimes Weather Centre; M. Larivière, A. Méthot and D. Bachand at the Québec Weather Centre; M. Mondou and L. Pelland at the CMC; G. Viau at Training Branch; N. Paulsen at the Ontario Weather Centre; N. Bargerie and C. Le Bot at Météo-France.

CLASSROOM CONNECTIONS

SCRIBE: An Interactive System for Composition of Meteorological Forecasts

Multiple Choice

Pick the best answer.

1. **What is the environmental problem the Canadian system SCRIBE works on?**
   A. Turning large amounts of complex distributed weather data into human readable weather bulletins in English and French.
   B. Public weather forecasting by human-AI cooperation in generating weather bulletins from weather station data.
   C. Automatically cross checking weather data from different weather stations.
   D. Deciding to sound the alarm for floods and tsunamis.
   E. A – C.
   F. None of the above.

2. **What AI methods are used in the SCRIBE weather system?**
   A. Semantic concepts.
   B. Hybrid AI with numerical and conceptual systems in combination.
   C. Case based reasoning.
   D. Rule based systems.
   E. Neural networks.
   F. A – D.

3. **What kind of data does this system work with?**
   A. Current (not historical) weather data sent from over 240 different stations.
   B. Distributed sensor data collected every 3 hours 365 days a year.
   C. Google and Facebook user input.
   D. Data in form of matrices.
   E. A, B and D.
   F. None of the above.

4. **What kinds of weather concepts does the AI system and user interface rely on?**
   A. Temperature.
   B. Wind direction and speed.
   C. Visibility concepts.
   D. Multi-concept storm descriptors like snow and thunderstorm mixed with ice.
   E. A – D.
   F. Cloudy with a chance of meatballs.

True or False

Please decide if each of the statements below are True or False.

5. Users can change or enter concepts in the user interface.

6. The system input uses objective weather element matrices from statistical analysis and standard meteorological model output.

7. The bulletins can be in French or English and have good grammar in each language.

8. The user can select different groupings of regions and bypass quality control.

9. The system is only run autonomously.

Answers can be found at the end of the book.

Chapter 13

Weather Forecasting

Retrieving Structured Spatial Information from Large Databases: A Progress Report

Eric K. Jones
Victoria University of Wellington, New Zealand

Aaron Roydhouse
Victoria University of Wellington, New Zealand

ABSTRACT

We describe ongoing work with MetVUW Workbench, a case-based reasoning system for intelligent retrieval and display of historical meteorological data. The system is intended to serve as a "memory amplifier" for meteorologists that allows them to rapidly locate and analyze past cases of interest.

MetVUW Workbench is distinguished by the large size of its case base, by its need to represent structured spatial information, and by its use of a relational database to store cases. This paper briefly describes some of the technical issues that follow from these design considerations, focusing on the role of the relational database.

1   INTRODUCTION

Effective exploitation of large archives of environmental data requires efficiently identifying the data that are relevant for a particular task. As environmental data are spatially distributed, identifying relevant data is frequently a problem of spatial information retrieval. This paper describes work in progress that addresses the problem of efficiently retrieving complex, structured spatial information from an archive of meteorological data.

The approach is implemented in MetVUW Workbench, a system for intelligent retrieval, analysis, and display of meteorological data [3, 4]. MetVUW Workbench is intended to serve as an intelligent assistant for weather forecasters and other meteorologists. Forecasters should

be able to use MetVUW Workbench to quickly retrieve past cases that are similar to the current weather situation, and to analyze and display the retrieved cases as an aid to forecast construction. Meteorology researchers should be able to use MetVUW Workbench to rapidly identify large numbers of examples of empirical phenomena of interest.

MetVUW Workbench can be thought of as a kind of case-based reasoning, system [6]. Each case comprises an *index label* that is used in case retrieval, together with raw data describing the weather situation at a particular moment in time. Index labels are structured collections of components representing weather systems and other high-level features of the weather situation in a case. Each component includes a symbolic description of the kind of system it represents (*e.g.* high-pressure system), geometrical descriptions of the system's layout in space (*e.g.* a polygonal approximation to its outer boundary), and numeric values for various parameters of the system (*e.g.* the observed maximum pressure). Spatial relationships between the components of the index label are also stored. Index labels are automatically derived off-line from ECMWF fields.

The raw data associated with a case include satellite imagery stored both in digital form and on laser disc, a document archive, and numeric fields from the European Center for Medium-range Weather Forecasting (ECMWF). The numeric fields include pressure, temperature, relative humidity, and wind speed, all of which are available for 14 different levels of the atmosphere. Cases are recorded at 12-hour intervals. MetVUW Workbench currently employs a portion of this numeric data that covers the Australasian region.

MetVUW Workbench currently possesses 3.5 years of data, or a case base of some 2500 cases. We anticipate that a further 10 years of data will soon be available to us, expanding the case base to about 10,000 cases. Within several years, re-analyses of historical data by the ECMWF and other organizations should produce data sets covering a period from World War II to the present, which would permit construction of a database of over 36,000 past cases.

The large size of this case base gives rise to special difficulties that are not faced by many other knowledge-based systems. In particular, the set of index labels is too large to conveniently hold in memory. For example, index labels for low and high pressure systems over the Australasian region currently occupy about 65 Mb. As the system is extended to incorporate more high-level features of weather situations, and as the period of time covered by the case base grows, storage requirements will further increase. We expect that a comprehensive collection of index labels for a 10-year data set covering the Australasian region will require on the order of 1 Gb to store.

To cope with these large storage requirements, MetVUW Workbench employs a relational database to store index labels. This approach is unusual in AI: most existing case-based reasoning systems have sufficiently small case bases that all indices can be stored in physical memory. Much of our research with MetVUW Workbench is concerned with the implications of this design decision. The remainder of this paper is structured as follows. Section 2 describes the architecture of MetVUW

Workbench. Section 3 exemplifies the structure of index labels in MetVUW Workbench. Section 4 discusses recent work to speed up case retrieval. Section 5 summarizes the current status of MetVUW Workbench, and outlines directions for future work.

2   THE ARCHITECTURE OF METVUW WORKBENCH

The use of a relational database naturally gives rise to a two-stage retrieval mechanism, as illustrated in Figure 1. The user interacts with the system via the *query constructor,* a graphical front end for constructing queries. Queries are built out of a vocabulary of high-level features of past weather situations. A sample query is shown in Figure 2. The query requests a complex low-pressure system over New Zealand with high-pressure systems to the east and west. The numbers in the center of each region indicate (1) the location of the pressure extremum and (2) the magnitude of the pressure difference between the mean sea-level pressure at that location and the pressure at the perimeter of the outermost enclosing region.

Once a query is formulated, case retrieval proceeds in two stages. In the first stage, the *case selector* exploits the machinery of a relational database to efficiently access cases whose index labels are likely to match a query. We use an advanced relational database called Postgres [8] to implement case selection. Case selection employs a number of sophisticated indexing strategies provided by Postgres, in particular, R-tree indexing of spatial information [1],

In the second stage of case retrieval, the cases identified by the case selector are passed to the *similarity assessor,* which uses a knowledge-intensive partial matching process to rank them according to how well they match the query. Those cases whose match quality falls below some threshold are discarded. Similarity assessment is discussed in detail in [5].

3   REPRESENTING INDEX LABELS

All representations of index labels in MetVUW Workbench are automatically extracted from the ECMWF data and stored in a Postgres relational database. Figure 3 depicts the representations of the low and high-pressure systems occurring in

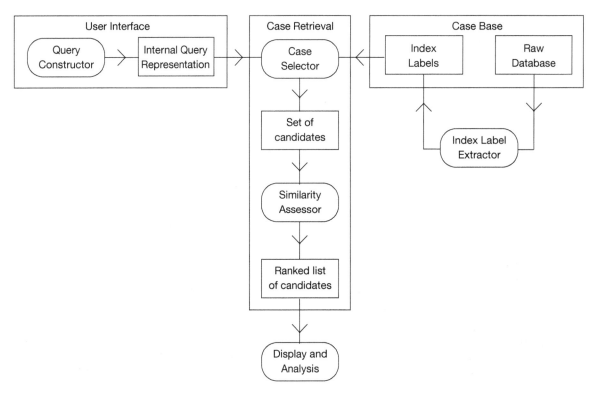

Figure 1. MetVUW Workbench's architecture for case retrieval.

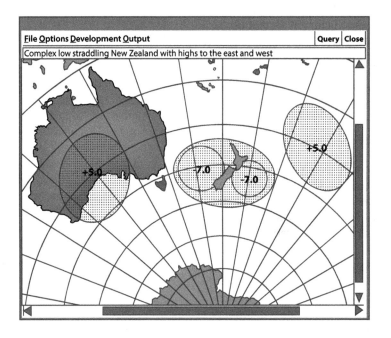

Figure 2. A query requesting a complex low-pressure system over New Zealand with high-pressure systems to the east and west.

the index labels for the two top-ranked cases that MetVUW Workbench retrieves in response to the query of Figure 2.

The index label is a qualitative representation of the key features of the mean sea-level pressure field that have the greatest meteorological significance. Closed curves in the index label correspond to isobars (contours of equal pressure). Only a few contours are stored, corresponding to (1) the major regions of high and low pressure in the case, and (2) the internal structure of these regions. For example, the contour labeled a in the top left-hand diagram of Figure 3 represents a low-pressure system with two subsidiary low-pressure systems, which are explicitly represented by additional contours labeled b and c. The system represented by c in turn contains two subsidiary low-pressure systems, represented by contours d and e. These contours are stored in a tree as depicted to the right of the diagram, and this tree structure is used during similarity assessment.

The Postgres representation of a portion of the index label depicted in the top diagram of Figure 3 is given in table 1. We only include the representation for the low-pressure systems in the index label. Regions of high pressure are stored using a similar scheme. Each case is allocated a unique identifier, stored using the "Case Id" field. Similarly, each region of low pressure has a unique identifier, stored using the "Reg. Id" field. For example, Reg. Id 1798644 corresponds to the region labeled a in the top diagram of Figure 3,

and Reg. Id 1798645 corresponds to region c. The location of the pressure minimum for each region, and the mean sea-level pressure at this location, are stored using the "Pres. Center" and "Min. Pres." fields. The "Perimeter" field holds a high-resolution polygon representing the outer boundary of the region. (For brevity, this field is omitted from table 1, but it is shown graphically in Figure 3.) A rectangular bounding box that approximates this polygon is stored in the "Bounding Box" field. This field is used for R-tree indexing during case selection. The "Peri. Pres." field holds the pressure at the perimeter of the polygon. The tree structure of complex low-pressure systems is encoded using the "Parent Id" field. The "Children" field of a region contains the number of immediate subordinate regions that it encloses.

4   CASE SELECTION

Case selection proceeds in two steps. In step 1 of case selection, Postgres queries are constructed and executed for each weather system in a user's query. The Postgres query for each high- or low-pressure system retrieves all regions in the case base that satisfy the following requirements:

1. The region has the same classification (high or low pressure) as the system in the query.

2. The region's bounding box overlaps the bounding box of the system in the query.

Reg. Id	Case Id	Parent Id	Pres. Center	Min Pres.	Bounding Box	Peri. Pres.	Children
1798643	1798631	––	(205.9,-47.0)	998.0	(201.3,-57.2,211.9,-41.5)	1002.0	0
1798644	1798631	––	(157.9,-44.6)	994.0	(131.5,-54.9,184.1,-34.7)	998.0	2
1798645	1798631	1798644	(172.0,-43.8)	993.0	(156.5,-47.1,183.1,-36.3)	996.0	2
1798646	1798631	1798645	(178.9,-44.8)	993.0	(173.9,-46.3,182.6,-41.7)	995.0	0
1798647	1798631	1798645	(165.2,-42.8)	992.0	(158.3,-46.5,172.0,-37.2)	995.0	0
1798648	1798631	1798644	(143.8,-45.5)	994.0	(136.7,-52.9,148.2,-41.9)	996.0	0
1798649	1798631	––	(102.0,-50.9)	979.0	(81.7,-66.3,123.6,-36.4)	992.0	2
1798650	1798631	1798649	(100.9,-45.3)	979.0	(98.2,-47.2,103.6,-43.4)	979.0	0
1798651	1798631	1798649	(103.2,-56.6)	967.0	(91.1,-63.3,113.9,-49.5)	979.0	0
1798652	1798631	––	(168.5,-67.9)	984.0	(159.5,-71.3,177.7,-66.5)	986.0	0
1798653	1798631	––	(213.0,-75.2)	972.0	(183.0,-83.5,258.8,-68.8)	982.0	0

Table 1. Portion of an index label describing low-pressure regions, excluding the "Perimeter" field.

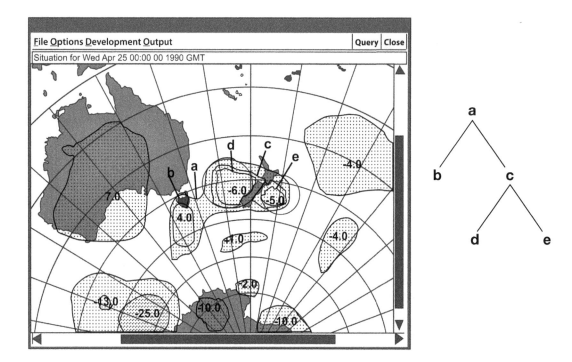

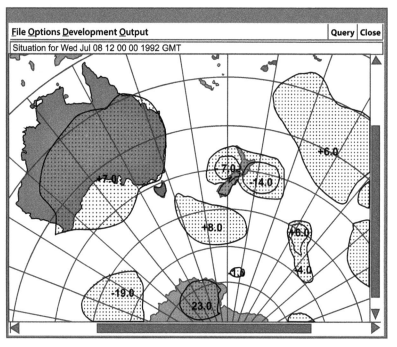

Figure 3. Graphical representations of two index labels. The tree illustrates the structure of the complex low-pressure system over New Zealand in the top index label.

3. The pressure extremum of the region is contained in the area of overlap between the region and the system in the query.

4. Similarly, the pressure extremum of the system in the query is contained in the area of overlap.

5. If the system in the query contains subordinate regions, then the corresponding region in the case has at least as many immediate subordinates.

Each Postgres query is implemented as a *select/project* operation. In step 2 of case selection, the sets of Case Id's retrieved in step 1 are intersected using a relational *join*, producing the set of cases that possess regions corresponding to every step 1 query. The output of this Postgres query is a list of Case Id's and is returned as the result of case selection.

4.1 SPEEDING UP CASE SELECTION

Case selection can be expensive, especially for queries involving a large number of weather systems, because although each weather system in the query may match many cases in the case base, there may be few cases that match all the weather systems in the query. For complex queries such as these, the *select/project* operations can be needlessly slow, because much computational effort is expended to construct temporary relations most of whose tuples will eventually be revealed to be irrelevant. Likewise, the *join* operation can be slow, because the cost of a *join* is proportional to the size of the individual relations to be joined.

To address these problems, we have developed a strategy to make the *select/project* operations more focused and retrieve fewer irrelevant tuples. The key idea is to introduce a new "summary" field into the index labels for each weather system in the case base to encode key features of nearby regions: their type (*e.g.* high or low pressure), their approximate location relative to the weather system in question, and their approximate spatial extent. Each *select/project* operation at step 1 of case selection then specifies both a particular weather system to retrieve and descriptions of any nearby regions in the query. The summary field in the index labels thus acts to quickly filter out tuples that would later be discarded anyway by the *join* operation at step 2.

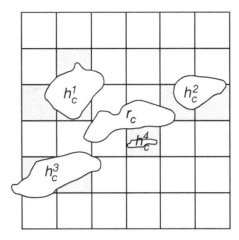

Figure 4. Graphical illustration of a bit-vector for the region r_c in a case. The shaded cells correspond to bits that are set to 1. In this example, the bit vector is `000000|010000 |110011|000100|110000|000000`. (Bits are allocated row by row, starting from the top left.)

In this fashion, it is hoped to increase the efficiency of case selection. The efficiency of step 1 should increase somewhat, because smaller temporary relations are constructed. The efficiency of step 2 should increase significantly, because the relations that need to be joined together are smaller.

We use bit vectors to encode summary descriptions of nearby regions, and we extended Postgres to support efficient computation of bit vector operations. For each region ρ of high or low pressure, a bit vector is allocated for each type of nearby region (*e.g.* high or low pressure). Each bit corresponds to a cell in a grid. The grid covers a region of the globe centered on ρ and is oriented along lines of latitude and longitude. Figure 4 illustrates the bit-vector representation for a region r_c of a hypothetical case. The bit vector is centered on r_c and encodes four nearby regions of high pressure, $h_c^1, ..., h_c^4$. A bit is set to 1 if a significant proportion of the corresponding cell in the grid is covered by a region of high pressure, otherwise the bit is set to 0.

During step 1 of case selection, the various Postgres *select/project* operations are augmented to take advantage of these bit-vector summaries. The *select/project* operation for retrieving a given region in the query only retrieves a region in a case if the bit vector for that region has bits set that correspond to the other regions in the query. Further details of this process are provided in [2].

4.2 EMPIRICAL EVALUATION

A preliminary evaluation of the utility of bit-vector representations in case selection has been carried out, using three representative queries. The queries request two, three, and four weather systems, respectively. Table 2 shows the percentage improvement in time efficiency as a consequence of employing the bit-vector approach.

No. of weather systems	Two	Three	Four
Step 1 *(select/project)*	-2%	-5%	10%
Step 2 *(join)*	6%	39%	71%
Overall	0%	12%	27%

Table 2: Percentage improvement using bit-vector representations

The results indicate some success for queries with more than two conjuncts, most of which comes from reduction in the cost of joins. It appears, however, that the impact on efficiency of the *select/project* operations is more limited. It seems that the major bottleneck for these operations is locating tuples in memory and testing whether they should be included in the resulting temporary relation. Comparatively little time is spent building the relation itself – that is, allocating space for the relation and copying tuples into it. Further speeding up the *select/project* operations remains a topic for future work.

5 SYSTEM STATUS AND FUTURE WORK

An initial prototype of MetVUW Workbench has been completed. Representation and retrieval of low- and high-pressure systems is fully implemented, together with software for displaying data associated with particular cases [7]. A preliminary evaluation of case selection has been carried out [4].

It remains to extend MetVUW Workbench to further high-level features of the mean sea-level pressure field such as ridges and troughs, and to apply these and similar techniques to other numeric fields such as wind speed and potential vorticity. It also remains to develop software to compute summary descriptions of the sets of cases that MetVUW Workbench returns. In addition, we intend to augment the system to allow queries involving temporal information; this task will be the focus of the next stage of our research.

Throughout the development process, we have maintained links with the Meteorological Service of New Zealand (MSNZ). Advice from MSNZ has played a valuable role in determining which aspects of low- and high-pressure systems are meteorologically significant and should therefore be included in queries. At a later date, we hope to actively involve MSNZ in the evaluation (and calibration) of similarity assessment.

6 CONCLUSION

Case-based reasoning is an increasingly important technology for developing knowledge-based systems [6]. MetVUW Workbench demonstrates that a relational database can be used to manage a large case base. This approach to the design of case-based reasoning systems should find ready application in the environmental sciences, where knowledge bases are often very large. Two particular contributions of our approach are as follows:

1. **An architecture for case retrieval.**
   Case retrieval in MetVUW Workbench is split into separate processes of case selection and similarity assessment. Case selection uses the efficient indexing and retrieval machinery of a relational database to quickly identify candidate cases for retrieval. Similarity assessment then analyses these cases in more detail, using a process of knowledge-intensive partial matching.

   This general architecture for case retrieval should prove useful in a wide range of large scale case-based reasoning applications.

2. **Summaries of spatial relationships**.
   A field summarizing the spatial relationships between each weather system and other nearby weather systems is stored as part of each index label. This summary field serves to speed up case selection. Summaries of this kind can be used to increase the efficiency of any retrieval task involving queries for sets of objects with spatial extent that bear some spatial relationship to one another.

ACKNOWLEDGEMENTS

This research was carried out in collaboration with James McGregor of the Institute of Geophysics at Victoria University of Wellington. The idea of using spatial relations to focus case selection arose during discussions with Peter Andreae and David Andreae.

REFERENCES

[1] A. Guttman. R-trees: A dynamic index structure for spatial searching. In *Proceedings of the 1984 ACM-SIGMOD Conference on Management of Data*. ACM-SIGMOD, June 1984.

[2] Eric K. Jones and Aaron Roydhouse. Efficient retrieval of structured spatial information from a large database. In *Proceedings of the AI'94 Workshop on Knowledge-based Systems in Natural Resource Management*, pages 49-69, Armidale, Australia, November 1994. Also available as Technical report CS-TR-94/20, Victoria University of Wellington. URL: ftp://ftp.comp.vuw.ac.nz/doc/vuw-publications/CS-TR-94/CS-TR-94-20.ps.gz.

[3] Eric K. Jones and Aaron Roydhouse. Intelligent retrieval of historical meteorological data. *AI Applications,* 8(3):43-54, 1994. Also available as Technical report CS-TR-93/8, Victoria University of Wellington. URL: ftp://ftp.comp.vuw.ac.nz/doc/vuw-publications/CS-TR-93/CS-TR-93-8.ps.gz.

[4] Eric K. Jones and Aaron Roydhouse. Iterative design of case retrieval systems. In *Proceedings of the AAAI-94 Workshop on Case-Based Reasoning*, pages 150-156, July 1994. Also available as Technical report CS-TR-94/6, Victoria University of Wellington. URL: ftp://ftp.comp.vuw.ac.nz/doc/vuw-publications/CS-TR-94/CS-TR-94-6.ps.gz.

[5] Eric K. Jones and Aaron Roydhouse. Spatial representations of meteorological data for intelligent retrieval. In *Proceedings of the Sixth Colloquium of the Spatial Information Research Centre, University of Otago, New Zealand,* pages 45-58, May 1994.

[6] Janet L. Kolodner. *Case-based reasoning.* Morgan Kaufmann, San Mateo, California, 1993.

[7] Aaron Roydhouse, Linton Miller, Eric K. Jones, and Jim McGregor. The design and implementation of MetVUW Workbench version 1.0. Technical Report CS-TR-93/7, Victoria University of Wellington, November 1993. URL: ftp://ftp.comp.vuw.ac.nz/doc/vuw-publications/CS-TR-93/CS-TR-93-7.ps.gz.

[8] M. Stonebraker and L. Rowe. The design of Postgres. In *Proceedings of the 1986 SIGMOD Conference on Management of Data*. ACM Press, May 1986.

CLASSROOM CONNECTIONS

Retrieving Structured Spatial Information from Large Databases

Multiple Choice
Pick the best answer.

1. **What environmental problem is the AI system working on here?**
   A. Analyze decades of multi-media meteorological data.
   B. Find answers to user queries about past meteorological cases of interest.
   C. Quickly locate and analyze specific meteorological data in the Australasian region over a period from World War II to present time.
   D. Automatically sort our recycling.
   E. A – C only.
   F. All of the above.

2. **What AI technologies are used in this system?**
   A. The random coin toss algorithm.
   B. Intelligent assistants / intelligent software agents.
   C. Intelligent search and retrieval using complex semantic indices.
   D. Hybrid AI: combining database technologies with case based semantic search methods.
   E. B – D.
   F. None of the above.

3. **What is case based data retrieval?**
   A. Case examples selected using a similarity assessment.
   B. Using existing relational database ideas where indices are semantic concepts, the match is similarity based and entries containing case examples with references to raw offline data.
   C. It uses intelligence to determine similarity assessment.
   D. Hybrid neural nets and concepts/rules that match concept indices.
   E. A – C.
   F. B – D.

True or False
Please decide if each of the statements below are True or False.

4. Weather and meteorology only look to the future.

5. Intelligent systems are needed for analyzing big data.

6. The purpose of the work is to study historical weather patterns.

7. The location of the data in this chapter is Europe and North Africa.

8. The MetVUW project was never tested.

Answers can be found at the end of the book.

Chapter 14

The Environmental Information Mall

Michael N. Huhns
Microelectronics and Computer Technology Corporation (MCC), USA

Munindar P. Sing
Microelectronics and Computer Technology Corporation (MCC), USA

Gregory E. Pitts
Microelectronics and Computer Technology Corporation (MCC), USA

ABSTRACT

The *Environmental Information Mall* is being developed for the dissemination of information about the environment, including information derived from the application of analytical tools to environmental data. This paper describes an implementation plan to create an environmental information forum situated on the National Information Infrastructure (NII). The success of this forum depends on the development of an ontology of environmental concepts, which will be used to enable the interoperation of data and analytical tools from a variety of independent sources. We describe tools for the creation and maintenance of the ontology, and then show how it can be used: by information sources to advertise their capabilities, by mediators to combine analytical tools with the data on which they operate, by end users to locate information, and by interfaces to fuse information from several sources. Development of the *Environmental Information Mall* has just begun, so there is as yet no implementation or results to describe.

1 THE VISION

Environmental awareness is in everyone's best interest. Businesses and consumers all benefit when products are manufactured, used, and ultimately disposed of in ways that are safe and beneficial for the environment. A key to achieving this awareness is to make environmental information widely available. However, much of the available environmental information is not reaching either the large or small business communities.

More than 15 federal organizations, numerous state and local agencies, and many private corporations are now actively engaged in producing or gathering environmental data, spanning efforts from "design for the environment" (DFE) to remediation. Currently, the data is impossible to monitor, let alone utilize. It is located at hundreds of distributed data sites and resides on numerous operating systems and configurations. Even if the data could be inventoried, wildly varying differences in quality, vocabularies, and operating platforms make it incredibly difficult for individuals and organizations to access and use it. Therefore, individuals and organizations cannot effectively take advantage of this information to minimize compliance costs, design for the environment, or reduce the impact of production processes. Also, without a high-level view of what information is being used and not used, they will frequently make shortsighted, reactive plans for future research.

A comprehensive project to couple the development and collection of environmental data with the dissemination of the information to the actual user groups could change all this. MCC has proposed that an *Environmental Information Mall* be established to make available the information needed for intelligent environmental decisions. The availability of myriad data and analysis tools would enable more sophisticated modeling and DFE processes, thereby reducing lifecycle environmental costs, and would facilitate industry and government access to resources and activities in the environmental area.

The *Environmental Information Mall* would provide an easily accessible source for environmental regulations, for analysis and solution of environmental and remediation problems, and for commerce in environmental technology and services. It will provide on-line, active manuals promoting environmental technologies. The resulting information will enable businesses and individuals to make intelligent environmental decisions. It would provide a means for the EPA to guide its own decision making and to use its resources in helping industry comply with environmental regulations. It would also provide a secure means to track, collate, analyze, and disseminate pollution prevention and remediation information.

2   REALIZING THE VISION

The establishment of an *Environmental Information Mall* is timely, because most of the needed technology components are now in place:

- **Communication Infrastructure** — fostered by the National Information Infrastructure program and implemented by telecommunication companies
- **Environmental Data** — collected by many government agencies, commercial organizations, and consortia
- **Environmental Analysis and Simulation Tools** — developed by many commercial organizations for executing on the above data.

These technology components are necessary for successful establishment of an *Environmental Information Mall,* but they are not sufficient. A remaining challenge is integration of the many repositories of data and varieties of analysis tools, which are mostly heterogeneous and independently maintained. These sources of information will be useful only if they can be easily accessed and readily applied. MCC, in concert with government and commercial sponsors, is creating an information forum situated on publicly available communication facilities, such as the Internet. The project will define a dynamic, distributed "information space" where disparate data, currently kept in myriad formats, can be placed and accessed logically. The information space must be sophisticated enough that information technology tools can be run against the data to make the information usable (both in form and in content). Finally, the operating parameters should be such that the maintenance and structure become self supporting.

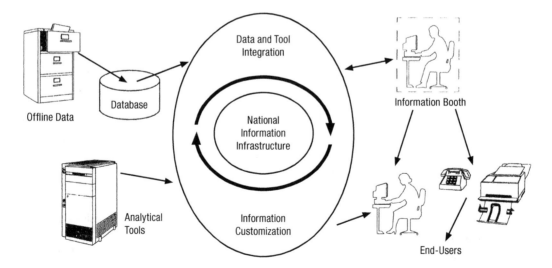

Figure 1. Conceptual View of the Relationship of Users to Environmental Data and Analysis Tools.

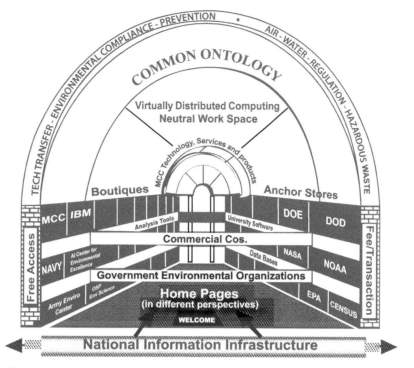

Figure 2. The architectural organization of the Environmental Information Mall.

To assist in this, MCC provides the necessary interoperation tools to:

- Incorporate new databases and other information resources into an open information environment
- Develop and maintain environmental domain ontologies
- Browse domain ontologies and available information resources
- Formulate queries, in terms of the domain ontologies, for accessing the resources

However, this technology must be adapted to the National Information Infrastructure, and then applied to existing resources. The result will be environmental information that is not only accessible, but also usable.

Application Domain. The Federal Government is aggressively seeking to assist small- and medium-sized businesses through a variety of mechanisms. Within DoD, the Manufacturing Centers of Excellence and the CALS Shared Resource Centers are attempting to provide information via the emerging electronic highway. Similarly, NASA has established Technology Outreach Centers, and the Department of Commerce, through the National Institute of Standards and Technology (NIST), is establishing Manufacturing Technology Centers (MTCs) and Manufacturing Outreach Centers (MOCs).

A key infrastructure component to all these technologies is an electronic link between sources of information and users of information. Once the linkage is established, however, providing or finding the relevant information in a timely fashion will be critical to the success of the program. The use of intelligent mediated information agents is needed by such a network. The most important type of information to be exchanged concerns environmental regulations, compliance, and remediation.

3 TECHNICAL CHALLENGES

Existing NII technology for accessing information from open information systems is insufficient because it relies on hardcoded links, does not mitigate heterogeneity, incorporates no semantics, and provides no fusion of results. In developing the current technology, the emphasis has been on finding text, not data or databases. Additional challenges involve the

- Amount of Data (finding needles in haystacks)
- Quality of Data
- Using the Data
  - Mediation to match tools to databases [Wiederhold 1992]

– Autonomous application of tools against databases.

4 PROJECT DESCRIPTION

The *Environmental Information Mall* will be assembled in a series of phases. When fully complete it will be a resource node on the NII that will be accessible via one of several "homepages" oriented toward specific user disciplines, *i.e.*, law, manufacturing, research, etc. Upon entering the *Mall*, users will be able to browse for both analysis tools and databases. An intelligent "sales clerk" or mentor will be available to assist users as they ask questions and browse the domains within the *Mall*. A key feature of the *Mall* will be the apparent ubiquitous nature of the analysis tools and databases. This will be accomplished by creation of a common ontology or context that can be viewed from several user perspectives [Guha 1990]. All of the tools and resources in the *Mall* will be related or mapped to the common ontology [Collet *et al.* 1991]. It becomes the unification, or the "walls" that define the *Mall*'s space. The ontology development will use MCC's Carnot technologies [Woelk *et al.* 1992].

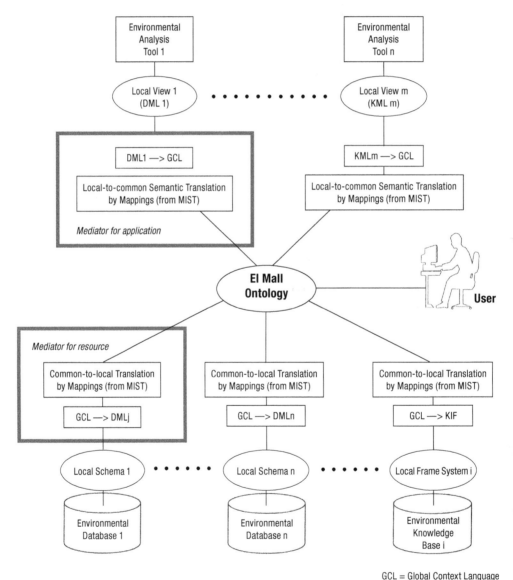

GCL = Global Context Language
DML = Data Manipulation Language
KML = Knowledge Manipulation Language
KIF = Knowledge Interchange Format

Figure 3. Environmental Information Mall Processes.

As users browse the *Mall*, they will identify sets of pertinent data, and the sales clerk will identify appropriate tools to run against the data to yield the specific information needed. The intelligent mentor will also apply a statistical probability or priority rating to inform the user of the likelihood of receiving the knowledge from the tools and databases accessed. The user will exit the *Mall* with just the information needed, not the torrents of data used for the analysis.

In order to accomplish this, the *Mall* will offer a neutral computing space of high-performance computing (HPC) facilities where the analysis tools can be applied to data from one or more databases. In doing so, the Mall will take advantage of the HPC program, which has put in place the ability for a virtual computation environment. The user will issue only a simple request to process the data using the identified tools, with known costs and temporal constraints.

An important aspect of the *Environmental Information Mall* is the ability to do commerce. While certain sets of data and tools will be available free of charge, others will incur a fee per transaction. Following free market principles, information and databases will be created, perhaps from public information, which address specialized information, or which present the data in particularly easy to use formats. These will have a higher usage rating, will score a higher probability of finding the information, and hence will be able to charge for their use. These "boutiques" will be the beginning of a class of facilities in the *Mall* that will become revenue generators for the developers. This, in turn, will attract other boutique creators and other listings of environmental databases and tools.

As mentioned earlier, the unifying feature of the *Mall* will be the common ontology. Hence, each database and tool provider will need to pay integration costs for mapping their system into the common ontology for the *Mall*. The revenue generated by users will both encourage further database creation and support the maintenance on the *Mall*'s ontology framework.

This concept involves the incorporation of many advanced information technologies, but as stated above, many of these technologies exist today and can be applied fairly rapidly. The *Environmental Information Mall* represents one of the more aggressive and comprehensive approaches to developing both a paradigm and a functional utility for creating a money-making enterprise on the NII and for helping enterprises comply effectively with environmental standards.

REFERENCES

[Collet *et al.* 1991] Christine Collet, Michael N. Huhns, and Wei-Min Shen, "Resource Integration Using a Large Knowledge Base in Carnot," *IEEE Computer*, Vol. 24, No. 12, Dec. 1991, pp. 55-62.

[Cutkosky *et al.* 1993] Mark R. Cutkosky, Robert S. Englemore, Richard E. Fikes, Michael R. Genesereth, Thomas R. Gruber, William S. Mark, Jay M. Tenenbaum, and Jay C. Weber, "PACT: An Experiment in Integrating Concurrent Engineering Systems," *IEEE Computer*, January 1993, pp. 28-38.

[Guha 1990] R. V. Guha, "Micro-theories and Contexts in Cyc Part I: Basic Issues," MCC Technical Report Number ACT-CYC-129-90, Microelectronics and Computer Technology Corporation, Austin, TX, June 1990.

[Neches *et al.* 1991] Robert Neches, Richard Fikes, Tim Finin, Tom Gruber, Ramesh Patil, Ted Senator, and William R. Swartout, "Enabling Technology for Knowledge Sharing," *AI Magazine*, Vol. 12, No. 3, Fall 1991, pp. 36-56.

[Wiederhold 1992] Gio Wiederhold, "Mediators in the Architecture of Future Information Systems," *IEEE Computer*, Vol. 25, No. 3, March 1992, pp. 38-49.

[Woelk *et al.* 1992] Darrell Woelk, Wei-Min Shen, Michael N. Huhns, and Philip E. Cannata, "Model-Driven Enterprise Information Management in Carnot." in Charles J. Petrie Jr., ed., *Enterprise Integration Modeling: Proceedings of the First International Conference*, MIT Press, Cambridge, MA, 1992.

CLASSROOM CONNECTIONS

The Environmental Information Mall

Multiple Choice

Pick the best answer.

1. **Why are Environmental Information Mall important?**
   A. Finding relevant data is time consuming and exhausting.
   B. Knowing compatibility of tools and data is a burden to solving already difficult problems.
   C. It gives AI systems a standard ontology to share across agencies and data.
   D. If data has already been analyzed, finding and sharing the results saves time.
   E. All of the above.

2. **Who would be interested in using an Environmental Information Mall?**
   A. Shoppers.
   B. Data analysts and decision makers.
   C. Government agencies, non-profits, schools and corporations.
   D. Gardeners, Parents and Environmentalists.
   E. B and C.
   F. A – D.

3. **What kinds of AI techniques are helpful in building an Environmental Information Mall?**
   A. Ontologies.
   B. Software agents.
   C. Meta-knowledge.
   D. Machine learning and cooperative software agents.
   E. Video Animation.
   F. A – D.

4. **What difficulties arise in using AI systems for Environmental Information Malls?**
   A. Machine learning needs to explain the conclusions it draws from the data.
   B. Ontologies can change as we learn more and new data sets are added.
   C. Meta-knowledge about data and tools must be also be updated.
   D. It can become our overlord.
   E. A – C.

True or False

Please decide if each of the statements below are True or False.

5. Globally, environmental data is hard to monitor because there are hundreds of data sites and many different operating systems, file formats and configurations.

6. A system that comprehensively disseminates relevant information benefits from a shared ontology that enables interoperation of analytical tools from a variety of independent sources.

7. Intelligent user interfaces that fuse information from several sources automatically gives users a powerful search tool.

8. Information sources that advertise their capabilities to intelligent agents can help users locate information.

9. Without a high level view of what information is used and not used we may make shortsighted, reactive plans for the future.

Answers can be found at the end of the book.

Chapter 15

Biodiversity and Ecosystem Catalogues

Biodiversity and Ecosystems NEtwork (BENE) —

The Challenge of Building a Distributed Informatics Network for Biodiversity

Leland Ellis
Texas A&M University, USA

Andrew Jackson
Texas A&M University, USA

Steve Young
Smithsonian Institution, USA

ABSTRACT

The Biodiversity and Ecosystems NEtwork (BENE) is a partnership enterprise, whose members share in the responsibility for providing distributed information about biodiversity and ecosystems via the world-wide Internet.

1 INTRODUCTION

Current estimates of the diversity of life (plant, animal, microorganisms) on Earth (biodiversity) range beyond the ~1.5 million species described to date up to perhaps as high as ~130 million species. Thus, the great majority of the diversity of life on this planet remains to be discovered and described (for discussion, see [Wilson, 1992]).

Given that biodiversity encompasses all of life on earth, the quality of life enjoyed by all depends critically on maintaining the proper balance between the use and conservation of these vast resources. In a practical sense, we humans very much depend on our environment to provide sufficient food and shelter, as well as products which impact upon our health (*e.g.*, ~40% of all pharmaceuticals are of plant origin).

And yet, current estimates of the ongoing loss of biodiversity are quite startling, *e.g.*, up to 10,000 species may disappear every year [Wilson, 1992]. Thus, unknown resources of inestimable value are lost without prior discovery, characterization and potential utilization [Lovejoy, 1994].

Furthermore, newspaper headlines often bring us startling reminders of how little we understand about some of the elements of our environment.

For example, it has been suggested that the emergence (or re-emergence) of quite devastating diseases (*e.g.*, the current outbreak of the Ebola virus in Zaire [Ebola, 1995]) may be the result of the (i) novel exposure of humans to these otherwise latent, hidden agents, or (ii) new imbalances in Nature resulting from the disruption of species habitats (for an extensive review and discussion, see [Garrett, 1994]).

1.1 INFORMATION ABOUT BIODIVERSITY

The study of biodiversity attracts the interest and commitment of a wide range of individuals, from diverse social, political and economic strata, including members of academe, government, corporations, non-government organizations, museums and herbaria, private foundations, and individual citizens. The data types of interest in this domain are also quite diverse, and include the specimens themselves (or samples or images of them), field notes of taxonomists, collections and repositories (herbaria and museums), results of basic research, geographic information systems (GIS), genome projects, valid taxonomic nomenclature, educational materials (including television), etc.

There are currently a number of available avenues by which information relevant to biodiversity can be accessed, including the telecommunications media (especially television), primary collections (museums and herbaria) themselves (often without computerization), desktop microcomputer records, relational databases, Email ListServer discussion groups, network resource locators (ftp, Gopher [Gopher, 1995] and WorldWide Web [WWW, 1995]), etc.

Thus, on all fronts, the domain of biodiversity constitutes an extremely broad challenge in terms of providing an infrastructure for information. National and international discussions of how to identify, manage and conserve the biota of the planet is an ongoing topic of discussion (see below).

2 BIODIVERSITY AND ECOSYSTEMS NETWORK

2.1 ORIGIN OF BENE

How does one begin to approach the notion of providing an interface to a vast variety of information to such an extensive and diverse user community? Thousands of people in the U.S. and the rest of the globe are concerned about conserving and sustainably using biodiversity and ecosystems. Hundreds of government units,

academic and other institutions, private-sector entities, non-governmental organizations, and other groups are involved.

In the Clinton/Gore Reinventing Government initiative to create a government that works better and costs less, building creative new networks to help people work together is seen as an important strategy for progress. BENE joins a number of other networks in the growing NetResults program [NetResults, 1995] of the National Performance Review [NPR, 1995].

BENE is designed to foster enhanced communications and collaborations among those interested in biodiversity conservation and ecosystem protection, restoration, and management.

BENE is a partnership enterprise, whose members share in the responsibility for providing biodiversity information via the world-wide Internet. The initial members of the BENE partnership are the (i) Environmental Protection Agency's Community Environmental Protection team [EPA, 1995], (ii) National Performance Review [NPR, 1995] NetResults Team, (iii) Smithsonian Institution [SI, 1995] and (iv) W.M. Keck Center for Genome Informatics (Institute of Biosciences and Technology, Texas A&M University) [Keck, 1995].

2.2 BENE INFRASTRUCTURE

The current computational infrastructure (Unix workstations) for BENE is housed at the Institute of Biosciences and Technology (Texas A&M University, Houston). In its initial year of activity, BENE has rapidly become a highly visible (international) network presence, which includes BENE resources for an (i) Email ListServer [BENE, 1995c], (ii) WWW server [BENE, 1995e], (iii) Gopher server [BENE, 1995d] and (iv) anonymous ftp server [BENE, 1995a].

BENE brings together a diverse set of participants, including many of those groups stated above, who communicate and exchange information via distributed Internet resources. In addition to the ongoing dialog on the BENE Email ListServer (whose archives are accessible via WWW HyperMail and a wais-indexed Gopher database; [BENE, 1995c]), BENE also provides a document archive [BENE, 1995b] to provide users with ready access to materials of interest (via WWW, Gopher and/or anonymous ftp).

One of the major initial functions of the BENE WWW server is to provide pointers to on-line repositories and collections of information elsewhere, in government, universities, museums, etc. (see [BENE, 1995g]).

In particular, it is probably impossible to even contemplate trying to single-handedly collect and archive all relevant information at a single site! Thus, we and others very much depend on widely distributing the load of such information gathering.

How much duplication is there in such efforts? How should such diverse activity be coordinated at the national and international levels? How does one develop meta-data and meta-indexes for this distributed information (see further below)?

These are very challenging questions, and daunting ones at present. Hopefully, we will capture the imagination of computer scientists to help us address these issues.

2.3 USER CONTRIBUTIONS

We actively encourage members of the BENE community to help us develop BENE resources by means of their direct participation.

For example, to help commemorate Earth Day '95 (April 22nd), we developed a HyperText Markup Language (HTML; [HTML, 1995]) form for users to use to construct BENE's Earth Day '95 WWW page [Earth Day, 1995a]. By means of this form [Earth Day, 1995b], users can easily fill in information (URLs, descriptive information, etc.) about activities of interest.

We are currently using a similar forms-based approach to solicit BENE community input for Oceans Day '95 [Oceans Day, 1995], and for a 'Help BENE to Grow' project (BENE, 1995f).

3 BENE OUTREACH

BENE works together with other organizations to provide a means by which primary collections can be given network access to a much larger audience.

For example, BENE has worked with a member of the Informatics staff (Alan Tucker) of the Missouri Botanical Garden in St. Louis to provide a remote host (at Keck-IBT) for extensive WWW and Gopher resources of the Garden, including a wais-indexed version of the TROPICOS database, which includes some 650,000 taxa [MBG, 1995]. A recent (and very lovely) addition to these materials is the Conspectus of the Vascular Plants of Madagascar (~35 MBytes, of which ~31 MBytes are gifs; [Madagascar, 1995]). These pages of the Garden

get an average of from 7,500 to 14,000 WWW events per week, attesting to the keen user interest in access to such materials [Stats, 1995].

Secondly, BENE has worked with systematic botanists (Hugh Wilson and Steve Hatch) on the Texas A&M University [TAMU, 1995] campus in College Station to provide electronic versions of several bodies of information, which is collectively accessible via the Texas A&M Plant Diversity Information Center WWW Home Page [PDIC, 1995], This page has pointers to the Texas Organization of Endangered Species (TOES) Plant Listing, the Department of Biology Herbarium and the Checklist of the Vascular Plants of Texas.

Thirdly, BENE is working with the National Biological Service (NBS; [NBS, 1995]) and the Association of Systematics Collections (ASC; [ASC, 1995]) to provide information about the ASC and its members.

In all of these outreach activities, BENE can be thought of as a precursory demonstration of some of the functionality proposed for the U.S. National Biodiversity Information Center (NBIC; [NBIC, 1995]).

In addition, BENE supports the goals of the NBS in its effort to lead development of the National Biological Information Infrastructure (NBII; [NBII, 1995]).

4 BIODIVERSITY INFORMATION NETWORK 21

How does one hope to coordinate such informatics activities on an international scale?

4.1 CONVENTION ON BIOLOGICAL DIVERSITY

One potential mechanism is the Biodiversity Information Network (BIN21; [BIN21, 1995]) which was established during the U.N.-sponsored Convention on Biological Diversity (CBD; Earth Day) in Rio de Janiero in 1992 [CBD, 1992]. BIN21 is an international network of information providers who strive both to facilitate the mobilization of information within their home countries, but also internationally between BIN21 nodes. At present, there are nodes in Australia (4), Brazil (the BIN21 Secretariat resides at the Base de Dados Tropical), Costa Rica, Ecuador, Finland (2), Italy, Japan, the United Kingdom and the United States (BENE is the only BIN21 node in the U.S.A.).

Examination of the WWW servers of the BIN21 nodes [BIN21, 1995] provides an extensive look at the approaches being taken internationally to provide a diverse audience with information relevant to the study of biodiversity and ecosystems. For example, the Environmental Resources Information Network [ERIN, 1995] in Australia is often cited as an excellent example of a very effective organization of information in this 'domain'.

4.2 CONVOCATION OF THE PARTIES

At the first Convocation of the Parties (CoP; a meeting of signatories of the CBD) in Nassau in November of 1994 [CoP, 1994], further discussion of a proposed 'Clearing House Mechanism(s)' (CHM) for world-wide biodiversity information was begun. In September/October, 1995, a workshop entitled Clearing House Mechanism on Biological Diversity – The Role of Special Interest Networks [CHM, 1995] is scheduled in Brazil (Campinas, Sao Paulo) to discuss the current state of BIN21 activities, the potential role of BIN21 in the CHM, and to plan an Informatics agenda for the next CoP (II) in Indonesia in November 1995.

5 FUTURE NEEDS AND CHALLENGES

5.1 SEARCHING INFORMATION SPACE

The biodiversity information domain is vast, and growing at a rate faster than any one person can absorb. We at BENE certainly see the need for new mechanisms to help users to find data and information of greatest interest to them.

A major requirement is for efficient as well as thorough cataloging of sources, *e.g.*, comprehensive and current lists of relevant information servers, including WWW, Gopher, ftp, Email ListServers and Internet Newsgroups. For example, how does a specialist in, *e.g.*, camels, locate discussion groups (*e.g.*, ListServers) devoted to camels.

Furthermore, there is a need to shield users from the need to track the proliferation of relevant resources, and to provide an integrated information space in which the user can search for biodiversity information of interest.

As an example, an information 'agent' might subscribe to all available, relevant Email ListServers, read all relevant Internet Newsgroups and archive and index the traffic for searching by

the user. These needs also extend to Webspace and Gopherspace, and require intelligent means for locating and ranking sources.

Automated guidance needs to be provided to help users direct their announcements and inquiries to the most appropriate resources.

WWW search tools such as Lycos [Lycos, 1995] and others [Searching, 1995] are a significant help as well. Most such search tools are limited to an environment rather than an information domain, however; *i.e.*, Lycos searches Webspace only; Veronica searches Gopherspace only, and so forth. Multi-domain and multi-depth search and indexing tools such as Harvest [Harvest, 1995] represent a welcome step towards the design of 'domain specific' indexing tools.

5.2 DATABASE TECHNOLOGY

The great majority of materials provided via the WWW rely on flat files (ascii text and gif images) organized in a Unix file system hierarchy.

On the other hand, we and others are also exploring the utility of relational or object-oriented databases to accommodate taxonomic data. For example, we have used the Object Data Environment (ODE) developed by Gehani and coworkers at AT&T Bell Labs [Agrawal and Gehani, 1989; Biliris, 1992] to develop a WWW client-based graphical-user interface, using the Common Gateway Interface (CGI) to the WWW [CGI, 1995]. In particular, we have developed prototypes for Classes for the TOES data (see above; [TOES, 1995]) as well as for TROPICOS data (Taxon and Specimen Classes; in progress). The addition of a query language to ODE (termed SWORD, expected in 1995) will provide new and expanded user interaction (more complex queries) with the underlying taxonomic data.

Given the great diversity of institutions and organizations engaged in the collection of biodiversity information, there is of course a great diversity in the database architectures employed. Ultimately, an end-user will require a means by which to direct a query, over the network, to multiple distributed databases simultaneously. Examples of such efforts in the Biodiversity community include the MUSE project (MUSE, 1995) and the CIESIN gateway (CIESIN, 1995).

5.3 SPATIAL DATA

Most of the data provided in today's information resources for biodiversity and ecosystems is ascii text and images.

However, there is already the recognition of the need to provide an interactive graphical-user interface to spatial data, as an intuitive interface by which to study and examine the distribution of, *e.g.*, species, geographically (see, *e.g.*, [MUSE, 1995]).

At present, the integration of GIS [*e.g.*, Antenucci *et al.*, 1991] with the WWW is just beginning (see, *e.g.*, [REGIS, 1995]). For the biological community, this is a daunting challenge, as the physical requirements to store the requisite information are enormous (hundreds of GBytes even for states and countries, ?Bytes for the Earth), the data formats are very numerous and unfamiliar, and the resulting strain on the current Internet infrastructure of using such distributed GIS interfaces is already apparent.

On the other hand, the computational challenge of dealing with spatial data is being addressed. In fact, two of the initial NSF/ARPA/NASA awards for Digital Libraries [DL, 1994] deal with these challenging issues: Project Alexandria at UC-Santa Barbara [Alexandria, 1994] and the UC-Berkeley Electronic Environmental Library Project [Berkeley, 1994] (see also Sequoia 2000 [Sequoia, 1994]).

Biologists interested in biodiversity are going to need much help indeed to consider and hopefully implement practical and usable GIS interfaces for our information systems.

6 INFORMATICS AND BIODIVERSITY

What is the impact of the current generation of informatics resources, including BENE, on the community concerned with biodiversity and ecosystems? Is there an impact on those who make decisions concerning the environment?

We are aware that computer scientists indeed concern themselves with the need and methods of evaluation of software and hardware systems that they deploy. While the requirements for the design of a biodiversity information network have certainly been considered in detail (*e.g.*, [Green and Croft, 1994], [NBIC, 1995]), we are unaware (at present) of any formal comparisons and critiques having been done for currently available biodiversity information resources. This is one of the important functions that would be expected of a national organization, *e.g.*, the NBIC (see above) – the U.S.A. currently has no such organization (cf. Australia's ERIN).

Given these limitations, and the early stage of BENE's development, we can only share our subjective impressions of how we believe that BENE is already making an impact.

First, BENE provides a communications mechanism which allows decision-makers to post draft documents for review and ask questions of the broad BENE audience. This can improve decision-making by opening up the process to a wider community and making the process more transparent to non-bureaucrats. These resources are complemented by recently introduced government resources and tools ([*e.g.*, [Thomas, 1995]), which now also provide ready public access to information about the legislative process in the United States Congress, *e.g.*, current deliberation about the Endangered Species Act.

Second, BENE is helping to display the wide range of biodiversity and ecosystem resources on the Internet, and implicitly indicate gap areas where information is not yet available (*e.g.*, documented data on extinctions which have taken place in the recent past). We believe that BENE is already helping to demonstrate the current state of practice in networked information delivery and thereby reduce the amount of duplication of effort and technological under-achievement among biodiversity and ecosystem information providers. Workshops that focus on the training of "information providers" meet with an enthusiastic audience, and have proven quite useful (*i.e.*, new resources subsequently come on-line; see, *e.g.*, [Workshop, 1994]).

Thus, we are confident that BENE is beginning to spur closer collaborations among information providers in Federal agencies, state governments, non-governmental organizations and academia. We certainly welcome input as to how to make us do so more effectively.

7 SUMMARY

By means of the activities summarized above, BENE is now actively involved in providing and facilitating the exchange of information for Biodiversity at the national and international (BIN21) levels.

On the one hand, the technology thus far utilized by BENE derives from today's network resource locators. Despite its success to date in reaching a large and diverse target audience, the limitations of this technology in terms of dealing with the vast amounts of information of interest is readily apparent.

We anticipate that 'next-generation' tools under

development in the Computer Science community (*e.g.*, agency, queries of distributed heterogeneous databases, knowledge discovery in databases, digital libraries [DL '95, 1995], etc.), will find future application in this domain of Biodiversity.

Furthermore, user communities such as BENE should provide important end-user communities and testbeds for next-generation informatics tools.

BENE welcomes discussions and interactions with this research community, and the opportunity to participate in this Workshop on Artificial Intelligence and the Environment [IJCAI, 1995].

ACKNOWLEDGMENTS

The BENE staff and computational resources at the Center for Genome Informatics, Institute of Biosciences and Technology, Texas A&M University (Houston) are supported by the W.M. Keck Foundation. We thank Staff Assistant Janis Bender for her continuing contribution to Keck-IBT activities.

REFERENCES

[Agrawal and Gehani, 1988] R. Agrawal and N. Gehani. Ode (Object Database and Environment): The Language and Data Model. In Proceedings of the ACM-SIGMOD 1989 International Conference on the Management of Data, pages 36-45, Portland, Oregon, May-June 1989.

[Alexandria, 1994] Alexandria Digital Library Home Page, University of California at Santa Barbara. http://alexandria.sdc.ucsb.edu/

[Antennucci *et al.*, 1991] John C. Antennucci, Kay Brown, Peter L. Croswell, Michael J. Kevany and Hugh Archer. *Geographical Information Systems – A Guide to the Technology.* Van Nostrand Reinhold, New York, 1991.[ASC, 1995] Association of Systematics Collections (ASC) WWW Home Page. http://straylight.tamu.edu/bene/systematics/asc/asc.html

[BENE, 1995a] BENE Anonymous ftp Server. ftp://keck.tamu.edu/pub/bene/

[BENE, 1995b] BENE Document Archive, http://straylight.tamu.edu/bene/home/bene.docs.html

[BENE, 1995c] BENE Email ListServer. http://straylight.tamu.edu/bene/listserv/benel-ist.html.
A hypertext archive of the list is also available (http://straylight.tamu.edu/bene/hypermail.html), as well as a wais-indexed archive via Gopher (http://straylight.tamu.edu/gopher/gopher.html)

[BENE, 1995d] BENE Gopher Server. http://straylight.tamu.edu:70/ll/.bene/

[BENE, 1995e] BENE World-Wide Web (WWW) Server Home Page. http://straylight.tamu.edu/bene/bene.html.

[BENE, 1995f] Help BENE to Grow http://straylight.tamu.edu/bene/NewURLs/NewURLs.html.

[BENE, 1995g] Biodiversity and Ecosystems Information. http://straylight.tamu.edu/bene/home/bene.information.html

[Berkeley, 1994] An Electronic Environmental Library Project Home Page, University of California, Berkeley. http://http.cs.berkeley.edu/~wilensky/proj-html/proj-html.html

[Biliris, 1992] A. Biliris. An efficient database storage structure for large dynamic objects. In *Proceedings of the Eighth International Conference on Data Engineering,* pages 301-308, Tempe, Arizona, May 1992.

[BIN21] Biodiversity Information Network 21. http://straylight.tamu.edu/bin2l/bin21.html

[CBD, 1995] Convention on Biological Diversity, Earth Summit, Rio de Janiero, Brazil, 1992. http://www.unep.ch/biodiv.html

[CGI, 1995] The Common Gateway Interface. National Center for Supercomputing Applications (NCSA), University of Illinois, Urbana-Champagne. http://hoohoo.ncsa.uiuc.edu/cgi/overview.html

[CIESIN, 1995] CIESIN Gateway – Data and Information Search and Access. Consortium for International Earth Science Information Network

(CIESIN).
http://www.ciesin.org/

[CoP, 1994] First Conference of the Parties. 28 November to 9 December, 1994. Nassau, The Bahamas.
http://www.iisd.ca/Hnkages/biodiv.html

[DL, 1994] NSF Awards Digital Libraries Research.
http://straylight.tamu.edu/home/nsf_dl.html

[DL '95] The Second International Conference on the Theory and Practice of Digital Libraries. June 11-13, 1995. Austin, Texas. http://bush.cs.tamu.edu/dl95/README.html

[Earth Day, 1995a] Earth Day '95, April 22nd.
http://straylight.tamu.edu/bene/EarthDay/Earth-Day.html

[Earth Day, 1995b], Earth Day '95 URL Submission Form.
http://straylight.tamu.edu/bene/EarthDay/Earth-Day-submit.html

[Ebola, 1995] The Ebola Page.
http://ichiban.objarts.com/ebola/ebola.html

[EPA, 1995] Environmental Protection Agency WWW Server Home Page.
http://www.epa.gov/

[ERIN, 1995] ERIN, Environmental Resources Information Network Home Page.
http://www.erin.gov.au/erin.html

[Garrett, 1994] Laurie Garrett, *The Coming Plague – Newly Emerging Diseases in a World out of Balance.* Farrar, Straus and Giroux, New York, 1994.

[Gopher, 1995] University of Minnesota Gopher.
gopher://gopher.micro.umn.edu:70/l

[Green and Croft, 1994] David G. Green and Jim R. Croft, *Proposal for Implementing a Biodiversity Information Network.* In *Linking Mechanisms for Biodiversity Information.* Proceedings of a Workshop for the Biodiversity Information Network, Base de Dados Tropical, Campinas, Sao Paulo, Brasil, 1994.

[Harvest, 1995] The Harvest Information Discovery and Access System. Department of Computer Science, University of Colorado.
http://harvest.cs.colorado.edu/

[HTML, 1995] HyperText Markup Language (HTML).
http://www.w3.org/hypertext/WWW/MarkUp/MarkUp.html

[IJCAI, 1995] IJCAI Workshop on Artificial Intelligence and the Environment, August 19, 1995. Montreal, Canada.
http://ic-www.arc.nasa.gov/ic/conferences/IJCAI-Enviroment.html

[Keck, 1995] W.M. Keck Center for Genome Informatics, Institute of Biosciences and Technology, Texas A&M University, Houston, Texas. http://straylight.tamu.edu/straylight.html

[Lovejoy, 1994] Thomas J. Lovejoy, Biodiversity: The Most Fundamental Issue. AUSTRALIAN ACADEMY OF SCIENCE, Tuesday, 1 March 1994.
http://kaos.erin.gov.au/life/general_info/love-joy.html

[Lycos, 1995] Lycos, Catalog of the Internet. Carnegie Mellon University.
http://lycos.cs.cmu.edu/

[Madagascar, 1995] Conspectus of the Vascular Plants of Madagascar, Missouri Botanical Garden.
http://straylight.tamu.edu/MoBot/FM/welcome.html

[MBG, 1995] Missouri Botanical Garden – Remote WWW and Gopher Servers at Keck-DBT.
http://straylight.tamu.edu/MoBot/welcome.html, gopher//:keck.tamu.edu:70/ll/.tropicos

[MUSE, 1995] Distributed Searches of MUSE Based Collections.
http://muse.bio.comell.edu/taxonomy/fish.html

[NBIC, 1995] U.S. National Biodiversity Information Center (NBIC).
http://straylight.tamu.edu/bene/nbic/nbic.html

[NBII, 1995] National Biological Information Infrastructure (NBII).
http://www.its.nbs.gov/nbii/

[NBS, 1995] National Biological Service, Department of Interior, WWW Home Page. http://www.its.nbs.gov/

[NetResults, 1995] National Performance Review (NPR) NetResults Team. http://www.npr.gov/NPR/html_NPR/NetResults.html

[NPR, 1995], National Performance Review (NPR). http://www.npr.gov/

[Oceans Day, 1995] Oceans Day '95, June 8th. http://straylight.tamu.edu/bene/OceansDay/OceansDay.html

[PDIC, 199] Plant Diversity Information Center, Texas A&M University. http://straylight.tamu.edu/tamu/pdic.html

[REGIS, 1995] Research Program in Environmental Planning and Geographic Information Systems (REGIS) Home Page. http://www.regis.berkeley.edu/

[Searching, 1995] Searching the WWW. http://straylight.tamu.edu/bene/home/bene.www.html

[Sequoia, 1994] Sequoia 2000 Home Page. http://www.sdsc.edU/0/Parts_Collabs/S2K/s2k_home.html

[SI, 1995] Smithsonian Institution, Washington, D.C. Home Page http://www.si.edu/

[Stats, 1995] User Statistics for the Straylight WWW Server at Keck-IBT. http://straylight.tamu.edu/home/ServerStats.html

[TOES, 1995] The W3ODE Interface to the Texas Organization for Endangered Species Plant Listing. http://keck.tamu.edu/cgi/ODE/toes.w3ode.html

[TAMU, 1995] Texas A&M University WWW Home Page. http://www.tamu.edu/

[Thomas, 1995] Thomas, Legislative Information on the Internet. http://thomas.loc.gov/

[Wilson, 1992] Edward O. Wilson, *The Diversity of Life*. Belknap Press of Harvard University Press, Cambridge, Massachusetts, 1992.

[Workshop, 1994] Biological Collections Information Providers Workshop. University of California, Berkeley, January 13-15, 1995. http://muse.bio.cornell.edu/workshop/description.html

[WWW, 1995] The International World-Wide Web Consortium. http://info.cern.ch http://www.inria.fr/ http://www.w3.org/

CLASSROOM CONNECTIONS

Biodiversity and Ecosystems Network (BENE)— The Challenge of Building a Distributed Informatics Network for Biodiversity

Multiple Choice

Pick the best answer.

1. What is the BENE project?
   A. Crowd sourced global data collective initiative for species cataloguing.
   B. GIS data products.
   C. A unified way of tracking the growth and decline of life on earth.
   D. A resource to track habitat destruction/construction and species decline/increase.
   E. A way to share notes about family pets on social media.
   F. A – D.

2. What kinds of biodiversity data is being shared in the BENE project?
   A. Field notes and specimens.
   B. Geographic information system.
   C. Satellite data.
   D. Pictures of clowns.
   E. A, B, and C.
   F. None of the above.

3. What makes sharing biodiversity data difficult?
   A. Many different data types and many different policies for access, formatting and sharing across agencies.
   B. There are too many species to count.
   C. The size of the data collective is vast and there are diverse standards for identification.
   D. Zebras don't like their pictures taken.
   E. A and C.

4. How is AI being used to help catalogue and share species data?
   A. Automatically locate and link related data on the internet.
   B. Many different countries can use the same AI software and naming conventions.
   C. Knowledge integration across spatial data interfaces.
   D. Self Driving Cars.
   E. A, B and C.

True or False

Please decide if each of the statements below are True or False.

5. Biodiversity tracking and indexing is essential in many kinds of environmental problems such as evidence for increases or decreases in number of species in an area.

6. Pictures of animals need meta-data to help automate ontology building and species identification, including the elimination of duplicate information.

7. Query answering across interconnected data collections is only for field notes.

8. Biodiversity data comes from all kinds of sources including social, political and economic members from governments, corporations, academia, private foundations, individual citizens, etc.

9. The data types from different collectives are uniformly formatted and semantically consistent.

Answers can be found at the end of the book.

Chapter 16

Automated Modeling of Complex Biological and Ecological Systems

Jeff Rickel
University of Texas, USA

Bruce Porter
University of Texas, USA

ABSTRACT

The ability to answer prediction questions is crucial in reasoning about physical systems. A prediction question poses a hypothetical scenario and asks for the resulting behavior of variables of interest. Prediction questions can be answered by simulating a model of the scenario. For complex biological and ecological systems, constructing a suitable model requires distinguishing relevant aspects of the scenario from irrelevant aspects. This paper provides criteria for making this distinction, and it presents an algorithm that uses these criteria to construct a suitable model for answering a given prediction question. The algorithm has been implemented in a modeling program called TRIPEL, and the paper summarizes an evaluation of TRIPEL in the plant physiology domain.

1 INTRODUCTION

The ability to answer prediction questions is crucial in reasoning about physical systems. The following question, from the plant physiology domain, illustrates the general form of a prediction question: "How would decreasing soil moisture affect a plant's transpiration[1] rate?" A prediction question poses a hypothetical *scenario* (*e.g.*, a plant whose soil moisture is decreasing) and asks for the resulting behavior of specified *variables of interest*, (*e.g.*, the plant's transpiration rate). An answer to a prediction question includes the desired predictions and, perhaps more importantly, an explanation of the assumptions and principles that justify the predictions. In biology and ecology, such questions are important for predicting the consequences

of natural conditions and management policies as well as for teaching biological and ecological principles. Because prediction is time consuming and error prone, and requires people with special knowledge, automation would be valuable.

A tool for answering prediction questions would be particularly useful for predicting the effects of global climate changes on plants and animals in specific regions. Answering these questions requires considerable knowledge: general principles of plant and animal physiology and species interactions as well as specific data on individual species, climatic events, and geologic formations. The central issue in answering prediction questions is constructing, from this wealth of information, a model that captures the important aspects of the scenario and their relationships to the variables of interest.

---

[1] Transpiration is the process by which water evaporates from the leaves.

This paper describes TRIPEL, a modeling program for answering prediction questions. Section 2 defines the modeling task. Section 3 presents TRIPEL's criteria for distinguishing relevant aspects of the scenario from irrelevant aspects. Section 4 describes the algorithm that uses these criteria to construct the simplest adequate model for answering a question.

While TRIPEL is designed to support a wide variety of domains, it has been extensively tested in the domain of plant physiology. Specifically, TRIPEL has been used to answer questions from the Botany Knowledge Base (Porter *et al.* 1988). The BKB is a large (over 200,000 facts), multipurpose knowledge base covering plant anatomy, physiology, and development. It was developed by a domain expert. Section 5 discusses the results of evaluating TRIPEL using the BKB.

Because the BKB covers many different physical phenomena at many levels of detail, constructing simple yet adequate models from it is a difficult task. The techniques that allow TRIPEL to perform this task efficiently are applicable throughout science and engineering, but they are especially useful for biology and ecology.

2   THE MODELING TASK

TRIPEL's inputs are a prediction question and domain knowledge. The question has two parts: the scenario and the variables of interest. The scenario includes physical objects, spatial relations among them, and *driving conditions*. Driving conditions specify the behavior of selected variables (*e.g.*, soil moisture is decreasing), their initial value (*e.g.*, the temperature is above the freezing point), or both.

TRIPEL uses the compositional modeling approach (Falkenhainer & Forbus 1991), in which the modeler's job is to select those elements of domain knowledge that are needed to answer the question. Our research focuses on building differential equation models, so the elements of domain knowledge are the *influences* that pertain to the scenario.

An influence is a causal relation between two variables, as in Qualitative Process Theory (Forbus 1984). The variables are real-valued, time-varying properties of the scenario (*e.g.*, soil moisture or the plant's transpiration rate). Each influence specifies that a variable, or its rate of change, is a function of another variable.

Conceptually, each influence represents a physical phenomenon in the scenario at some level of detail. Typically, an influence represents the effect of a process (*e.g.*, the amount of water in the plant is negatively influenced by the rate of transpiration) or a factor that affects a process's rate (*e.g.*, the rate at which the plant absorbs water from the soil is positively influenced by the level of soil moisture). To emphasize their role in modeling, we call the set of all influences that pertain to the scenario the *candidate influences*.

TRIPEL's output, the *scenario model,* is the subset of candidate influences that are relevant to the question. Another program, the Qualitative Process Compiler (Farquhar 1994), built on QSIM (Kuipers 1986), simulates the scenario model starting from the initial state of the scenario. This simulation generates the predictions that are needed to answer the question. A colleague at the University of Texas is developing a program that will use the model and simulation results to answer the question and explain the answer.

3   MODELING CRITERIA

When the domain knowledge is extensive, as with plant physiology, it will describe many phenomena in the scenario, some at multiple levels of detail. Thus, there are two fundamental issues in modeling. First, the modeler must decide which phenomena are relevant to the question and which can be ignored. Second, for each relevant phenomenon, the modeler must choose a relevant level of detail. A candidate influence is relevant if it represents a relevant level of detail for a relevant phenomenon.

3.1   SCOPE

Of the many phenomena in any scenario, only a few are needed to answer any particular question. For example, of the many processes at work in a plant, the question about decreasing soil moisture only requires a model of the plant's water regulation processes. The *scope* of a model is the set of phenomena it covers.

There are two types of irrelevant phenomena. The first type, insignificant phenomena, can be ignored because they do not significantly influence the variables of interest. For instance, in our example, growth processes can be ignored because they do not significantly influence the transpiration rate.

The second type of irrelevant phenomena are those that can be treated as *exogenous*. For instance, in our example, the processes that regulate soil moisture (*e.g.*, rain and evaporation from the soil) can be treated as exogenous. Although exogenous phenomena *do* significantly influence the variables of interest, they are nonetheless irrelevant to the question; they do not help predict the effects of the driving conditions (in our example, decreasing soil moisture) on the variables of interest.

To choose a suitable scope for the model, the modeler must eliminate both types of irrelevant phenomena. To eliminate insignificant phenomena, the modeler must eliminate both types of irrelevant phenomena. To eliminate insignificant phenomena, the modeler needs criteria for recognizing insignificant influences. By pruning insignificant influences, the modeler disconnects the model from all the insignificant phenomena in the scenario.

TRIPEL determines whether an influence is significant using time scale information. Processes cause significant change on widely disparate time scales. For example, in a plant, water flows through membranes on a time scale of seconds, solutes flow through membranes on a time scale of minutes, and growth requires hours or days. In TRIPEL, each influence that represents an effect of a process may have associated knowledge specifying the fastest time scale on which the effect is significant. Before constructing the scenario model, TRIPEL automatically determines a suitable *time scale of interest* for the question (Rickel & Porter 1994). The time scale of interest allows TRIPEL to conclude that any candidate influence operating on a slower time scale is insignificant. This significance criterion is used by human modelers in many domains, including biology, ecology, and many branches of engineering (Gold 1977; O'Neill *et al.* 1986; Saksena, O'Reilly, & Kokotovic 1984).

To eliminate exogenous phenomena, the modeler needs criteria for choosing the exogenous variables of the model. Exogenous variables are those variables in the model whose behavior is determined by influences that are outside the scope of the model. All other variables in the model are *dependent*, their behavior is determined by influences in the model. Thus, the exogenous variables constitute the boundary of the model, separating the model from exogenous phenomena in the scenario. For instance, in our example, by

treating soil moisture as an exogenous variable, the processes that regulate soil moisture are excluded from the model.

To determine whether a variable in the model can be treated as exogenous, TRIPEL uses two criteria. First, by definition, the variable must not be significantly influenced, in the scenario, by any other variable in the model. One variable significantly influences another if there is a chain of candidate influences leading from the first variable to the second and every influence in the chain is significant. Second, note that the objective in a prediction question is to predict the effects of the *driving variables* on the variables of interest. A driving variable is one whose behavior or initial state is specified in the question (in our example, soil moisture). To meet that objective, the modeler must ensure that the exogenous variables do not separate the model from the driving variables of the question. Therefore, a variable in a model can be treated as exogenous only if it is not significantly influenced, in the scenario, by any driving variable of the question. TRIPEL tests these two criteria using a graph connectivity algorithm on the candidate influences (Rickel & Porter 1994).

In summary, TRIPEL eliminates irrelevant phenomena from the scope of the model by pruning insignificant influences (using time scale information) and by choosing suitable exogenous variables for the model. Phenomena that do not significantly influence the variables of interest, or that influence the variables of interest only through exogenous variables, are not included in the model (at any level of detail).

3.2 LEVEL OF DETAIL

The domain knowledge may provide multiple levels of detail for many phenomena in the scenario. For example, water in the plant can be treated as an aggregate, or the water in the roots, stem and leaves can be modeled individually. Similarly, processes can be aggregated. For example, the chemical formula for photosynthesis summarizes the net effects of its component reactions. Also, the dynamics of a process can often be summarized by its equilibrium results. For example, when the level of solutes in a plant cell changes, the process of osmosis adjusts the cell's water to a new equilibrium level. If the dynamics of this process are irrelevant, the modeler can simply treat the level of water as an instantaneous function of the level of solutes. Each of these types of alternatives arises in many areas of science and engineering.

For each relevant phenomenon in the scenario, the modeler must choose a suitable level of detail. Irrelevant details complicate simulation and make the resulting explanation less comprehensible, so the modeler must choose the simplest level of detail that is adequate for answering the question.

TRIPEL has several criteria for choosing the level of detail. First, some approximations may be invalid in the context of the question. For example, process dynamics can only be summarized by their equilibrium result if the process reaches equilibrium very quickly relative to the time scale of interest. TRIPEL includes a variety of general principles for recognizing that a level of detail is invalid or inadequate for a question.

Second, TRIPEL includes coherence criteria. These ensure that the level of detail chosen for different phenomena in the model are compatible. The coherence criteria also ensure that the model does not include different levels of detail for any single phenomenon.

Finally, for those alternatives that are adequate for the question and coherent with other parts of the model, TRIPEL chooses the one that leads to the simplest adequate model. While any simplicity criteria could be used, TRIPEL defines one model as simpler than another if it has fewer variables. The number of variables in a model is a good heuristic measure of the complexity of simulation and of the model's comprehensibility.

In summary, the domain knowledge often provides alternative levels of detail for relevant phenomena, and the modeler must determine which level is relevant. In TRIPEL, a level of detail is relevant if it is adequate for answering the question, coherent with other elements of the model, and it leads to the simplest adequate model.

4   MODELING ALGORITHM

Each candidate influence represents some phenomenon at some level of detail, so TRIPEL's criteria for choosing scope and level of detail allow it to determine the influences that should be included in the scenario model. This section explains TRIPEL's algorithm for selecting the relevant influences.

TRIPEL conducts a best-first search for the simplest adequate scenario model for the question. Each state in the search space is a *partial model*, a model whose scope may not include all relevant phenomena. A partial model may contain *free variables* (variables not yet chosen as exogenous

or dependent). The initial state in the search is a partial model consisting only of the variables of interest, all free. The successor function, described below, extends the scope of a partial model to include any additional phenomena relevant to the free variables, possibly adding new free variables. A partial model has multiple successors when there are alternative levels of detail for the new phenomena. A partial model is pruned from the search if it is incoherent (*i.e.*, violates the coherence criteria) or invalid (*i.e.*, includes an invalid level of detail); any extension of an incoherent/invalid partial model is also incoherent/invalid. The search ends when an adequate model is found that is at least as simple as all remaining partial models; these partial models can only grow. The simplicity criterion (*i.e.*, number of variables in the model) also serves as the evaluation function for the best-first search.

The successor function, **extend-model**, extends the scope of a partial model. **Extend-model** first determines whether all the free variables in the partial model can be exogenous, as described in Section 3.1. If so, it marks each one as exogenous and returns the resulting model, which is now complete. Otherwise, it chooses a free variable that must be dependent, and it determines all combinations of candidate influences on that variable that include every significant influencing phenomenon at some level of detail (multiple combinations arise from alternative levels of detail for these phenomena). **Extend-model** returns a set of new partial models, each the result of extending the original partial model with one of the combinations.

To extend the original partial model with a combination of candidate influences, **extend-model** adds the influences to the model, marks the chosen free variable as dependent, and adds any new free variables to the model. The new free variables are those variables referenced by the new influences but not already in the model (*e.g.*, an influencing variable).

This algorithm is guaranteed to return the *simplest* adequate scenario model whenever an adequate scenario model exists. To see this, note that each partial model represents all its extensions. Thus, the initial partial model in the search represents all scenario models that include the variables of interest. Conceptually, the guarantee results from the following strategy:

- From the space of all possible scenario models, the algorithm repeatedly prunes away models until only a single scenario model (if any) remains.

- It never prunes a scenario model unless either (1) the model is inadequate for the question or (2) if the model is adequate, there is an adequate scenario model still under consideration (*i.e.*, that is an extension of a partial model on the search agenda) that is at least as simple.

For the details of the proof, see (Rickel 1995).

5   EVALUATION

To evaluate TRIPEL, we tested it on a variety of prediction questions concerning the physiology of a prototypical plant. The questions were generated by a domain expert. Each question specifies the qualitative behavior of one variable (*e.g.*, soil moisture is decreasing) and asks for the resulting behavior of another (*e.g.*, transpiration rate).

The domain knowledge was provided by the Botany Knowledge Base (BKB) (Porter *et al.* 1988). The BKB is a large (over 200,000 facts), multipurpose knowledge base covering plant anatomy, physiology, and development. It was developed by a domain expert. The BKB provides 691 variables representing properties of a plant and its environment (soil and atmosphere), and it provides 1507 candidate influences among them. The candidate influences cover many different types of processes, including water regulation, metabolism, temperature regulation, and transportation of gasses and solutes. These processes operate on many different time scales. Many phenomena covered by the BKB are represented at multiple levels of detail, as described in Section 3.2.

The evaluation, described in detail in (Rickel 1995), suggests that TRIPEL is already an effective modeling program. Despite the size of the BKB, TRIPEL typically generates simple, adequate models, as judged by a domain expert. Models ranged in size from 3 variables to 93 variables, and more than half had fewer than 20 variables. Furthermore, the knowledge TRIPEL requires to construct these models is fundamental plant physiology knowledge that is natural for a domain expert to encode.

The evaluation also identified the most important limitation of TRIPEL: its criterion for determining whether one variable significantly influences another should be more sophisticated. Currently, TRIPEL concludes that one variable significantly influences another if there is a chain of influences connecting them and every influence in the chain is significant on the time scale of interest. The evaluation suggests that TRIPEL should also consider extra time lags due to the length of the chain or the spatial distance it covers. Due to this limitation, TRIPEL sometimes chooses a time scale of interest that is too fast, and it sometimes includes irrelevant elements in models. TRIPEL is designed to easily incorporate additional criteria for determining the significance of influences and chains of influences, so the main challenge for future research is simply to formulate the criteria.

6   RELATED WORK

The modeling programs of Falkenhainer and Forbus (1991), Nayak (1994), and Iwasaki and Levy (1994) are most similar to TRIPEL. The program of Falkenhainer and Forbus is notable for its contrasting method of selecting the scope, and Nayak's program is notable for its contrasting method of constructing a model (it builds an overly complex model and then repeatedly simplifies it). The modeling algorithm developed by Iwasaki and Levy is most similar to TRIPEL's algorithm, although their algorithm cannot automatically choose exogenous variables. For a detailed comparison between TRIPEL and these programs, see (Rickel & Porter 1994) and (Rickel 1995).

7   FUTURE WORK

To model physical systems as complex as ecosystems, TRIPEL will need a sophisticated ability to distinguish significant and insignificant phenomena. Time scale is an extremely valuable criterion, especially in biology and ecology, but humans also use many other criteria. As mentioned earlier, TRIPEL is designed to easily incorporate additional significance criteria, so the main challenge is simply to formulate new criteria.

Generating predictions about complex biological and ecological systems will also require the ability to reason with varying levels of quantitative detail. The issues that TRIPEL addresses are important for both numerical and qualitative simulation. In principle, TRIPEL supports either method, because Farquhar (1993) showed how both numerical and qualitative models can be constructed from influences. However, TRIPEL has only been used to generate qualitative models. In the future, we would like to use it to generate numerical models as well.

8 CONCLUSIONS

To provide a reliable, comprehensible answer to a prediction question, a modeler must choose the simplest adequate scenario model. TRIPEL employs several criteria to distinguish relevant aspects of the scenario from irrelevant aspects. These criteria guide a best-first search through the space of models. Our evaluation indicates that TRIPEL effectively identifies those aspects of the scenario that are relevant to answering each question.

REFERENCES

Falkenhainer, B., and Forbus, K. D. 1991. Compositional modeling: Finding the right model for the job. *Artificial Intelligence* 51:95-143.

Farquhar, A. 1993. *Automated Modeling of Physical Systems in the Presence of Incomplete Knowledge.* Ph.D. Dissertation, Artificial Intelligence Laboratory, University of Texas. Technical Report AI93-207.

Farquhar, A. 1994. A qualitative physics compiler. In Proceedings of the *Twelfth National Conference on Artificial Intelligence (AAAI-94),* 1168-1174. Menlo Park, CA: AAAI Press.

Forbus, K. D. 1984. Qualitative process theory. *Artificial Intelligence* 24:85-168.

Gold, H. 1977. *Mathematical Modeling of Biological Systems.* New York: John Wiley and Sons.

Iwasaki, Y., and Levy, A. Y. 1994. Automated model selection for simulation. In *Proceedings of the Twelfth National Conference on Artificial Intelligence (AAAI-94)*, 1183-1190. Menlo Park, CA: AAAI Press.

Kuipers, B. 1986. Qualitative simulation. *Artificial Intelligence* 29:289-338.

Nayak, P. P. 1994. Causal approximations. *Artificial Intelligence* 70:277-334.

O'Neill, R.; DeAngelis, D.; Waide, J.; and Allen, T. 1986. *A Hierarchical Concept of Ecosystems.* Princeton, NJ: Princeton University Press.

Porter, B.; Lester, J.; Murray, K.: Pittman, K.; Souther, A.; Acker, L.; and Jones, T. 1988. AI research in the context of a multifunctional knowledge base: The botany knowledge base project. Technical Report AI88-88, University of Texas at Austin.

Rickel, J., and Porter, B. 1994. Automated modeling for answering prediction questions: Selecting the time scale and system boundary. In *Proceedings of the Twelfth National Conference on Artificial Intelligence (AAAI-94),* 1191-1198. Menlo Park, CA: AAAI Press.

Rickel, J. 1995. *Automated Modeling of Complex Systems to Answer Prediction Questions.* Ph.D. Dissertation, Department of Computer Science, University of Texas at Austin.

Saksena, V.; O'Reilly, J.; and Kokotovic, P. 1984. Singular perturbations and time-scale methods in control theory: Survey 1976-1983. *Automatica* 20(3):273–293.

CLASSROOM CONNECTIONS

Automated Modeling of Complex Biological and Ecological System

Multiple Choice

Pick the best answer.

1. **Why is it helpful to use AI to automatically create qualitative models for environmental systems?**

   A. Because many physical systems and their relations to other physical systems are ill defined and well suited to qualitative models, and we need to ask lots of questions about the physical systems in different scenarios.

   B. It increases our ability to understanding and predict environmental events by using methods that speed up the modeling and question-answering about physical systems that changing conditions.

   C. Because there is an overwhelming amount of information related to questions about biological and ecological physical systems and an AI system that automatically and quickly generates a model to answer questions with only the information that relates to your question makes it fast, and therefore it becomes possible to ask many more questions in a given time period.

   D. It helps predict and manage outcomes of potential changes in physical systems because the answer to a prediction question explains the chain of connections between the assumptions and consequences of assumptions made about the physical system.

   E. Because machine learning can't explain its decisions to us and we need common sense to model important relations among ill-defined physical systems.

   F. All of the above.

2. **What is the input to the automatic model generating system?**

   A. A question to answer.

   B. Knowledge about a physical system such as plant physiology.

   C. Measurements.

   D. Principles about the physical system.

   E. A, B, and D.

   F. None of the above.

3. **How does the AI system create a model?**

   A. It analyses the question and determines which principles of knowledge are needed.

   B. It builds the model with only the knowledge and principles that relate to the question.

   C. It has a qualitative model of causes.

   D. It has knowledge representing cause and effect phenomena of physical systems, such as the rate at which a plant absorbs water from the soil is positively affected by the amount of water in the soil.

   E. A – D.

   F. Only C.

4. How does the AI system find the scope of knowledge related to a question?

A. It guesses.

B. It uses knowledge about physical phenomena to determine relevance, cause and effect influence, and level of detail.

C. It creates a list of candidates and eliminates knowledge that is not related.

D. B and C.

E. None of the above.

5. Can the system always generate the simplest model?

A. It can as long as there is a candidate model that relates to the question.

B. There is a mathematical proof that if a model exists the system can pick the simplest.

C. No, because sometimes a question cannot be answered with the knowledge it has so there is no model.

D. All of the above.

6. Can this AI system be used on physical systems other than plants?

A. Yes, because its algorithms are not about plants but about how to build a model from knowledge that answer a user's questions.

B. Yes, because it determines candidate solutions based on level of detail, relevance, time and other factors, not on plant physiology.

C. Yes, because it is programmed to build models related to a question and pick the simplest model, not to know about plants.

D. All of the above.

E. Biology and ecology do not need models, only plants need models.

True or False

Please decide if each of the statements below are True or False.

7. Prediction questions can be answered by simulating a model of the scenario related to the question.

8. To automatically create a model of the scenario related to your question, the AI system must distinguish relevant from irrelevant aspects of information related to the question scenario.

9. The AI system uses multiple levels of detail for phenomena in a question scenario.

Answers can be found at the end of the book.

Shorts

Chapter 17

Automating the Detection of Environmental Crime

Jon W. Robinson
Goddard Space Flight Center, USA

Nick Short
Goddard Space Flight Center, USA

Robert Cromp
Goddard Space Flight Center, USA

ABSTRACT

Due to personnel constraints, the violation of many environmental regulations goes undetected or is detected long after the damage has been done. This paper will propose the use of AI and remote sensing technology to detect land use changes in restricted areas such as wetlands, National Parks etc. It will incorporate the local communities' educational institutions in the process, providing an education bonus as well.

Satellite remote sensing has already been used to detect water theft in the southwestern United States. Aerial photography has been used to document draining and agricultural use on the edge of the Everglades National Park. In addition, timber theft has been a recurring problem in National and State forests.

We propose to use the Intelligent Information Fusion System, IIFS, to combine map information delineating wetlands with digital terrain data, satellite imagery and ground based observation to detect illicit land use change and theft of natural resources.

This will combine building an expected property profile for areas of concern such as forests and wetlands and then scanning new data for unexpected changes. The property profile will include expected spectral characteristics along with measures of the geometric pattern and frequency data. Neural networks and rule based systems will be used to classify and characterize new data as it is acquired. The rule-based system will be used to schedule further automated processing and/or schedule human-supervised analysis.

The model for implementation will involve direct broadcast of TM data (possibly SPOT as well) as the satellite passes overhead along with realtime processing to identify areas that deserve special attention: either further computer analysis of the image or an on-site visit.

In our model, the direct down link for each area will be hosted by local consortiums of colleges, universities and high schools. The analysis, processing and ground truthing will be carried out by students. A spin-off benefit is that students would learn map reading, spatial analysis, analytical skills and develop a better understanding of what is going on in their communities.

Chapter 18

The EOSDIS Production Environment:

Distributed Capacity Management
and Production Scheduling

Bruce Barkstrom
NASA Langley Research Center, USA

ABSTRACT

The Earth Observing System (EOS) and its Data and Information Systems (EOSDIS) provide one of the most interesting environments for dealing with data that we are likely to find in the information sciences. This long-term enterprise will of course be ingesting, archiving, and distributing much larger quantities of remotely sensed data than any agency has previously attempted. A significant part of EOSDIS is concerned with converting the raw data from a variety of instruments into more understandable information. This paper will discuss the system capacity planning and management for EOSDIS, particularly as it applies to the more plannable parts of EOS-DIS data production. Given the job stream that these plans involve, this paper will also discuss the nature and possible solutions for the planning and scheduling tasks in a geographically distributed system, where a variety of enterprises may interact with the system. Because instruments sometimes act in strange ways and because the Earth can surprise our algorithms, just-in-time planning and hierarchical scheduling appear to offer some useful perspectives on what we have to do.

Chapter 19

Objects in the Intelligent Information Fusion System

Keith Wichman
NASA Langley Research Center, USA

ABSTRACT

NASA Goddard, Code 935 is developing the Intelligent Information Fusion System (IIFS) to help scientists combat the problem of having too much data to search. It provides the basis for doing queries on the data in terms the scientists understand. The complexity of modeling the remote sensing domain is such as to make relational databases undesirable. The IIFS is an attempt to provide a scalable system that will handle searches into terabytes and petabytes of data. The OODB allows the use of unique indices that are not available in the relational databases. For instance, Sphere Quadtrees (SPT) allow a spherical representation of the Earth that is more appropriate for world-wide coverage. The SQT has already been incorporated into the IIFS as a spatial search mechanism. The database serves as a test bed for trying various search techniques. Its object-oriented design allows for easy alterations to the strategies used for querying. The combination of a well-designed model, the performances of the object-oriented database and the use of specialized search techniques should provide a system that will grow into its role of managing petabytes of data.

About the Editor

DR. C. L. MASON has a Ph.D. in Computer Science with a concentration in Artificial Intelligence. She has extensive experience working on extreme data analysis involving hybrid AI automation technologies for structured, unstructured and sensor data analysis. Dr. Mason has worked in corporate and government settings on applications involving data integrity, integration and feature extraction. She proposed the first US (AAAI) and international (IJCAI) symposiums on AI and the Environment, bringing together many kinds of scientists, AI researchers and engineers. At NASA Ames she worked with the robotics team that sent the first tele-operated undersea robot to Antarctica. Using a kind of AI that is spread across a network of machines called Distributed Artificial Intelligence (DAI), Dr. Mason helped astronomers create a new way of gathering data 24/7 (called pass-the-star) using a global network of robotic telescopes. Her early work on DAI focused on a global monitoring system for treaty verification in nuclear weapons testing, and won the AAAI award for Outstanding Contribution to the Field of DAI. As a research scientist at UC Berkeley, Dr. Mason

began studying health and human sciences along with AI. These studies led to her idea of emotion as a form of intelligence and the first AI programming language to represent emotion. It also led to the concept of artificial compassionate intelligence. Her studies on human sciences with experts from the US, China, Japan and India were the basis for key research on mind body computation for the New York Times Bestseller, *How to Build A Mind*. They are also the basis for a series of self care education classes she taught in the Stanford Hospital, clinics and community as well as the development of a public resource for sustainable, scalable healthcare, www.21stcenturymed.org. Dr. Mason's work on AI at NASA, UC Berkeley and Stanford along with studies in human sciences inspired innovations in AI such as the first AI programming language with emotion and the concept of artificial compassionate intelligence. She appears in the Australian National Museum for Pioneering Women with Dr. Anna Lichtenberg for starting a CS Department in the Australian Outback. Dr. Mason can be reached at cmason@cmason.us.

Thanks

AT THE TIME, when we all began these AI and Environment projects, we did not realize just how important this work would eventually become. So, the thanks we offer today is especially heartfelt. Big or small, in the beginning, or at the end, or consistently… it all mattered – and in fact, it still matters.

This book is created with modern book-making software and hardware. It's being printed with Harvard Book Store's book-making robot, and it's being created by individuals rather than a large publishing house. And as it turns out book-making entails a surprising amount of work to ensure that the final product actually looks like a book.

To the people who helped to create the original content, I thank every single author. Their names appear in the front of the book, under a dedicated section that I titled, "The Pioneers." I would also like to thank the International Joint Conference on Artificial Intelligence, the Association for the Advancement for Artificial Intelligence, the Canadian Meteorological Organization and the Canadian Society for Computational Studies of Intelligence. Thank you to the reviewers and committee members, Palma Blonda, Cindy Mason, Stan Matwin, Erik Jones, Jim Peak, Nick Short and Roger King.To Henry Lieberman a special thank you for pitching in at Montreal.Thanks to colleagues and staff at NASA Ames who voluntarily helped in the middle of budget cuts, especially Megan Eskey, Ken Lindsay and Boris Rabin. A special thanks to NASA colleague Michael Hall as well as friends at the National Research Council.

In recreating the papers as a volume for digital publication* many people helped to repair text and images, especially Cat Schaad, for helping to keep the texts as the authors prepared it as much as possible, changing fonts in order to make the printed version legible and for e-book production formats. Without her skills, this volume would not have happened. Throughout this process there are many people to thank –graphic artists Mehede, Andew, Dawood, Valmir Morina, and Bill Daul helped in reconstructing images. A super thanks to Tyler Kemp Benedict for an amazing job proof reading and fact checking. Many thanks to philosopher and fellow writer Andrew Porter for sharing his scanner, printer and dinner table.Thank you to Rogelio Marquez, Victoria Evans and the CS students at U.C. Santa Cruz for the idea of adding the Classroom Connections that makes this volume so much more.

Thank you to my colleagues Miquel Sànchez-Marrè, Anne Ruimy, Cris Puentes, Tierney Thys, Richard Waldinger, Harold Boley, Marsali Hancock, Hans Thomas, Stan Matwin, and Roger King for a positive shared vision and for your moral support. The groundwork for most of this idea was laid while crossing the pacific from Los Angeles to Sydney, so to captain Sven, I send heart thanks and warm winds. Thanks to my advisors (and esp. Rowland Johnson), Chris Green, and Joe Morgan. To Berkeley friends Curt, Emily, Jackie, Charlie, Leo and Cleo, and a wide range of friends in Palo Alto that are too many to count, I would like to thank you all. To all of the people I may have missed, thank you.

We recreated the documents as carefully and thoroughly as possible.

Answers to Classroom Connections

Part I
Boots on the Ground

CHAPTER 1
MULTIPLE CHOICE
(1.1) E
(1.2) F
(1.3) F

TRUE/FALSE
(1.4) T
(1.5) T
(1.6) T
(1.7) T
(1.8) T

CHAPTER 2
MULTIPLE CHOICE
(2.1) E
(2.2) D
(2.3) D

TRUE/FALSE
(2.4) T
(2.5) T
(2.6) T
(2.7) T
(2.8) T

CHAPTER 3
MULTIPLE CHOICE
(3.1) E
(3.2) F
(3.3) F
(3.4) E

TRUE/FALSE
(3.5) F
(3.6) T
(3.7) T
(3.8) T
(3.9) T

CHAPTER 4
MULTIPLE CHOICE
(4.1) F
(4.2) E
(4.3) F

TRUE/FALSE
(4.4) T
(4.5)T
(4.6) T
(4.7) T

CHAPTER 5
MULTIPLE CHOICE
(5.1) D
(5.2) D
(5.3) D
(5.4) E

TRUE/FALSE
(5.5) T
(5.6) T
(5.7) T
(5.8) T
(5.9) F

CHAPTER 6
MULTIPLE CHOICE
(6.1) E
(6.2) F
(6.3) E

TRUE/FALSE
(6.4) T
(6.5) T
(6.6) T
(6.7) T
(6.8) T
(6.9) F

CHAPTER 7
MULTIPLE CHOICE
(7.1) E
(7.2) E
(7.3) E
(7.4) E

TRUE/FALSE
(7.5) T
(7.6) F
(7.7) T
(7.8) F
(7.9) T

CHAPTER 8
MULTIPLE CHOICE
(8.1) E
(8.2) E
(8.3) F

TRUE/FALSE
(8.4) T
(8.5) T
(8.6) T
(8.7) T
(8.8) F

CHAPTER 9
MULTIPLE CHOICE
(9.1) F
(9.2) F
(9.3) F

TRUE/FALSE
(9.4) T
(9.5) T
(9.6) T
(9.7) T
(9.8) T

Part II
Data Data Everywhere

CHAPTER 10
MULTIPLE CHOICE
(10.1) F
(10.2) F
(10.3) E

TRUE/FALSE
(10.4) T
(10.5) T
(10.6) T
(10.7) T
(10.8) F

CHAPTER 11
MULTIPLE CHOICE
(11.1) F
(11.2) F
(11.3) E

TRUE/FALSE
(11.4) T
(11.5) T
(11.6) T
(11.7) T
(11.8) T
(11.9) T

CHAPTER 12
MULTIPLE CHOICE
(12.1) E
(12.2) F
(12.3) E
(12.4) E

TRUE/FALSE
(12.5) T
(12.6) T
(12.7) T
(12.8) T
(12.9) F

CHAPTER 13
MULTIPLE CHOICE
(13.1) E
(13.2) E
(13.3) E

TRUE/FALSE
(13.4) F
(13.5) T
(13.6) T
(13.7) F
(13.8) F

CHAPTER 14
MULTIPLE CHOICE
(14.1) E
(14.2) F
(14.3) F
(14.4) E

TRUE/FALSE
(14.5) T
(14.6) T
(14.7) T
(14.8) T
(14.9) T

CHAPTER 15
MULTIPLE CHOICE
(15.1) F
(15.2) E
(15.3) E
(15.4) E

TRUE/FALSE
(15.5) T
(15.6) T
(15.7) F
(15.8) T
(15.9) F

CHAPTER 16
MULTIPLE CHOICE
(16.1) F
(16.2) E
(16.3) E
(16.4) D
(16.5) D
(16.6) D

TRUE/FALSE
(16.7) T
(16.8) T
(16.9) T